For Marx
Against Althusser

Current Continental Research
is co-published by
The Center for Advanced Research
in Phenomenology
and
University Press of America, Inc.

This is Brendan's book.

CURRENT CONTINENTAL RESEARCH 201

John O'Neill

FOR MARX
AGAINST ALTHUSSER
And Other Essays

1982

Center for Advanced Research in Phenomenology
& University Press of America, Washington, D.C.

Library of Congress Cataloging in Publication Data

O'Neill, John, 1933-
    For Marx against Althusser, and other essays.

    (Current continental research ; 201)
    Includes bibliographical references and indexes.
    1. Marx, Karl, 1818-1883—Addresses, essays, lectures.
2. Althusser, Louis—Addresses, essays, lectures.
3. Communism and philosophy—Addresses, essays, lectures.
I. Title. II. Series.
HX39.5.O58   1982   335.4'01   82-17353
ISBN 0-8191-2815-5
ISBN 0-8191-2816-3 (pbk.)

Acknowledgements

Ch.1: THE HUMAN CONTEXT, Vol.6, No.2, 1979, pp.385-89; Ch.2: SITUATING MARX, ed. Paul A. Wilson, London: Chaucer Press, 1972; Ch.3: ETHICS, Vol.77, No.1, Oct. 1966, pp.38-49; Ch.4: PHILOSOPHY AND PHENOMENOLOGICAL RESEARCH, Vol.25, No.1, Sept. 1964, pp.64-84; Ch.5: SOCIAL RESEARCH, Vol.43, Winter 1977, pp.837-44; Ch.6: PROCEEDINGS OF THE XIVth INTERNATIONAL CONGRESS OF PHILOSOPHY, Vienna: Herder, 1968, Vol.2: pp.96-103; Ch.9: CANADIAN JOURNAL OF SOCIAL AND POLITICAL THEORY, Vol.2, 1978, No.2, pp.31-62; Ch.10: PHILOSOPHY OF THE SOCIAL SCIENCES, Vol.11, No.3, Sept. 1981, pp.281-302.

PREFACE

Over the years, I have argued for the view that Marx's thought cannot be separated from itself. Any attempt to break into the intertextuality of Marx's philosophy, economics, history and sociology, or to separate him from Hegel and the classical economists, merely results in crude reductions of Marx's achievement. I do not say that we cannot "reread" or "rethink" Marx. In doing so, however, we must be careful to remember that Marx himself set a standard for rereading and rethinking. I hope that by collecting these essays in a volume unencumbered by other sociological and literary concerns of mine, they will be more readily available to serious students of the issues with which they are concerned.

This is also an occasion to thank Paul Sweezy who sent me to study with his friend Paul Baran at Stanford University, California in 1957. My debt to the two Pauls is enormous.[1] I should also say that in the last decade it has been impossible to think about Marx without coming to terms with the work of Jürgen Habermas.[2] The argument of many of these essays was first presented in the following universities whose collegiality and hospitality it is a pleasure to recall: The London School of Economics and Political Science, Nuffield College, Oxford and Cambridge University; the Free University of Berlin, The University of Poitiers, University of Lund, The University of Louvain, The Hebrew University of Jerusalem, The University of Rome, The Center for Post-Graduate Studies, Dubrovaik, Yugoslavia; and in the United States, Purdue University, The University of Kentucky, The University of Arizona, Michigan State University and New York University. Finally, I would like to thank the Walter and Henry Gordon Charitable Foundation for a generous grant that supported several of my endeavors in the last few years.

Toronto 1982

1.   See my remembrance of Baran as a teacher in "To the Memory of Paul Alexander Baran", MONTHLY REVIEW, Vol. 16, Number 11, March 1965, pp. 120-123; and my "Introduction: Marxism and the Sociological Imagination", in Paul A. Baran, THE LONGER VIEW: Essays Toward A Critique of Political Economy, Edited by John O'Neill, New York and London: Monthly Review Press, 1969.

2.   John O'Neill, Edited and with an introduction, ON CRITICAL THEORY. New York: The Seabury Press, 1976.

Table of Contents

CHAPTER 1

FOR MARX AGAINST ALTHUSSER

Nowadays everybody reads Marx. Or at any rate, many people are ready to read books about Marx, preparatory to reading Marx himself. Everyone admits that it is not easy to read Marx. Marx did not always write very well, much of his writing is polemical in the worst sense and his magnum opus, CAPITAL, apart from being unfinished except for the first volume, is not readable for most people unfamiliar with the categories of Hegelian logic. At best CAPITAL influences the consciousness of the proletariat only in as much as it is read sentimentally, as the history of their misery. Beyond that it is a tissue of conceptual and logical errors that make it the bastard child of economic philosophy or, worse still, of philosophical economy. Nevertheless, despite the increasing disenchantment with socialist reality in the East, and the apparent containment of Marxism in the West, Marx continues to be read. We have Marx in our bones. 'Of course', as Althusser remarks:

> . . . we have all read, all do read CAPITAL. For almost a century, we have been able to read it every day, transparently, in the dramas and dreams of our history, in its disputes and conflicts, in the defeats and victories of the workers' movement which is our only hope and our destiny. Since we 'came into the world,' we have read CAPITAL constantly in the writings and speeches of those who have read it for us, well or ill, both the dead and the living, Engels, Kautsky, Plekhanov, Lenin, Rosa Luxemburg, Trotsky, Stalin, Gramsci, the leaders of the workers' organizations, their supporters and opponents: philosophers, economists, politicians. We have read bits of it, the 'fragments' which the conjuncture had 'selected' for us. We have even all, more or less, read Volume One, from 'commodities' to the 'expropriation of the expropriators.'[1]

CAPITAL, then, is not merely a piece of crabbed economic analysis. It is an ethnography of our daily lives in which the texture of experience is interwoven with the realities of property, power and money that determine for us the rhythms of ease and misery, not just in our daily schedules but in the division of the earth into dominions and colonies. In such a world, to think at all is to presuppose the pain and exploitation of one's fellow men, and to do so responsibly is to subscribe to a tradition of thought in which reason thirsts for justice. It is to draw one's substance

---

1. Louis Althusser and Etienne Balibar, READING CAPITAL, transl. Ben Brewster, New York: Pantheon Books, 1970, p. 13.

from the legacy of the Enlightenment, to experience the bondage of reason without revolution, to join the struggle of men everywhere who believe in the Utopian service of knowledge to justice. For this reason, then, CAPITAL fixes in the Marxist mind as a monumental effort to tie together the misery of the day's labor with a vision of science and justice. And this is the peculiar burden of the Marxist mind--to analyze appearances and yet to submit to the palpable and everyday vision of social justice.

At first sight it looks as though Althusser's project is to understand the Marxist mind, to enter into its vision, perhaps to sit with Marx in the museum, to try to understand this persistent effort within the very storm of history, to read history and politics as a story of reason and the emancipation of the masses. Only such an approach is adequate to the hermeneutic task of the Marxist mind confronted with the history and politics of its own revolutionary intervention, which has itself separated reason and freedom in ways it could not foresee. Marxists are inveterate readers not because they belong, as some argue, to a stranded sect of millenarian and chiliastic believers, but because Marxists are humanists. That is why Marxists read all history as the history of class struggle. That is why, à la Hegel, they believe that there are times when universal history passes through the eye of the needle, when the proletarian revolution concretizes the 'future-philosophy of the world' into the 'world-future of philosophy. . . .' It is for the same reason that in the midst of these world-shaking events Marxists continue to read and to write.

But in the next breath Althusser means to put an end to so much reading and writing, by reading CAPITAL, once and for all, line by line, in the original German(!), while pretending that this is only an exercise in ambiguity, embracing the existential responsibilities of its own interpretative effort. Each of us must read Marx, because of our times, just as we look at the sky for tomorrow's weather. But, Althusser continues:

> some say it is essential to read CAPITAL to the letter. To read the text itself, complete, all four volumes, line by line, to return ten times to the first chapters, or to the schemes of simple reproduction and reproduction on an enlarged scale, before coming down from the arid table-lands and plateaux of Volume Two into the promised land of profit, interest and rent. And it is essential to read CAPITAL not only in its French translation (even Volume One in Roy's translation, which Marx revised, or rather, rewrote), but

also in the German original, at least for the fundamental
theoretical chapters and all the passages where Marx's key
concepts come to the surface. [2]

Thus, what the very history of CAPITAL shows to be impossible,
indeed even more impossible than Marx's own efforts to put
CAPITAL into a finished form, is now to be settled by Althusser
and his associates. Together this small band feels confident
enough of its place in history to provide a reading of CAPITAL
that will reduce the readings of Lenin, Lukacs, Luxemburg and
Gramsci to the abortive wastes of premature theorizing.

I

Althusser's method is to destroy the unity of Marx's theoretical
initiative by raising the question of whether the 'object' of
CAPITAL is economics or history, and thus to rediscover Marx's
own philosophy behind his back, so to speak, in order to reduce
it to the science of dialectical materialism. But this is a conclusion that we must reach more slowly and in pace with
Althusser's own reflections upon 'reading' CAPITAL. For what is
curious in Althusser's enterprise is the way he manages to reach
positivist conclusions from what is an apparently phenomenological
starting-point sensitive to the issues that we have raised so far.

However paradoxical it may seem, I venture to suggest that
our age threatens one day to appear in the history of human
culture as marked by the most dramatic and difficult trial of
all, the discovery of and training in the meaning of the
'simplest' acts of existence: seeing, listening, speaking,
reading--the acts which relate men to their works, and to
those works thrown in their faces, their 'absences of
works.'[3]

We owe it to Marx, Nietzsche, and Freud that we now comprehend
a work, a culture or a period through the 'absence of its concept', by which it accomplishes something more and something less
than its agents intended. A structuralist reading, Althusser
argues, is not the 'innocent reading' of the young Marx, sweep-
ing away 'concrete' appearances in order to reveal the 'abstract'
essence of economics, politics and history guided by a scriptural
reading of Hegel's Absolute Knowledge and Marx's own escha-
tology. The young Marx is still trapped in the religious myth of
reading the book of nature as the revelation of an alienated
human essence. His philosophy of history remains a theodicy, an
ideological reading that has still to become a science of history,

2. IBID., pp. 13-14

3. IBID., pp. 15-16.

4 FOR MARX AGAINST ALTHUSSER

and this is the shift that occurs in CAPITAL: 'By discovering that the truth of history cannot be read in its manifest discourse, because the text of history is not a text in which a voice (the Logos) speaks, but the inaudible and illegible notation of the effects of a structure of structures.'[4]

Already we are enmeshed in Althusser's own reading of texts, in his own way of deciding the presence and absences in Marx's work. I shall argue that Althusser's reading of CAPITAL is from the very beginning[5] determined by a method of exorcism that expels what is there in the name of what is not there, to make room for what is not there in the name of Marx's 'object'. It is therefore necessary to intercept Althusser at the very beginning, i.e., the question of what is absent and what is present in an author's work must determine the responsibility of our reading. Thus we must be conscious that Althusser's reading of CAPITAL first of all suppresses its humanistic impulse. This, however, is tantamount to a political reading of Marx since it separates in the name of theoretical autonomy the unity of Marxist praxis that has become troublesome to the Soviet bloc. In other words, we need to be aware of the organization of background and foreground that determines our reading of the text and the 'context' of CAPITAL. It is the 'break' between Hegel and Marx that makes Althusser conscious of what he calls his 'culpable reading' of Marx,. Although he presents this 'break' as the fulfilment of Marx's Promethean critique of philosophy, whose death is the birth of Marxist science, Althusser disavows the humanist intentions that justified the revolt of Prometheus and the pathos of his interminable suffering. Althusser wants no more caricatures of the Promethean Marx chained to a suffering mankind: Marx is to be a scientist, despite himself: 'To break with the religious myth of reading: with Marx this theoretical necessity took precisely the form of a rupture with the Hegelian conception of the whole as a "spiritual" totality, to be precise, as an expressive totality.'[6] Once Marx had broken with Hegel's spiritualization of history he was free from the religious myth of history as the expression of the human senses, of the voice of the heart, of the ear of man that discerns in Being a Logos and a Truth.

But this is surely an unmusical reading of Marx. Marx did not argue that religion is simply an illusion, a distorted way of seeing what science produces as knowledge. Religion is the expression of man's generic nature, which cannot be reduced to an object except through another, a master of a class, just as it can only

4. IBID., p. 17.

5. LIRE LE CAPITAL presupposes the exercise undertaken in POUR MARX, Paris: Francois Maspéro, 1966. See Chapter 2.

6. READING CAPITAL, p. 17.

achieve selfhood through others in recognition and community. Religion is the expression of man's generic being under social and historical conditions that alienate man from his own legacy. Religion is not a simple failure to see things; it is the vision of the failure of things where man is concerned.

> Religious suffering is at the same time an expression of real suffering and a protest against real suffering. Religion is the sign of the oppressed creature, the sentiment of a heartless world, and the soul of soulless conditions. It is the opium of the people.
>
> The abolition of religion as the illusory happiness of men, is a demand for their real happiness. The call to abandon their illusions about their conditions is a call to abandon a condition which requires illusions. The criticism of religion is, therefore, the embryonic criticism of this vale of tears of which religion is the halo.[7]

It is not a question of reducing religion to economic causes but of being able to see that the expressive being of man, in other words man's metaphysical nature, is such that the domains of religion, politics, economics, and art resonate in each other, even though each has a distinctive valence in the social structure of any given historical period. What Marx understands by the critique of ideology is the effort to situate each of the praxes of economics, politics, and philosophy within a historical milieu from which they cannot be abstracted, but to which they are not simply reducible. This is, of course, what Marx established in his 'Theses on Feuerbach' and the GERMAN IDEOLOGY, which Althusser treats, however, as prescientific efforts in Marx's theoretical development.

Again we must not overlook the way Althusser reduces the problem of the historical vision of critical reason which occupied Marx throughout his early and later works to an epistemological critique of naive realism and its simple-minded logic of vision. In terms of this argument Marx failed to understand the scientific departure in his own reading of classical economics, because he treated those texts as a given in which it remained only for him to correct certain theoretical gaps as failures of vision, without being able to present an adequate account of his own implicit theoretical advance.

7. Karl Marx, "Contribution to the Critique of Hegel's Philosophy of Right," in EARLY WRITINGS, transl. and ed. T. B. Bottomore, New York: McGraw-Hill, 1964, p. 43.

This single logic of sighting and oversight thus reveals itself
to us as what it is: the logic of a conception of knowledge in
which all the work of knowledge is reduced in principle to
the recognition of the mere relation of vision; in which the
whole nature of its object is reduced to the mere condition of
a given. What Smith did not see, through a weakness of
vision, Marx sees; what Smith did not see was perfectly
visible, and it was because it was visible that Smith could
fail to see it while Marx could see it. We are in a circle--we
have relapsed into the mirror myth of knowledge as the
vision of a given object or the reading of an established
text, neither of which is ever anything but transparency
itself--the sin of blindness belonging by right to vision as
much as the virtue of clear-sightedness--to the eye of
man.[8]

Althusser's reading of Marx's theoretical departure with respect
to classical economics, whose significance allegedly escaped Marx
himself, must be understood as the departure Althusser himself
seeks to introduce into the Party's own history of naive realist
determinations of socialist theory. It is, I would argue, the
absence of Althusser's own object that veils his efforts to clarify
the theoretical autonomy of the domains of history, economics,
and politics in terms of his critique of realist epistemology and
Hegelian idealism. Having raised the ghost of naive realism,
Althusser proceeds to give an account of the nature of theoretical
abstraction or concept formation which reduced the literal notion
of abstraction from concrete particulars to a permanent absurdity.
This is an exercise that may be therapeutic for the Party mind
bulldozed by socialist realism. But it is hardly a serious epistemological issue in Marx, who considered it a good part of 'la misère
de la philosophie' to which idealists and realists may both contribute, in as much as they overlook the genesis of ideas within
specific historical praxis.

Monsieur Proudhon has very well grasped the fact that men
produce cloth, linen, silks, and it is a great merit on his
part to have grasped this small amount. What he has not
grasped is that those men, according to their powers, also
produce the social relations amid which they prepare cloth
and linen. Still less has he understood that men, who
fashion their social relations in accordance with their material
mode of production, also fashion ideas and categories, that
is to say the abstract, ideal expression of these same social
relations. Thus the categories are no more eternal than the
relations they express. They are historic and transitory
products. For M. Proudhon, on the contrary, abstractions

8. READING CAPITAL, p. 19.

and categories are the primordial cause. According to him, they, and not men, make history. The abstraction, the category taken as such, i.e., apart from men and their material activities, is of course immortal, unmoved, unchangeable, it is only one form of the being of pure reason; which is only another way of saying that the abstraction as such is abstract. An admirable tautology!

Thus, regarded as categories, economic relations for M. Proudhon are eternal formulae without origin or progress.[9]

This early text is resonant with what Althusser calls 'a second and quite different reading' in which, as he says himself, the argument in terms of the logic of vision yields to a critique, not of the failures of vision in Marx's predecessors, but of their failure to perceive what they did see, namely, the field of production. The notion of the 'production' of theory constitutes a problematic that it is the task of critical theory to comprehend. Althusser argues, however, that Marx himself, although he unwittingly provided the answer to this problematic, was unable to pose its question explicitly because he remained tied to the field of classical economics:

> This restoration of an utterance containing emptinesses and this production of its question out of the answer enable us to bring to light the reasons why classical economics was blind to what it nevertheless saw, and thus to explain the non-vision inside its vision. Moreover, it is clear that the mechanism whereby Marx is able to see what classical economics did not see while seeing it, is identical with the mechanism whereby Marx saw what classical economics did not see at all--and also, at least in principle, identical with the mechanism whereby we are at this moment reflecting this operation of the sighting of a non-sight of the seen, by reading a text by Marx which is itself a reading of a text of classical economics.[10]

II

We must ask, therefore, what is the question to which Althusser's own symptomatic epistemology is an answer? For there is surely something backward looking in Althusser's lengthy reductio ad absurdum of naive realism, as well as his insistence upon an epistemological break between Hegel and Marx. Indeed it is the

9. Marx to P. V. Annenkov, Brussels (28 December 1846), in K. Marx and F. Engels SELECTED CORRESPONDENCE 1846-1895, New York: International Publishers, 1934, pp. 14-15.

10. READING CAPITAL, pp. 23-24.

latter effort that increases the relentlessness of Althusser's
critique of naive realism--which is otherwise not a serious issue
for Marx, supposing we derive any sense from the THESES ON
FEUERBACH. Moreover, since the yield of Althusser's reading of
CAPITAL is simply the apparent recovery of the theoretical
autonomy of the domains of economics and politics, but at the
expense of Marxist humanism and historicism which provided a
principle for the ordering of these domains, we can only conclude
that Althusser's epistemology ultimately answer the question of
theoretical autonomy in terms of a parti pris, or a jeu de mots, in
which the Party is the unconscious method of the 'production' of
socialist theory. In other words, Althusser reduces the autonomy
of socialist theorizing to the 'savage practice' of Party praxis,
while appearing to save its autonomy as a productive effort,
irreducible to other productions, such as the imperative of
politics and economics. In this way Althusser succeeds in bar-
barizing Marx's THESES ON FEUERBACH with a gloss on Lenin's
political praxis:

> That is how Lenin responded to the prophecy in the XI
> Thesis, and he was the first to do so, for no one had done
> it before him, not even Engels. He himself responded in the
> 'style' of his philosophical practice. A wild practice [une
> pratique sauvage] in the sense in which Freud spoke of a
> wild analysis, one which does not provide the theoretical
> credentials for its operations and which raises screams from
> the philosophy of 'interpretation' of the world, which might
> be called the philosophy of denegation. A wild practice, if
> you will, but what did not begin by being wild.[11]

Let us be clear about what is at issue in Althusser's attempt to
sever the connection between the synchronic and diachronic
structures contained in the theory of historical materialism. If
'Marxism is not a species of historicism' then we may neglect
Lenin's reading of Hegel in order to orient himself at a critical
juncture in the history of imperialism and nationalist revolutions.
But the theoretical brilliance of Lenin's analysis of imperialism lies
in his grasp of national liberation movements as products of the
world economy created by monopoly capitalism which, provided the
proletariat can transform imperialist wars into civil wars, becomes
a genuinely revolutionary period. Thus Lenin was able to reject
the Revisionists and Opportunists in the International because
they failed to understand how the class implications of
imperialism, when grasped in their specific dialectical implications,

---

11. Louis Althusser, LENIN AND PHILOSOPHY AND OTHER ESSAYS, transl.
Ben Brewster, New York: Monthly Review Press, 1971, p. 66.

were favorable by means of civil war to the proletarian revolution, in Russia and elsewhere. Lukács has the same view as
Merleau-Ponty of Lenin's political practice, separating it entirely
from what others might regard as Realpolitik:

> Above all, when defining the concept of compromise, any
> suggestion that it is a question of knack, of cleverness, of
> an astute fraud, must be rejected. 'We must,' said Lenin,
> 'decisively reject those who think that politics consists of
> little tricks, sometimes bordering on deceit. Classes cannot
> be deceived.' For Lenin, therefore, compromise means that
> the true developmental tendencies of classes (and possibly of
> nations--for instance, where an oppressed people is con-
> cerned), which under specific circumstances and for a
> certain period run parallel in determinate areas with the
> interest of the proletariat, are exploited to the advantage of
> both. [12]

In the postscript to his essay on Lenin, Lukács repeats the
argument for the unity of Lenin's theoretical grasp of the political
nature of the imperialist epoch and his practical sense of proletarian politics. In trying to express the living nature of that
unity in Lenin's own life, he describes how Lenin would learn
from experience or from Hegel's LOGIC according to the situation,
preserving in himself the dialectical tension between particulars
and a theoretical totality. What Althusser fails to make clear is
how by turning to Hegel Lenin sought to find a way to avoid
making theory the mere appendage of State practice, while
reserving a more creative political role to practice than the retro-
active determination or revision of ideology. But this means that
Marxist materialism can never be the simple enforcement of
political will, any more than political will can be exercised without
a theoretical understanding of the specific class relations it presupposes. Thus Lenin remarks:

> The standpoint of life, of practice, should be first and
> fundamental in the theory of knowledge. . . . Of course, we
> must not forget that the criterion of practice can never, in
> the nature of things, either confirm or refute any idea
> completely. This criterion too is sufficiently 'indefinite' not
> to allow human knowledge to become 'absolute,' but at the
> same time it is sufficiently definite to wage a ruthless fight
> against all varieties of idealism and agnosticism. [13]

   12.   Georg Lukács, LENIN: a study on the unity of his thought, transl.
Nicholas Jacobs, London: NLB, 1970, p. 79.

   13.   Quoted in Alfred Schmidt, THE CONCEPT OF NATURE IN MARX, transl.
Ben Fowkes, London: NLB, 1971, pp. 118-119.

Of course in these later Hegelian formulations Lenin is modifying his own revision of Engel's dialectical materialism as set forth in MATERIALISM AND EMPIRIO-CRITICISM, thereby rejoining the challenge set to this work by Lukacs's own HISTORY AND CLASS CONSCIOUSNESS, as well as Karl Korsch's MARXISM AND PHILOSOPHY, both published in 1923. Lukács's essay on Lenin was published on the occasion of the latter's death in 1924. What died with Lenin was orthodox Marxism, although its dead hand was to be upon socialism for another thirty years or more. Orthodox scientific Marxism was completely undermined with Lukács's insight into the historically determined praxis of science. But while it is clear that scientific socialism was unready for Lukacs, the same must be said of the West, where only today is the critique of scientific praxis entering into a properly reflexive or critical social science. In HISTORY AND CLASS CONSCIOUS-NESS Lukács made it clear that living Marxism is inseparable from its idealist and Hegelian legacy. This split Russian and Central European Marxism. Today it is the core of neo-Marxist critical theory as developed by Horkheimer, Marcuse, and Adorno. What emerges from these developments is that the Hegelian concept of totality furnishes a matrix for the integration of ethics and politics through the restless dynamics of man's attempt to measure his existential circumstances against the ideal of his human essence, which he achieves through the struggle against self and institutional alienations. The Hegelian Marxist totality is thus the basis for the integral humanism of Marxist social science.[14]

These developments, whose complexity we can hardly pretend to have raised in any historical depth, are effectively 'purged' by Althusser's notions of an 'implicit' reading. That is to say, in taking account of Lenin's reading of Hegel between 1914 and 1916 Althusser argues that in effect Lenin stripped the LOGIC to its scientific core already arrived at in MATERIALISM AND EMPIRO-CRITICISM without the benefit of Hegel, except in as much as he had already read him in reading the first chapter of CAPITAL! Furthermore, the ultimate theoretical gain from this scientific 'purge' of the LOGIC is that the subject of CAPITAL is a process without a subject, namely, a structure and not a historical process of alienation.[15] Thus Althusser concludes by reversing Lenin's judgement that an understanding of CAPITAL is impossible without Hegel's LOGIC with the verdict: 'For a hundred and fifty years no one has understood Hegel! To understand Hegel one must have thoroughly studied and understood Marx's CAPITAL.'

14. See Chapter 6.

15. Louis Althusser, "Lénine devant Hegel" LENINE ET LA PHILOSOPHIE SUIVI DE MARX ET LENINE DEVANT HEGEL, Paris: Francois Maspéro, 1972.

According to Althusser, though this is hardly news and is certainly more Hegelian than he seems to think, the specificity of scientific Marxism lies in its theory of the overdetermination of social structures, which accounts for their features of simultaneous complexity and unity. Such 'structures' in dominance are the only proper referents of the notion of unity or totality in Marxist theory. The theory of the overdetermination of social structures, he argues, has nothing in common either with the Hegelian unity of essence and its alienated appearances or with the monistic causality of material determinism. The Hegelian unity relentlessly negates the differences that never exist-for-themselves and therefore can never determine any practical policy that could materially affect the development of the spiritual unity of its essence.

> My claim is that the Hegelian totality: (1) is not really, but only apparently, articulated in 'spheres'; (2) that its unity is not its complexity itself, that is, the structure of this complexity; (3) that it is therefore deprived of the structure in dominance which is the absolute precondition for a real complexity to be a unity and really the object of a <u>practice</u> that proposes to transform this structure: political practice. It is no accident that the Hegelian theory of the social totality has never provided the basis for a policy, that there is not and cannot be a Hegelian politics.[16]

Thus Althusser's structuralist redefinition of the theory of historical materialism, severed from its roots in Hegel and Feuerbach, serves to suppress the history of socialist theory that continuously reconnects in revolutionary ways with a Hegelian politics pitted against the alienation of socialist and capitalist rationality. The new context of socialist theory is the convergence of the processes of technical rationality and bureaucratic relations of production in industrial societies, capitalist or socialist. In this context the social sciences adopt cybernetics or synchronic models of social structure, on the analogue of the information processes that are the typical output, as well as input, of such systems. In other words, it is the production process of advanced industrial societies that, as Marcuse has argued, is thoroughly 'ideological.' The industrial ideology of both capitalist and socialist societies is predicated upon a technological rationality that ignores the substantive values of humanist reason. The technique of this denial is the suppression of history and the denial of Utopia. But history and Utopia are the roots of critical reason.

---

16. Louis Althusser, FOR MARX, transl. Ben Brewster, New York: Vintage Books, 1970, p. 204.

Althusser's reading of CAPITAL ignores the way Marx's meta-
economics structure CAPITAL as a <u>critique</u>. This means that
CAPITAL is not simply a scientific work produced by the distinction between essences and appearances. This would serve only to
separate it from common sense knowledge, but not from classical
economics. Nor is the distinction between essence and appearance
reducible to Marx's distinction between the ideological superstructure and its economic substructures. This again is a feature of
historical materialism that does not distinguish it from classical
sociology. <u>The critical question</u> in CAPITAL, but also in every
work of Marx, is how is it possible that the being who produces
everything should produce his own nonbeing? This question is
raised in CAPITAL as a question about the nature of the
historical and social distance between the absence of man and the
presence of man. Marx's method is clearly structuralist in his
analysis of the socioeconomic conditions of the absence of man,
i.e., the historical structure of surplus-value. But what makes
his theoretical grasp of the structures of suplus-value critical is
precisely its <u>historicist confrontation</u> between the order of
scientific <u>theory</u> and the social <u>praxis</u>, which produces scientific
knowledge in the course of its own dynamics. [17]

> While it may be said, therefore, that the categories of bour-
> geois economy contain what is true of all other forms of
> society, the statement is to be taken <u>cum grano salis</u>. They
> may contain these in a developed or crippled or caricatured
> form, but always essentially different. The so-called
> historical development amounts in the last analysis to this,
> that the last form considers its predecessors as stages
> leading up to itself and always perceives them from a single
> point of view, since it is very seldom and only under certain
> conditions that it is capable of self-criticism; of course, we
> do not speak here of such historical periods as appear to
> their own contemporaries to be periods of decay. The
> Christian religion became capable of assisting us to an objec-
> tive view of past mythologies as soon as it was ready for
> self-criticism to a certain extent, <u>dynamei</u>, so to speak. In
> the same way bourgeois political economy first came to under-
> stand the feudal, the ancient and the oriental societies as
> soon as the self-criticism of bourgeois society had com-
> menced. In as far as bourgeois political economy has not
> gone into the mythology of identifying the bourgeois system
> purely with the past, its criticism of the feudal system

    17. My conception of Marx's structuralism is similar to Godelier's view, al-
though not sharing either his agreement with Althusser of his view that the
diachronic shift between social structures is a matter only of scientific analysis
without benefit of Marx's humanism and historicism. Cf. Maurice Godelier,
"Remarques sur les concepts de structure et de contradiction," ALETHEIA, 4 (May
1966), pp. 228-236.

against which it still had to wage war resembled Christian criticism of the heathen religions or Protestant criticism of Catholicism. [18]

In this passage from Marx's discussion in the GRUNDRISSE of the method of political economy, we see that the notion of critique rests upon the transformation of a social order in which the new social system, for example capitalism, is the absent concept in the horizon of the mercantile practices still embedded in feudalism but seeking outlets in the towns, the nation-state, and Protestantism. [19]   The absence of man in the feudal world is framed in terms of the rationalist critique of authority and tradition that opens up the realm of individual conscience to gear with the new experience of society as a field of individual interest, subject only to market forces.   Under capitalism, the presence of man is the emergence of the individual and the absence of divinely ordained states.   It is just here, however, that the critique contained in CAPITAL reveals its full force by showing that the class structure of bourgeois individualism is precisely the absence of man as a human being.   Classical economics is therefore the direct expression of the absence of true humanism under capitalist conditions.   The impersonal laws of commodity production and exchange relationships conceal the specific class relations of production that make possible the simultaneity of exchange and exploitation, i.e., the expropriation of labor by capital.   Marx's critique of classical political economy, however, is not contained as such in the elaboration of the concepts of labor-value, exploitation, and surplus-value.   Nor is it wholly exhausted in the revelation of the specific historical and constitutional preconditions of the economic exchange between labor and capital as commodities. Marx's critique of political economy is essentially a humanist critique of the absence of man and his world-alienation produced through the subjectivization of the principle of property.

Under the guise of recognizing man, political economy, whose principle is labor, carries to its logical conclusion the denial of man.   Man himself is no longer in a condition of external tension with the external substance of private property; he has himself become the tension-ridden being of private property.   What was previously a phenomenon of being external to oneself, a real manifestation of man, has now become the art of objectification, of alienation.   This political economy seems at first, therefore, to recognize man with his independence, his personal activity, etc.   It incorporates

18.   Karl Marx, THE GRUNDRISSE, transl. and ed. David McLellan, New York: Harper and Row, 1971, p. 40.

19.   Karl Marx and Fredrich Engels, THE GERMAN IDEOLOGY, Moscow: Progress Publishers, 1964, Part 1.

private property in the very essence of man, and it is no
longer, therefore, conditioned by the local or national
characteristics of private property regarded as existing
outside itself. It manifests a cosmopolitan, universal activity
which is destructive of every limit and every bond, and
substitutes itself as the only policy, the only universality,
the only limit and the only bond. But in its further development it is obliged to discard this hypocrisy and to show
itself in all its cynicism. It does this, without any regard
for the apparent contradictions to which its doctrine leads,
by showing in a more one-sided fashion, and thus with
greater logic and clarity, that labor is the sole essence of
wealth, and by demonstrating that this doctrine, in contrast
with the original conception, has consequences which are
inimical to man. Finally, it gives the death-blow to ground
rent; that last individual and natural form of private
property and source of wealth existing independently of the
movement of labor, which was the expression of feudal
property but has become entirely its economic expression and
is no longer able to put up any resistance to political
economy. (The Ricardo School.)[20]

III

Every reading of history stands to be judged by history. This is
not the conclusion of a historical determinism, as it might seem,
but is rather a statement of the problematic of the philosophy of
history. It calls for an account of the relation between knowledge and action in which we must avoid both the scientism of
simplistic realism and the nihilism of subjective relativism, which
equally destroy the hermeneutic of reason in history. Marxist
rationalism is more than an epistemology because it is concerned
with the human meaning of knowledge, and is therefore always
critical with respect to the uses of science. At the same time
Marxism does not reduce knowledge to a class practice because
this would barbarize its humanist aims. We must avoid altogether
the idea that history is governed either by scientific laws or by
an occult logic that makes human events rational, whatever the
appearances. But this means we need a proper conception of
human knowledge and the historical space in which it unfolds.
Hegel and Marx between them have taught us that the human
spirit does not exist outside of history, any more than history
itself can unfold except as the externalization (Entäusserung) of
human subjectivity. Idealism and materialism are false alternatives. They fail to describe the constitution of historical space

        20.   Karl Marx, "Economic and Philosophical Manuscripts," in EARLY
WRITINGS, New York: International Publishers, 1964, p. 148.

as a praxis determined by the affinity of choices (<u>Wahlver-</u>
<u>wandtschaft</u>) men make in their economic, political and <u>religious</u>
lives. This is how we read Marx's conception of the subjectivization of the productive forces of nature into the master concepts
of <u>labor</u> in classical economics and of <u>faith</u> in the Protestant
religion.

> Engels is right, therefore, in calling Adam Smith the <u>Luther</u>
> <u>of</u> <u>political</u> <u>economy</u>. <u>Just</u> <u>as</u> <u>Luther</u> <u>recognized</u> <u>religion and</u>
> <u>faith</u> as the essence of the real <u>world</u> and for that reason
> took up a position against Catholic paganism; just as he
> annulled <u>external</u> religiosity while making religiosity the
> <u>inner</u> essence of man; just as he negated the distinction
> between priest and layman because he transferred the priest
> into the heart of the layman; so wealth external to man and
> independent of him (and thus only to be acquired and con-
> served from outside) is annulled. That is to say, its
> <u>external</u> and <u>mindless</u> <u>objectivity</u> is annulled by the fact that
> private property is incorporated in man himself, and man
> himself is recognized as its essence. But as a result, man
> himself is brought into the sphere of private property, just
> as, with Luther, he is brought into the sphere of
> religion. [21]

Thus the cultural pluralism that Althusser seeks to establish
through his 'culpable reading' of Marx lies there for any innocent
reader who has not burdened himself with Althusser's 'epistemological break' and its spurious separation of Marxist humanism
from Marxist science. The pluralism inherent in Marx's economic
and philosophical conception of capitalism is not the opposite of a
unified interpretation of history sought by Marxist social science.
But neither is it a covert appeal to the political independence of
the ideological superstructure that now determines socialist
history. On the contrary, the methodological pluralism in
historical materialism attest the solidarity of the realms of
economics, politics, law, and religion within a praxis that is a
qualitative relation between man, society, and nature. Thus a
Marxist reading of history is an initiation into the whole of human
history and all of its facets; it is, in short, a humanist education
(<u>Bildung</u>).

The problematic of Marxist theory is <u>not</u> the role of humanism in
Marxist science. On the contrary it is the role of Marxist science
in humanism. For humanism is not a science but a form of conduct. It is 'a reason <u>within</u> unreason', as Merleau-Ponty says.
Of course humanism remains an idle wish, a palace surrounded by
hovels, unless it joins with science and politics. But as we have

---

21. IBID., pp. 147-148.

learned from Weber, these are uneasy vocations for which science may teach us responsibility in the place of faith, but neither certainty nor the abandonment of hope, because the question of the meaning of human experience continuously transforms our history. Thus there can never be a science of history, but only a series of 'responsible readings' that are not entirely disjunctive because the human present does not leap out of the past any more than it faces the future as a void.

> There is no history where the course of events is a series of episodes without unity, or where it is a struggle already decided in the heaven of ideas. History is there where there is logic within contingence, a reason within unreason, where there is a historical perception which, like perception in general, leaves in the background what cannot enter the foreground but seizes the lines of force as they are generated and actively leads their traces to a conclusion. This analogy should not be interpreted as a shameful organicism or finalism, but as a reference to the fact that all symbolic systems--perception, language and history--only become what they were although in order to do so they need to be taken up into human initiative.[22]

Thus Marx himself understood that the 'mathematical' reading in the method of classical economics is dependent upon the axioms of continuity and exchangeability, or the algebra of money, which imposes an objective unity upon the subjective and social processes of alienation. The objectivism of classical economics is the truly 'culpable' reading of a historical and social system that Marx reads 'innocently' as the absence of man. But this means that Marx's critique of political economy is not based upon a literal reading in anything like the positivistic sense that Althusser intends with respect to CAPITAL. Marx's reading of classical economics, like Hegel's reading of the history of philosophy, is a phenomenology of the tradition of rationality, of the history of reason and unreason. Therefore the object of CAPITAL is not its topic, i.e., the analysis of the structures of surplus-value formation, but its objective, namely the recovery of the subjective axioms of objectification in alienated and nonalienated modes of expression. That is to say, Marx's theoretical enterprise is governed by a rationalist philosophy of history which determines positively and negatively the critical stages of human development. Thus the Marxist reading of history is essentially a violent reading in contrast to the mathematical reading of classical economics, whose vision is ultimately that of the stationary state in a world of surrounding misery and poverty. The violence of

---

22. Maurice Merleau-Ponty, "Materials for a Theory of History," THEMES FROM THE LECTURES AT THE COLLEGE DE FRANCE 1952-1960, transl. John O'Neill Evanston, Ill.: Northwestern University Press, 1970, pp. 29-30.

Marxism is the violence of the turning-points in human history. For the same reason, CAPITAL is not what Marx is writing <u>about</u>, because the sense of its analysis feeds off the next stage of human development. This only haunts the text in the language of moral criticism, but is essential to it, if we are to 'see through' the analysis to the form of life that socialism inscribes in the grammar of history through the vocabulary of revolution. The question that CAPITAL seeks to answer is: What is the human meaning of capitalism? It then proceeds to unfold this question in the grammar of structuralist economics. Through this procedure Marx uncovers the absence of man's human presence in the asceticism of the labor/capital exchange system that is implicitly made the unreal inversion of the ideal value of man for man.

Habermas has argued that Marx's phenomenology is inadequate because he reduced the synthesis of the moral and political grammar of the human ideal to the materialist synthesis of species reproduction.[23]   But this, of course, is the product of Habermas's own reduction of historical materialism, which creates the need to recover the absence of men by turning in part to Hegel and Freud. We shall consider this argument in the next chapter. The failure to read the absence of man in Marx's texts is itself a historical and political failure.[24]   This mode of reading is the method that is truly the enemy of the open society. It is the weapon of the Party with its back to history and the education of mankind. It destroys the myth of humanity that cannot be made a science, because science itself is dependent upon the humanist faith in Reason, however much science forgets its own history. Thus Althusser's scientism is the ultimate violence of an unhistorical reading of Marx in place of the authentic violence of a reading that is the necessity of the orientation of reason amid unreason.

23.   Jürgen Habermas, KNOWLEDGE AND HUMAN INTERESTS, transl. Jeremy Shapiro, Boston: Beacon Press, 1971, p. 42.

24.   Habermas himself provides for the conclusion in his essay "Toward a Theory of Communicative Competence," in RECENT SOCIOLOGY NO. 2, PATTERNS OF COMMUNICATIVE BEHAVIOR, ed. Hans Peter Dreitzel, New York: Macmillan, 1970. This essay in fact makes it necessary to remark that my specific criticism of KNOWLEDGE AND HUMAN INTERESTS is that it fails to recognize that the interest in autonomy and responsibility (Mundigkeit), which Habermas treats as the foundation of social and political dialogue, is in principle determined by a rationalist philosphy of history, as I have argued here.

CHAPTER 2

HABERMAS AND ALTHUSSER ON
THEORY AND CRITICISM IN MARX

Our times are characterized by a Marxism of fact and documentation which is in danger of becoming a revolutionary pastime if not
a contribution to the counterrevolutionary structure of repressive
communication which guarantees the success of liberal criticism.
If this is not to be the case, then surely the phenomenal expansion of the Marx business and the thriving academic careers
which it supports must provide a resource as well as an occasion
for reflection upon the nature of Marxist critique. For unless we
make Marx's own notion of critique thematic in the treatment of
his work we shall risk reducing its unity and development to the
contingencies of world politics and bibliographical discoveries
which make of Marx an intellectual dope and of Marxism nothing
but a series of historical and political pratfalls.

Here I shall be concerned with Habermas' argument[1] that Marx
is not sufficiently critical because he lacks an adequate concept of
reflection. I think I can answer this argument by showing that
the Hegelian and Marxist conceptions of critique are inseparably
tied to the ground of <u>embodied</u> <u>consciousness</u> and the reflexive
structures of <u>language</u>, <u>work</u> and <u>recognition</u>. Moreover, so far
as the unity of this conception is concerned, I think it can be
shown to be the generative principle of Hegalian phenomenology
and as such the legacy upon which Marx never ceased to draw.

I shall first try to defend the Hegel-Marx notion of critique
against the arguments of two critical theorists, Habermas and
Althusser. The latter is, of course, not usually considered a
critical theorist. But I would argue that Althusser's problematic[2], namely, the nature of Marxist 'theory', lies precisely
within the concerns of critical theory. I would then like to
conclude with some remarks on the problem of the unity or
totality of Marx's thought and the practice of Marxology in terms
of a more general phenomenological approach to theory and
criticism.

I shall argue for a notion of critique which derives the auspices
of theoretical reflection in the social sciences from Hobbes rather

---

1. Jürgen Habermas, KNOWLEDGE AND HUMAN INTERESTS, translated by
Jeremy J. Schapiro, London: Heinemann Educational Books, 1971.

2. Louis Althusser, FOR MARX, translated by Ben Brewster, New York:
Vintage Books, 1970. It is important to consult the glossary to the text for the use
of Althusser's basic concepts and his own interpretations of them.

than Kant, and from there to Hegel and Marx. I do not mean to
ignore Kant; that is hardly possible. But I mean to show that
there is a materialist as well as idealist source of critical theory.
From the outset then, my own argument makes an appeal to a
notion of critical reflection which is not to be decided and certainly can never be arrived at by reading texts in the ordinary
sense. The criteria for the latter activity are something else and
important enough in establishing the texts of Marx, for example,
given his manner of work and the stray history of his publication. But it is a mistake to imagine that the question of Marx's
own theoretical auspices can be established by stripping away all
other interpretations through an appeal to texts overlooked,
misconstrued, or only recently available. Now I cannot excuse
myself from this confusion. But I would now argue that there is
no escape from the phenomenon of the multiplicity of interpretations of Marx or Plato, or Christianity. The alternative is either
to regard the history of thought as a colossal error or else as a
gradual approximation to the truth in which everyone does his
bit, so that although the whole labor is Sisyphean, it is manage-
able and even pleasant in parts. Conventional criticism in this
case would amount to a series of minor labor disputes but not a
babel of tongues.

The problem which must be the concern of critical theory is its
reflexive awareness of the competing authoritative grounds for the
recommendation of its own procedures. What makes Hobbes,
Hegel, and Marx critical theorists is their awareness of the
essential ambivalence in the authoritative grounds of the corpus
of social science knowledge which takes individual interest as
axiomatic in the treatment of man and nature. This central
theme, which is generally known as the Hobbesian problem of
order, is set in the state of nature or civil society precisely
because these are the conditions which portray the ambivalence of
knowledge once a purely utilitarian conception of man and society
is projected as a daily practice. I believe Hobbes interposed a
divine fiat to solve the escalation of convention and the extreme
subjectivization of the bases of social order inherent in his vision
of the future of market society.[3] However, for a while at
least, the Hobbesian problem was largely determined by metaphysical pathos. Thus, Locke and Smith appeared to settle the

3. I am aware that this is a controversial assertion. Cf. A. E. Taylor, "The
Ethical Doctrine of Hobbes," and Stuart M. Brown, Jr., "The Taylor Thesis; Some
Objections," in HOBBES STUDIES, edited by Keith C. Brown, Oxford: Blackwell,
1965, pp. 35-55 and 57-71 respectively; as well as Michael Oakeshott, "The Moral
Life in the Writings of Thomas Hobbes," in RATIONALISM IN POLITICS AND OTHER
ESSAYS, London: Methuen, 1962, pp. 248-300; and Leo Strauss, THE POLITICAL
PHILOSOPHY OF HOBBES, Chicago: University of Chicago Press, 1963; Howard
Warrender, THE POLITICAL PHILOSOPHY OF HOBBES, Oxford: Clarendon Press,
1957.

corpus of utilitarian knowledge upon the principle of the identity
of interests, thereby launching the special sciences of psychology
and economics, though at the expense of politics and sociology.
So long as the authoritative grounds of the nature of theorizing
as _instrumental rationality_ held, then it provided for a self-
interested conception of man and of nature and society as
resources merely, or exchangeable utilities. In other words, the
instrumental auspices of the utilitarian corpus of knowledge determined its basically reductionist conception of the nature of society
and politics, strengthened by a nominalist epistemology which
cleared the ground for individual agency. So much is clear
(although, as we shall see, it is thoroughly obscured by
Habermas) from even a preliminary conception of what Marx
achieved in his critique of classical political economy and summarized in the theory of historical materialism. Moreover, it
cannot be sufficiently stressed that the only science Marx dealt
with critically was economics. Indeed, it is the principal contribution of what is called historical materialism to reveal critically
the theoretical grounds of utilitarian economics.

> Nor is it an accident that economics became an independent
> discipline under capitalism. Thanks to its commodity and
> communications arrangements capitalist society has given the
> whole of economic life an identity notable for its autonomy,
> its cohesion and its exclusive reliance on immanent laws.
> This was something quite unknown in earlier forms of
> society. For this reason, classical economics with its system
> of laws is closer to the natural sciences than to any
> other. . . . Its concern, as Engels put it, is with laws that
> are only understood, not controlled, with a situation in
> which--to quote Engels again--the producers have lost con-
> trol of the conditions of life of their own society. As a
> result of the objectification, the reification of society, their
> economic relations have achieved complete autonomy, they
> lead an independent life, forming a closed, self-validating
> system. Hence it is no accident that capitalist society be-
> came the classical terrain for the application of historical
> materialism. [4]

I remarked earlier that I considered Hobbes more important than
Kant in raising the question of the reflexive grounds of the
corpus of social science knowledge.[5] Let me elucidate that

    4. Georg Lukács, HISTORY AND CLASS CONSCIOUSNESS, Studies in Marxist
Dialectics, translated by Rodney Livingstone, London: Merlin Press, pp. 231-232.

    5. Although he focuses upon the problem of recognition, as I would call it,
and not the rational auspices of the corpus of social science knowledge, it is in-
teresting to find some support for my thesis in Fred R. Dallmayr, "Hobbes and
Existentialism: Some Affinities," THE JOURNAL OF POLITICS, XXXI, No. 3 (August
1969), pp. 615-640.

comment briefly before considering Kant's claim and the respective
arguments of Habermas and Althusser that Marx's positivism
undermines his own critical effort. What I take to be the basis of
the Hobbesian problem (why I do so must itself be open to reflection, and I shall return to this in my concluding remarks) is
Hobbe's awareness, his nasty vision, that the axiomatization of
individual interest had produced a conception of rationality which
made insoluble the problem of human recognition except through
such ironies as those of LEVIATHAN itself with its mechanical
metaphors and divine definitions. Indeed, the problem of recognition has remained endemic to the corpus of utilitarian knowledge
since Hobbes and has defined the problematic of social science
knowledge ever since. Thus, what makes Marx, Durkheim,
Toennies, and Weber, for example, classical theorists is their
preoccupation with this particular problematic. What would show
the differences between them would be the degree to which they
achieve a reflexive awareness of the primacy of the problem of
recognition in the determination of the role of knowledge in the
instrumental and ritual orders of conduct and society. I think
that while we probably owe more to Parsons for the categorical
distinctions involved, and for their analytic discrimination in the
history of classical social theory, his naïve instrumental conception of knowledge leads him to play down the classical problem of
recognition, of class struggle and alienation which have been
basically Marxian themes and thereby the concern of Durkheim
and Weber.

So much for a first indication of the way in which the problematic
of the authoritative grounds of the corpus of utilitarian knowledge, and specifically classical economics, is to be understood as
essentially a problem of the relation between the cognitive and
expressive interests in domination, recognition and freedom. In
other words, the crisis of the positivist sciences has always been
endemic to the utilitarian culture grounded in the authoritative
auspices of instrumental rationality.

Kant's questions, What can I know? What ought I to do? What
may I hope for? were raised from the very start in the tradition
of reflexive theorizing since Hobbes, precisely because such
questions are constitutive features of the culture through which
they arise. More precisely, modern society consists of these
questions which Kant settled by presuming upon the positivity of
science. Nor should we overlook that Kant's Copernican revolution competes with the Industrial and French Revolutions as
paradigmatic occasions for reflection upon the authoritative
auspices of the corpus of social and political knowledge. However

we read Kant,[6] Hegel and Marx could both argue that Kant's separation between the noumenal and phenomenal worlds made it impossible for him to discover the concrete historical mediations for the transvaluation of human practice. The limits of science are the limits of abstract space and time which are outside of human time and place whose synthetic unity is constituted by human presence, through memory of the past and the projection of a future. In short, science itself presupposes the historicity of mind as set out in Hegel's PHENOMENOLOGY. This does not mean, however, that scientific knowledge is not a major advent in the organization of human practice. But it can never furnish laws for human society of the same order as the scientific con- stitution of nature because of the distinctly reflexive features of human consciousness and its socially situated practices. Indeed, it is precisely the pretention of specific scientific rationalities, such as economics to separate themselves from other substantively rational modes of knowledge and interest which Marx attacked as ideology. Marx's distinction between the ideological superstruc- ture and the substructure of relationships of production is not a reductionist argument for the simple reason that what Marx is concerned with is <u>human production</u> which is <u>as such</u> rational and moral. But this means that every mode of production is simul- taneously a stage-specific mode of <u>domination</u> and <u>recognition</u>.[7] That is the critical core of the theory of historical materialism.

Nevertheless, Habermas has argued that whereas Hegel and Marx in their early work moved beyond Kant through the dialectic of recognition and its mediations in work and language, they respec- tively fell into the aberrations of the identity of absolute know- ledge and historical materialism. The result, according to Habermas, is that Marxism reduces the fundamental conditions for human emancipation and critical reflection to the mode of technical rationality and instrumental control. The error of this reduction is allegedly clear in Marcuse's attempts to discover a basis for critical theory in the face of the ideological nature of modern

6. Heidegger's reading of Kant would modify this judgment, putting greater stress on Kant's conception of the interplay between consciousness and the objects of experience. "Kant's questioning about the thing asks about intuition and thought, about experience and its principles, i.e., it asks about man. The question 'What is a thing?' is the question "Who is man?" That does not mean that things become a human product (<u>Gemachtes</u>), but, on the contrary, it means that man is to be understood as he who always already leaps beyond things, but in such a way that this leaping beyond is possible only while things encounter and so precisely remain themselves--while they send us back behind ourselves and our surface. A dimension is opened up in Kant's question about the thing which lies between the thing and man, which reaches out beyond things and back behind man." Martin Heidegger, WHAT IS A THING?, translated by W. B. Barton, Jr., and Vera Deutsch, Chicago: Henry Regnery Company, 1967, p. 244.

7. Karl Marx, ECONOMIC AND PHILOSOPHIC MANUSCRIPTS OF 1844, translated by Martin Milligan, edited with an Introduction by Dirk J. Struick, New York: International Publications, 1964, Estranged Labor.

technology and its social mode of repressive desublimation,[8] which appears to have becalmed any proletarian revolution.

Althusser, on the other hand, is concerned with the political and philosophical consequences of Marxism governed by the alternations of ideological humanism and positivistic material determinism which allegedly are the endemic regressions of Marxian theorizing.

It cannot be my purpose here to show how Marx developed his account of the manner in which the features of bourgeois civil society, the split between public and private action in the pursuit of utilitarian values and the organization of the social relations of production around given modes of production, are consistent with the ideological essence of private property and its possessive individualism.   The point that needs to be emphasized is that Marx's critical analysis is in no way outmoded by the findings, whether of Marcuse or Habermas, that the dominant mode of capitalist consciousness is now technical rationality.   The corporate organization of capitalism remains attached to a subjective agenda that simultaneously privatizes experience and dominates a multinational world environment in a manner which is not instrinsically different from the operation of capitalism first grasped by Marx in the ECONOMIC AND PHILOSOPHIC MANUSCRIPTS of 1844 and the COMMUNIST MANIFESTO OF 1847.

Marx's critique of classical economics, by challenging the authoritative auspices of instrumental rationality on moral grounds, revealed the categorical structure of land, labour, and capital, or rent, wages, and profits to be destructive of the human forms of language, work and community.   This is the sense of the paradox of the alienation of man through the universalization of his property of laboring which transforms the world and human nature itself into a calculus of being.

> The subjective essence of private property--private property as activity for itself, as subject, as person--is labour. It is therefore evident that only the political economy which acknowledged labour as its principle (Adam Smith), and which no longer looked upon private property as mere condition external to man--that it is this political economy which has to be regarded on the one hand as a product of the real energy and the real movement of private property. (It is a movement of private property become independent for itself in consciousness--the modern industry as Self.)-- as a product of modern industry--and on the other hand, as a force which has quickened and glorified the energy and

----

8.   Jeremy Shapiro, "From Marcuse to Habermas," CONTINUUM, VIII (1970), pp. 65-76.

development of modern industry and made it a power in the realm of consciousness. [9]

Marx, as we can see, was perfectly aware of the ideological and reflexive feature of modern industry constituted through the subjective auspices of labour and property. In the continuation of the passage I have just quoted, he concludes with a vision of the subjective grounds of capitalist property which is just as surely the intuition that later made Weber's fortune.

To this enlightened political economy, which has discovered within private property the subjective essence of wealth, the adherents of the money and mercantile system, who look upon private property only as an objective substance confronting men, seem therefore to be fetishists, Catholics. Engels was therefore right to call Adam Smith the Luther of Political Economy. Just as Luther recognized religion-- faith--as the substance of the external world and in consequence stood opposed to Catholic paganism--just as he superseded external religiosity by making religiosity the inner substance of man--just as he negated the priests outside the layman because he transplanted the priest into laymen's hearts, just so with wealth: wealth as something outside man and independent of him, and therefore as something to be maintained and asserted only in an external fashion, is done away with; that is, the external mindless objectivity of wealth is done away with, with private property being incorporated in man himself and with man himself being recognized as its essence. But as a result man is brought within the orbit of private property, just as with Luther he is brought within the orbit of religion. Under the semblance of recognizing man, political economy, whose principle is labour, rather carries to its logical conclusion the denial of man, since man himself no longer stands in an external relation of tension to the external substance of private property, but has himself become this essence of private property. What was previously being external to oneself--man's externalization in the thing--has merely become the act of externalizing--the process of alienating. [10]

Habermas traces the defects in Marx's conception of social theory to a relapse on the part of both Hegel and Marx with respect to Kant's critical achievement of revealing the antinomy of certain knowledge and the irrationality of its content. Kant himself was unable to grasp the nature of the historicity of knowledge and action which is the ground of the antinomy of rational knowledge.

9. ECONOMIC AND PHILOSOPHIC MANUSCRIPTS of 1844, p. 128

10. IBID, pp. 128-129.

This was Hegel's contribution, revealing the weakness of Kant's positivist assumption of the certainty of Newtonian science. Hegel's development of Kant consists in his conception of critical knowledge as the historical genesis of self-reflexive knowledge in the context of the cultural formation of the human species. Kant started from the positive a priori of an unhistorical subject whose cognitive formation is axiomatically that of Newtonian science. The weakness of the tradition of doubt from Descartes to Kant, as Hegel sees it, is that the tradition of methodical doubt is removed from the dialectical life of the self-knowledge of reason determined by specific historical praxes, and thus falls inevitably into the positivist assumptions of a specific category of knowledge, namely, science. Ultimately then, Kant's critical theory remains phenomenologically naïve from Hegel's standpoint because it fails to raise the question of the practice of science in itself to a question for us as reflexive theorists of human knowledge and practice. Hegel's transcendental phenomenology, unlike Kant's, is thus a wholly historical reconstruction of the processes of individual development, the universalization of the history of mankind, and the reflection of the cultural forms of absolute mind in religion, art, and scientific knowledge.

Habermas's remarks on the transition from Hegel to Marx are important for their difference with Althusser over the significance of Marx's THESES ON FEUERBACH. At the same time, Habermas introduces his own version of an epistemological disjunction--in this case with critical theory--within the ECONOMIC AND PHILO-SOPHIC MANUSCRIPTS, which results in Marx's progressively positivist conception of social theory. In the first thesis on Feuerbach, Marx corrected previous materialist theories with the Hegelian comment that materialism overlooks that objects are the product of human praxis. But then, according to Habermas, Marx understood praxis solely as the 'process of material exchange', without any relation to other symbolic syntheses, in particular, ideology, science, and politics. 'On the one hand', he says,

> Marx conceives of objective activity as a transcendental accomplishment; it has its counterpart in the construction of a world in which reality appears subject to conditions of the objectivity of possible objects of experience. On the other hand, he sees this transcendental accomplishment as rooted in real labour (Arbeit) processes. The subject of world constitution is not transcendental consciousness in general but the concrete human species, which reproduces its life under natural conditions. That this 'process of material exchange' ('Stoffwechselprozess') takes the form of processes of social labour derives from the physical constitution of this

natural being, and some constants of its natural environment.[11]

Habermas succeeds in cutting off Marx from critical theory by
reducing the synthesis of symbolic structures contained in the
theory of historical materialism to a crude form of technological
and biological determinism.   Once again, it would be tedious to
marshal texts for this criticism.   To put it as sharply as possible, let us simply say that Habermas' argument involves reading the ECONOMIC AND PHILOSOPHIC MANUSCRIPTS in a totally
reductive sense, that is to say, as a literally materialist synthesis
of economics and philosophy! The result of Habermas' materialist
reduction is to deprive Marx's conception of the critique of
political economy of any claim to constitute critical theory.[12]
As Habermas presents it, historical materialism is a strictly
materialist synthesis achieved solely at the level of the material
production and appropriation of products.   Habermas is clear
enough that Marx regarded nature as a category of human praxis,
and that Marx is in this sense more Kantian than materialist.
'But nature . . . taken abstractly, for itself--nature fixed in
isolation from man--is nothing for man.[13] But he reduces the
transcendence of human praxis to the invariant relation of the
species of a tool-making animal to its natural environment, despite
the historical restructuring of that relation through ideological
critique and class-conscious revolutionary action which together
constitute what Marx understood by historical materialism.   By
insisting that Marx tied the reflexivity of social science knowledge
to the system of instrumental action, Habermas is able to argue
that historical materialism lacks any adequate conception of critical
theory and rests ultimately on a positivist epistemology.

Thus in Marx's works a peculiar disproportion arises between
the practice of inquiry and the limited philosophical self-
understanding of this inquiry.   In his empirical analyses
Marx comprehends the history of the species under
categories of material activity and the critical abolition of
ideologies, of instrumental action and revolutionary practice,
of labour and reflection at once.   But Marx interprets what
he does in the more restricted conception of the species'
self-reflection through work alone.   The materialist concept
of synthesis is not conceived broadly enough in order to
explicate the way in which Marx contributes to realizing the

11.   KNOWLEDGE AND HUMAN INTERESTS, p. 27.

12.   Lest my argument seem to rely too much on the early writings, whereas
Habermas draws freely from early and later writings, see Marx's discussion of the
method of political economy in THE GRUNDRISSE, edited and translated by David
McLellan, New York: Harper and Row, Publishers, 1971, pp. 33-35; 65-69.

13.   ECONOMIC AND PHILOSOPHIC MANUSCRIPTS OF 1844, p. 19.

intention of a really radicalized critique of knowledge. In
fact, it even prevented Marx from understanding his own
mode of procedure from this point of view.[14]

Habermas and Althusser arrive by different paths at the same
conclusion with respect to Marx's faulty grasp of the nature of
critical theory. In the case of Habermas, the question is whether
we need to accept his reductionist account of the materialist
synthesis.[15] Similarly, we shall need to question whether
Althusser's positive interpretation of historical materialism as a
theory of the overdetermination of social structures really adds
anything to Marx. With respect to both critics we shall have to
ask whether the different ways in which each professes to complement Marx's conception of economics with a theory of politics,
allegedly lacking in Marx, constitutes the full development of
critical theory needed to ground Marx's conception of the relation
between philosophy and praxis.

Although Habermas does not explicitly confront the question of
the significance of Marx's ECONOMIC AND PHILOSPHIC MANU-
SCRIPTS, his interpretation of certain passages, and the progression which he derives from them, is tantamount to a stand on
the debate which they have inspired and allows for a comparison
between himself and Althusser. If Habermas is right, there can
be no question of any critical role for the ECONOMIC AND
PHILOSOPHIC MANUSCRIPTS with respect to the industrial praxis
of socialist society because the only critique contained in them is
the substitution of an instrumentalist or pragmatic theory of
knowledge for Hegelian idealism. It follows that Marx could not
formulate any critical reflection upon the status of the natural
sciences in relation to the science of man called for in the
MANUSCRIPTS, because Marx insisted on reducing human science
to the positivist study of the laws of social development along the
path of human emancipation.

Having stripped Marx's argument of its political framework,
Habermas then argues that the materialist synthesis needs to be
combined with a moral synthesis of critical-revolutionary action.
Thus Habermass succeeds in separating Marx from Hegel to point
out the necessity of rejoining Marx with Hegel in order to produce an adequate critical theory. A number of comments are
called for with regard to these two moves. In the first place,
Habermas suppresses the connection between Marx's analysis of

14. KNOWLEDGE AND HUMAN INTERESTS, p. 42.

15. For a nonreductionist account of Marx's critical theory see Trent Schroyer,
"Toward a Critical Theory for Advanced Industrial Society," RECENT SOCIOLOGY
No. 2, edited by Hans Peter Dreitzel, New York: The Macmillan Company, 1970,
pp. 210-234.

alienation and class struggle, which is pervasive of the early writings, central to the ECONOMIC AND PHILOSOPHIC MANU-SCRIPTS and never set apart either in the GRUNDRISSE of CAPITAL, not to mention the COMMUNIST MANIFESTO, which deserves more serious consideration than that of a pamphlet. But Hegel fares no better in Habermas's hands when it comes to putting Marx and Hegel together again. Whereas it is obvious that the dialectic of recognition is central to the PHENOMEN-OLOGY OF MIND, Habermas insists upon restricting its role to Hegel's early theological and political writings. Thus we have a very special version of the young Hegel and young Marx, each separated from the totality of their respective corpus.[16] It is on the basis of this reading of the Hegel/Marx relationship that Habermas formulates his own claim to a comprehensive critique of social science knowledge:

> Unlike synthesis through social labour, the dialectic of class antagonism is a movement of reflection. For the dialogic relation of the complementary unification of opposed subjects, the re-establishment of morality, is a relation of <u>logic</u> and of <u>life</u> <u>conduct</u> (<u>Lebenspraxis</u>) at once. This can be seen in the dialectic of the moral action developed by Hegel under the name of the <u>struggle</u> <u>for</u> <u>recognition</u>. Here, the sup-pression and renewal of the dialogue situation are recon-structed as a moral relation. The grammatical relations of communication, once distorted by force, exert force them-selves. Only the result of dialectical movement eradicates this force and brings about the freedom from constraint contained in dialogic self-recognition-in-the-other; in the language of the young Hegel, love as reconciliation. Thus, it is not unconstrained intersubjectivity itself that we call dialectic, but the history of its repression and re-establishment. The distortion of the dialogic relation is subject to the causality of split-off symbols and unified grammatical relations; that is, relations that are removed from public communication, prevail only behind the backs of subjects, and are thus empirically, coercive.[17]

16. The "existentialist" reading of Hegel destroys the unity of the PHENO-MENOLOGY OF MIND and the basic complementarity of Hegel's corpus with Marx's work. See Ch. 6.

17. KNOWLEDGE AND HUMAN INTERESTS, pp. 58-59. Actually, Habermas's complete theory also depends upon making Freud's notion of surplus repression the real basis of the revolutionary-critical theory of communication. Since it would require another essay to deal with this argument, I can only cite the passage in which Habermas gives everything to surplus repression and nothing to Marx's theory of the historical structures of surplus value. "Marx was not able to see that power and ideology are distorted communications, because he made the assumption that men distinguished themselves from animals when they began to produce their means of subsistence. Marx was convinced that at one time the human species elevated itself above animal conditions of existence by transcending the limits of animal intelligence and being able to transform adaptive behavior into instrumental action. Thus what

It would be tiresome to document the misinterpretations and fundamental alteration introduced by Habermas into the relation-ship between Hegel and Marx. Indeed, in general I prefer to document more intensively the arguments of Habermas and Althusser, respectively, since I imagine these are frequently more difficult to many than the notorious Hegel and Marx. All the same, I cannot simply counter in a declarative way that Habermas's improvement upon Hegel and Marx is superfluous, any more than I think this of the questions raised for Marxian theory by Althusser. On the contrary, I think both are adding babies to the Marxian bathwater which then becomes even more and not less essential to their displacement. The fundamental question, then, is the critical status of the theory of historical materialism. Habermas argues that Marxian social theory reduces the nexus of communicative interaction to instrumental action, which is then understood to determine reflection ideologically, so that critical theory is nothing but a critique of ideology lacking any positive phenomenological basis for a science of man and human value. According to Habermas, 'Marx did not develop this idea of the science of man. By equating critique with natural science, he disavowed it. Materialist scientism only reconfirms what absolute idealism had already accomplished: the elimination of epistemology in favour of unchained universal "scientific knowledge"--but this time of scientific materialism instead of absolute knowledge.[18]

Habermas's conclusion must be confronted at least briefly with an attempt to formulate the theory of historical materialism as a critical expression of the antinomy of the mathematical and value

interests him as the natural basis of history is the physical organization specific to the human species under the category of possible labor; the tool-making animal. Freud's focus, in contrast, was not the system of social labor but the family. He made the assumption that men distinguished themselves from animals when they succeeded in inventing an agency of socialization for their biologically endangered offspring subject to extended childhood dependency. Freud was convinced that at one time the human species elevated itself above animal conditions of existence by transcending the limits of animal society and being able to transform instinct-governed behavior into communicative action. Thus what interests him as the natural basis of history is the physical organization specific to the human species under the category of surplus impulses and their canalization: the drive-inhibited and at the same time fantasizing animal. The two-stage development of human sexuality, which is interrupted by a latency period owing to Oedipal repression, and the role of aggression in the establishmen of the superego make man's basic problem not the organization of labor but the evolution of institutions that permanently solve the conflict between surplus impulses and the constraint of reality. Hence Freud does not investigate primarily those ego functions that develop on the cognitive level within the framework of instrumental action. He concentrates on the origins of the motivational foundation of communicative action. What interests him is the destiny of the primary impulse potentials in the course of the growing child's interaction with an environment, determined by his family structure, on which he remains dependent during a long period of upbringing." IBID., pp. 282-283. See "Review Symposium on Habermas," PHILOSOPHY OF THE SOCIAL SCIENCES, volume 2, No. 3, September 1972.

    18. IBID., p. 63.

concepts of nature governing bourgeois natural science, which through the institution of the reification of commodities and human relationships furnishes the model of classical economics. Of course, such an interpretation involves the rejection of Engels' much disputed positivistic formulation of historical materialism. The passages which I quoted earlier from the ECONOMIC AND PHILOSOPHIC MANUSCRIPTS are fundamental to the revelation of the subjective sources of the massive objectivity of commodity production and the laws of economics. Furthermore, they illustrate the dependency of the ontological abstraction of exchange values upon the subjective reduction of human nature to the single value of labor. The other side of this, clearly, is the implicit theory of value, that is to say, of human nature and social organization, contained in the notion of use-value and its historical production.[19] Marx's critique of classical political economy is methodologically in no way below the level of reflexive critical theory. It rests upon the same intuition of the limited nature of the formal presuppositions of objective knowledge. But instead of bringing its argument to bear on mathematics or physics, it deals with the science of economics and the relativity of the institutional arrangements that make the natural sciences an analogue for economics. The error contained in Engels' positivist endorsement of scientific praxis is that he overlooks the alienation of objectivity separated from its subjective sources in the historical decision to treat nature, as Heidegger would say, 'mathematically',[20] an error, which Marx and Engels made patent when it came to the status of the economics laws of capitalist society. In other words, Marx and Engels ordinarily were very clear that the 'objectivity' of capitalist conduct depended upon the reification or alienation of the motives for accumulation and class oppression internalized as the objective basis for situated vocabularies of economic action. Thus, between Adam Smith and Hegel the subject of historical action is latent with the dialectical possibility of the humanization of nature as the larger project, into which the naturalization of man enters as a necessary secondary but alienated structure. This is the final positive conclusion of the ECONOMIC AND PHILOSPHIC MANU-SCRIPTS and it remains the philosophical underpinning of all of Marx's work which is inseparable from his critique of political economy.

Industry is the actual, historical relationship of nature, and therefore of natural science, to man. If, therefore, industry is conceived as the _exoteric_ revelation of man's

19. Lezek Kolakowski, "Karl Marx and the Classical Definition of Truth," in his TOWARD A MARXIST HUMANISM, Essays on the Left Today, translated from the Polish by Jane Zielonko Peel, New York: Grove Press, Inc., 1968, pp. 38-66.

20. WHAT IS A THING?, B I, 5.

essential process, we also gain an understanding of the
human essence of nature or the natural essence of man. In
consequence, natural science will lose its abstract material--
or rather, its idealistic--tendency, and will become the basis
of human science, as it has already become the basis of
actual human life, albeit in an estranged form. One basis
for life and another basis for science is a priori a lie. The
nature which develops in human history--the genesis of
human society--is man's real nature, hence nature as it
develops through industry, even though in an estranged
form, is true anthropological nature.[21]

With these last remarks I should now turn to Althusser's argument which is raised in the first instance, obviously, by my
insistence on the unity and significance of Marx's early works and
thus the denial of any effective epistemological break (coupure
epistémologique).[22] I do not intend to respond to Althusser's
argument over the epistemological break in Marx by means of a
fresh analysis of the sequence of Marx's texts.[23] This is in
part because, despite its length, Althusser's own argument is
only apparently so derived and is in reality much more dependent
upon the larger question of the Marxian problematic[24] and the
relation between theorizing and ideology which, for the rest, joins
with my own broad concern with the reflexive grounds of the
corpus of social science knowledge.

Althusser's FOR MARX is concerned with the 'critical death' of
Marxist philosophy in the Soviet Union and the French Communist
Party, the latter's milieu being as narrowly construed as to allow
for no references to Kojéve, Jean Wahl, Jean Hyppolite, or
Maurice Merleau-Ponty and only scant remarks on Sartre's
CRITIQUE DE LA RAISON DIALECTIQUE.

Perhaps most glaring is Althusser's silence with respect to the
works of Lukács and Korsch, both available in French and thus
once again central to the present argument. Korsch's MARXISM
AND PHILOSOPHY, as well as Lukács HISTORY AND CLASS
CONSCIOUSNESS of course, make patent Althusser's strange
combination of critical theorizing and theoretical regression. But,
once again, it is hardly to the point to cite different textual
sources against Althusser, for this no longer responds to the
sense of the grounds of theorizing, which I want now to invoke

21.   ECONOMIC AND PHILOSOPHIC MANUSCRIPTS OF 1844, pp. 142-143.

22.   FOR MARX, p. 249.

23.   For Althusser's organization of Marx's writings around the epistemological
break of 1845, see IBID, pp. 33-38, 256-257.

24.   IBID., pp. 51-86, 253-254.

in a final understanding of the notion of critique. This would require that we display our differences with Althusser as conjunctures of biography and politics, that is to say, as essays in the phenomenology of mind, determined retrospectively yet committed to the human contingency.

Althusser's own conception of his earlier approach to Marxist theorizing is self-consciously aware of the positivist fallibility which subtly pervades the concept of Marxist critique based upon the scientific reduction of its philosophical auspices. He states this in the following introspection in which we need to sense the interweaving of philosophical beginnings with Marx's own youthful proclamation of the death of philosophy.

So we contorted ourselves to give philosphy a death worthy of it: a philosophical death. Here again we sought support from more texts of Marx and from a third reading of the others. We proceeded on the assumption that the end of philosophy could not but be critical, as the sub-title of CAPITAL proclaims that book to be of Political Economy: it is essential to go to the things themselves, to finish with philosophical ideologies and to turn to the study of the real world-- but, and this we hoped would secure us from positivism, in turning against ideology, we saw that it constantly threatened 'the understanding of positive things', besieged science and obscured real characteristics. So we entrusted philosophy with the continual critical reduction of the thread of ideological illusions, and in doing so we made philosophy the conscience of science pure and simple, reduced it completely to the letter and body of science, but merely turned against its negative surroundings that could reduce them to nothing. Thus philosophy was certainly at an end, but it survived none the less as an evanescent critical consciousness for just long enough to project the positive essence of science on to the threatening ideology and to destroy the enemy's ideological phantasms, before returning to its place amongst its allies. The critical death of philosophy, identified with its evanescent philosophical existence, gave us at last the status and deserts of a really philosophical death, consummated in the ambiguous act of criticism. Now philosophy had no fate other than the consummation of its critical death in the recognition of the real, and in the return to the real, real history, the progenitor of men, of their acts and their thoughts. Philosophy meant retracing on our own account the Young Marx's critical Odyssey, breaking through the layer of illusion that was hiding the real world from us, and arriving at last in our native land: the land of history, to find there at last the rest afforded by reality and science in concord under the perpetual vigilance of criticism. According to this reading, there

could no longer be any question of a history of philosophy;
how could there be a history of dissipated phantasms, of
shadows traversed? The only history possible is that of
reality, which may dimly arouse in the sleeper incoherent
dreams, but these dreams, whose only continuity is derived
from their anchorage in these depths, can never make up a
continent of history in their own right. Marx said to himself
in THE GERMAN IDEOLOGY: 'Philosophy has no history.'
When you come to read [my] essay 'On the Young Marx' you
will be able to judge if it is not still partly trapped in the
mythical hope for a philosophy which will achieve its
philosophical end in the living death of a critical consciousness. [25]

Who has not read Marx this way? All that separates us from
Althusser, surely, is only his ulterior motives in locating this
Promethean reading of Marx in CAPITAL, instead of throughout
Marx from the time of his dissertion, ON THE DIFFERENCE
BETWEEN THE DEMOCRITEAN AND EPICUREAN PHILOSOPHY OF
NATURE. Is there, then, no progression in Marx's thought?
There is indeed; and on this Althusser has written with very
genuine phenomenological insight, if I may say so without inten-
tion to convert. Let us leave aside Althusser's ulterior motive,
namely, his desire to stem the tide of revisionism since the
Twentieth Party Congress, although this may be a suggestion
which is thoroughly inimical to the unity of theory and praxis.
However that may be, Althusser's arguments for the specificity of
Marxist theory can just as well be treated in terms of his proposed 'reading' of the shift in the problematic of Marx's thought
which makes for a radical separation between its ideological
humanism and its theoretical formulation of the historical structures of overdetermined contradictions. [26] This epistemological
break, as Althusser calls it, represents a decisive departure from
Marx's early dependence upon Hegel's critique of bourgeois civil
society, as well as Feuerbach's materialistic critique of Hegel
which so enchanted Marx and Engels prior to the GERMAN
IDEOLOGY, when they 'settled' their philosophical consciousness.
Actually, Althusser wants to argue that the young Marx 'was
never strictly speaking a Hegelian', and that the first dependency, so obvious, I would think, in the dissertion and the
ECONOMIC AND PHILOSOPHIC MANUSCRIPTS, belongs only to
the very early period of his 'disordered' consciousness, and then
only functioned to produce the 'prodigious "abreaction"' required
for its dissolution. To be exact, according to Althusser, Marx's
philosophical consciousness was first Kantian-Fichtean and then

25. FOR MARX, pp. 29-30.

26. IBID., pp. 200-216, 255.

Feuerbachian, that is to say, ideological until 1845 and thereafter scientific.

The potential regression of Marxist theory arises more than anything else from its interpretation in terms of the Hegelian notion of unity or totality. In this respect Althusser's argument is far below the level of Habermas's treatment of the relation between Hegel and Marx. However, Althusser also argues, as does Habermas, that there is a permanently positivist deficiency in Marx's concept of social theory and that there is a critical necessity to revive Marxist philosophy without which the demise of theoretical Marxism or its subordination to political opportunism is a certainty.

According to Althusser, though this is hardly news, and is certainly more Hegelian than he seems to think, the specific theoretical advance which belongs properly to Marx is his theory of the overdetermination of social structures which accounts for their features of simultaneous complexity and unity. Such 'structures in dominance' are the only proper referents of the notion of unity or totality in Marx's thought. Marx's theoretical advance in the analysis of social structures allows us to account for the relative autonomy of superstructures while nevertheless attributing determination in the last instance to the substructure, according to the overdetermination or value-added effect of the specifically antagonistic or nonantagonistic contradictions which dominate the system at any stage of its development. The theory of the overdetermination of social structures has nothing in common, therefore, with the Hegelian unity of essence through its alienated appearances or with the monistic causality of material determinism. The Hegelian unity relentlessly negates differences which never exist for themselves and therefore can never determine any practical policy which would materially affect the development of the spiritual unity of the Hegelian essence. 'My claim', argues Althusser,

> is that the Hegelian totality: (1) is not really, but only apparently, articulated in 'spheres'; (2) that its unity is not its complexity itself, that is, the structure of this complexity; (3) that it is therefore deprived of the structure in dominance (structure à dominante) which is the absolute precondition for a real complexity to be a unity and really the object of practice that proposes to transform this structure: political practice. It is no accident that the Hegelian theory of the social totality has never provided a basis for a policy that there is not and cannot be a Hegelian politics. [27]

27. FOR MARX, p. 204.

It hardly bears comment that a simplistic theory of economic determinism makes an enigma of the whole notion of Marxist political practice. What does deserve to be noticed is that Althusser's attribution of the theory of structural overdetermination to Marx, which is easily enough found in Marx, is derived much more from a gloss on Lenin's political practice, that is to say, it harks back to a time when Soviet political and economic life had not yet frozen in the grip of Party dictatorship. However, I shall return to Althusser's interpretation of Lenin's political philosophy in my concluding remarks on critical biography.

I should now take up Althusser's more important plea, whatever its derivation, for a reflexive theoretial awareness or philosophical consciousness in Marxism. It is the role of theory, he aruges, to formulate problems which already exist in Marxian political practice. However, a theoretical transformation requires a genuine theoretical labor in which there is an advance in knowledge and simultaneous critique of illusions. Thus it is the proper task of reflexive theory to examine the conditions which constitute the validity of its relevance to political practice, i.e., the transformation of social relations, or to economic practice, i.e., the production of goods and services. Now it is essential to recognize that theory itself qua theoretical practice falls among the economic, political, and ideological practices to which it is relevant. As such, theoretical practice includes ideological and prescientific theoretical practices, as well as scientific knowledge. It is therefore the specific task of theoretical practice to advance by means of distinct epistemological breaks with prescientific and ideological practices, in which it generally inheres. The explicit consciousness of the transformation of the domains of knowledge is what Althusser calls theory:

> So theory is important to practice in a double sense: for 'theory' is important to its own practice directly. But the relation of a 'theory' to its practice, in so far as it is at issue, on condition that it is reflected and expressed, is also relevant to the general Theory (the dialectic) in which is theoretically expressed the essence of theoretical practice in general, and through it the essence of the transformations, of the 'development' of things in general.[28]

Whereas Feuerbach denounced the speculative illusion in Hegel, Althusser argues that the essence of Marx's critique of Hegel is that Hegel denies the reality of theoretical practice, i.e., the genuine labor of the Notion. Thus, Hegel inverts the order of autogenesis between the levels of abstract and concrete reality,

28. FOR MARX, p. 169 and the qualification of this definition of Theory in the glossary, p. 256.

reducing the concrete generalizations of experience to the purely ideological universality of the Idea. However, Marx understood that the transformations of the concrete generalizations of fact or experience (Generality I) require particular theoretical transformations (Generality II) of the special sciences in order to be raised to the level of knowledge or science (Generality III). For these reasons, it is absolutely essential that Marx's theoretical advance over Hegel not be expressed as the <u>inversion</u> of Hegel's dialectical method, for this would leave Marxian theoretical practice essentially ideological and cut its roots with political intervention or the joining of knowledge and freedom.

> To sum up: if we recognize that scientific practice starts with the abstract and produces a (concrete) knowledge, we must also recognize that Generality I, the raw material of theoretical practice, is qualitatively different from Generality II, which transforms it into 'concrete in thought', that is, into knowledge (Generality III). Denial of the difference distinguishing these two types of Generality and ignorance of the priority of Generality II (which works) over Generality I (which is worked on), are the very bases of the Hegelian idealism that Marx rejected: behind the still ideological semblance of the 'inversion' of abstract speculation to give concrete reality or science, this is the decisive point in which the fate of Hegelian ideology and Marxist theory is decided. The fate of Marxist theory, because we all know that the deep reasons for a rupture--not the reasons we admit, but those that act--will decide for ever whether the deliverance we expect from it will only be the expectation of freedom, that is, the absence of freedom, or freedom itself.[29]

We see then that both Habermas and Althusser find Marxian theory liable to a positivist regression from which it can be rescued only by a critical conception of theorizing able to deal with the relative autonomy of symbolic and communicative structures. The source of these criticisms lies in the concern with the one-dimensionality of experience in industrial societies, whether capitalist or socialist, which forces an ideological unity of theory and practice that threatens to absorb genuine critique. The problem here, I suggest, is that of the end of history in the sense that the corporate economy, on the one hand, and the Party bureaucracy, on the other, destroy the space-time coordinates of genuine political action, dialogue, and criticism. But these are the essential elements of political life, the enduring Hellenic ideal which pervades Hegel's thought and Marx's ideal of the Commune. Althusser is able to twist these theoretical

29. IBID., pp. 191-192.

developments around the notion of <u>historical delay</u>[30] by which
he means that Marx, Engels, and Lenin, as well as Lukács and
Gramsci, were all philosophically premature in their views. The
same concept, according to Althusser, allows us to understand
that the union of Marxian theory with the workers' movement was
likewise premature for previous stages of socialist history. In
each case the deviations involve the attempt to push philosophy
ahead of Marxist science. However, Althusser will render justice
where history denied it by reinstating the philosophical and
political unity of Lenin's thought! The rest of Althusser's argument can only be summarized. It results in the reduction of
philosophy to the zero point of the epistemological intervention
contained in the eleventh thesis on Feuerbach: 'Die Philosophen
haben die Welt nur verschieden <u>interpretiert</u>; es kommt darauf
an, sie zu <u>verändern</u>.' Althusser interprets this thesis to
deprive philosophy of any proper domain. Having lost its one-
sidedness, philosophy acquires the task of representing the class
struggle in the realm of <u>theory</u> (the theoretical systems of particular sciences). Thus philosophy is neither (critical) theory
nor science, but a political-theoretical intervention of behalf of
the interests of the class struggle, a

> pratique sauvage au sens où Freud parle d'une analyse
> sauvage, qui ne fournit pas les titres théoriques de ses
> operations, et qui fait crier la philosophie de 'l'interpreta-
> tion' du monde, qu'on peut nommer philosophie de la dénéga-
> tion. Pratique sauvage tant qu'on voudra, mais qu'est-ce
> qui n'a pas commencé par être sauvage?[31]

We have reached two opposing conclusions as to the nature of
political life and the role of critical theory. Althusser returns
theory to the savage practice of the Hobbesian state which provided the very occasion for political theorizing. Habermas, on
the other hand, returns to the moral dialectic of recognition as
the framework of a theory of political dialogue and communication.
In each case what we witness is an appeal to different theoretical
grounds in the determination of the corpus of social science
knowledge. The argument has proceeded in terms of a variety of
interpretations of Marxian social theory and its Hegelian sources,
including my own attempt to display historical materialism as a
critique of the 'mathematical' auspices of classical political economy
and its imputations of individual conduct and social order.

Althusser argues that it will not do to display a variety of interpretations of man's thought, or of the corpus of social science

30. Louis Althusser, LENINE ET LA PHILOSOPHIE, Paris: François Maspero,
1969, pp. 30-31.

31. IBID., p. 55.

knowledge, as though there were any stage that was ideologically neutral. The development of social science thought must be determined by its own internal problematic, i.e., to understand its answers we must understand the <u>question</u> of <u>its questions</u>. That question is always the question posed to knowledge by its times--or the problem of order and recognition, as we have called it, determined according to the specificity of its historical and political context. But I think that 'the question of its questions' for social science knowledge is also a biographical question which determines each theorist's conception of the bases of order and recognition. Thus, the task of critical theory is the recognition of the processes of individual as well as social self-formation (<u>Bildung</u>). For this I believe Hegel's PHENOMENOLOGY OF MIND still serves as a paradigm of the integration of the structures of biological, social, and libidinal values which constitute the human project. It is this Hegelian legacy which is the treasure of Marxist critical theory. I hold Hegel in this regard for the reason that it was he who took over Hobbes's vision of man's bodily organization and its competitive felicity and built its capacities of reason, fear, and speech into a covenant with the whole of humanity and not just a convenient article of peace in an essentially unstable social order.

The differences I have referred to in the interpretations of Marx, must, as I have said earlier, be treated as problematic. Not, of course, in the sense that they invite despair over the trained stupidity of commentators. Such a reaction would not simply be unkind; it leaves totally unresolved what it is to read a text. Although I have disagreed with Althusser's procedures with respect to Marx, I do believe, that apart from its restriction to Marxist theory, the following statement of Althusser's expresses superbly the intentionality of criticism.

> That this definition (of Marxist theory) cannot be <u>read</u> directly in Marx's writings, that a complete prior critique is indispensable to an identification of the location of the real concepts of Marx's maturity; that the identification of the location of the real concepts of Marx's maturity; that the identification of these concepts is the same thing as the identification of the location of the real concepts of Marx's maturity; that the identification of these concepts is the same thing as the identification of their location; that all this critical effort, the absolute precondition of any interpreta-tion, in itself presupposes activating a minimum of pro-visional Marxist theoretical concepts bearing on the nature of theoretical formations and their history, that is, a theory of epistemological history, which is Marxist philosophy itself; that this operation in itself constitutes an indispensable circle in which the application of Marxist theory to Marx

himself appears to be the absolute precondition of an understanding of Marx and at the same time as the precondition
even of the constitution and development of Marxist
philosophy, so much is clear. But the circle implied by this
operation is, like all circles of this kind, simply the dialectical circle of the question asked of an object as to its
nature, on the basis of a theoretical problematic which in
putting its object to the test puts itself to the test of its
object. That Marxism can and must itself be the object of
the epistemological question, that this epistemological question can only be asked as a function of the Marxist
theoretical problematic, that is necessity itself for a theory
which defines itself dialectically, not merely as a science of
history (historical materalism) but also and simultaneously as
a philosophy, a philosophy that is capable of accounting for
the nature of theoretical formations and their history, and
therefore capable of accounting for itself, by taking itself as
its own object. Marxism is the only philosophy that
theoretically faces up to this test.[32]

The intentionality of criticism, as I see it, is a structure of
reading and writing, of second-order speech, which is never a
simple correction of what was said but a contribution in the same
direction of meaning through which the critic memberships his
own sense of a text in a community of truth. The anonymity of
knowledge is in this sense never a goal but a means only of the
establishment of truth. Hence disputes, errors, persuasions, and
corrections are never neutral, for what is at stake is the claim to
embed in a community of knowledge. Of course, none of this is
acceptable to the one-world epistemologists who look upon Marxism
and its squabbles as the latest or most widespread of human
follies. But this overlooks that the claim to truth is a call to the
freedom of the other and is inseparable from its dialogic constitution. That is why we read and think and talk and argue--not
endlessly but because of the inexhaustible depth and variety of
human culture to which we are always latecomers.

In terms of these general remarks, we can look upon the differences between Althusser, Habermas, and myself, as well as our
intellectual development, revisions, and the like, as different
institutions of a community of knowledge determined by theological, political, and sociological valencies which alternate between the extraversion of method and the introversion of self-
understanding. These are not simple contradictions; we never
cease to make of our moods objective frameworks and these in
turn never hold without enthusiasm. This is the hermeneutic
circle within which the question of the unity, youthfulness, and
maturity of Marx's thought, arises only as the question of the

32. FOR MARX, pp. 38-39.

significance of the life of <u>any</u> thinker.   For there is no privileged
standpoint from which either Marx himself or ourselves as inter-
preters could see or fail to see what he had in mind, except as
the production of its sense within this same hermeneutic circle
and the conjucture of meaning and facticity which makes it
impossible for us ever to foreclose upon its sense.   But that is
the very same thing as the opening of thought or the opportunity
it provides each of us for our inscription, our place in work of
the culture of truth, beauty, and justice, which is the determinate opening of philosophy to practice.

CHAPTER 3

MARXISM AND MYTHOLOGY:
PSYCHOLOGIZING CAPITAL

It seems incredible that anyone could read CAPITAL and overlook
the moral vision which furnishes the driving energy for such a
colossal documentation and analysis of the conditions of unau-
thentic existence in industrial, capitalist society. Yet it is
argued that if Marx was a social scientist, as most Marxists claim
for him, then he cannot have been a moral philosopher. Indeed,
many Marxists themselves have thought that a moral philosophy
had no part in scientific socialism. But gradually a certain
disenchantment with the political experience of socialism has
produced a number of attempts to rejuvenate Marxist metapolitics
with fresh interpretations of the original humanism of Marx.[1]
The current revolution of the philosophical framework of Marxian
thought, however, is seriously prejudiced by the view that
Marxian social philosophy is speculative in the worst sense, a
view compounded by a method of pseudopsychological explanation.
The latter approach is perhaps best developed in Professor R. C.
Tucker's treatment of philosophy and myth in Marx,[2] which
likewise provides inspiration for the comparison of Marx's
intellectual achievement with that of the drama of St Paul's vision
on the road to Damascus.[3]

It would not be difficult to show that Marx's sociological analysis
of religion is not on the same level as the phenomenon it treats.
Similarly, even if one were to grant the similarity between the
subsequent fate of Marx's writings and the tendency of original
religious teachings to become dogmatized in the process of institutionalization, one could easily show the difference between
religious teachings, written or unwritten, and Marx's studies in
the fields of economics, sociology, and political history. But in
practice the characterization of Marxism as a religious phenomenon
rarely goes beyond the level of metaphors which are not adequate
to the phenomenon of religion itself, let alone Marxian social
science. The serious basis of the attempt to denigrate the status
of Marxian social science rests ultimately upon an epistemological
argument, and it is at this level that it must be engaged.

1.   Daniel Bell, 'The Rediscovery of Alienation,' JOURNAL OF PHILOSOPHY,
LVI, no. 24 (November 1959), 933-952.

2.   R. C. Tucker, PHILOSOPHY AND MYTH IN KARL MARX' New York:
Cambridge University Press, 1961.

3.   Louis J. Halle, 'Marx's Religious Drama,' ENCOUNTER, XXV, No. 4
(october 1965), 29-37.

Tucker assumes that Marxism is not a scientific theory. It is in
part a philosophy and in greater part a myth. In so far as it is
philosophical, theoretical Marxism is concerned with the ethical
problem of good and evil. But, according to Tucker, Marx
cannot be classified as a moral philosopher because he fits no
obvious category in the history of Western philosophy. Marx is
at best a moralist, one concerned with good and evil, but never
in terms of a systematic inquiry into the nature of the supreme
good considered as problematic. Marx is, so we are to believe, a
moralist opposed to moral philosophy. Accordingly, Marx can be
understood only as a 'moralist of the religious kind.' Such is the
nature of the philosophical element in Marxian social theory. But
this element is outweighed by the mythical component in Marxism.

Tucker's theory of the nature of myth and, consequently of
Marxian social theory, its that 'something by nature interior is
apprehended as exterior, that a drama of the inner life of man is
experienced and depicted as taking place in the outer world.' By
contrast with myth, the attitude of philosophy is to represent
external processes as developments of an inner self. This is
exemplified in Hegel's introjection of the world-spirit and Marx's
critical substitution of a human species-self in place of the
Absolute Spirit. But Marx proceeds to mythologize his philosophical intuition by projecting onto the external world his image
of the human species-self and by going on to explain the
dynamics of self-alienation in terms of supposedly external social
forces of alienation.

> Whereas philosophy had once arisen against a background of
> myth, here myth arose against a background of philosophy--
> the Hegelian philosophy. A phenomenology of spirit, in
> which the world was consciously represented as a subjective
> process of realization of a world-self, became first a new
> phenomenology in which Marx pictured the world as a pro-
> cess of realization of a human species-self. This was done
> consciously and without mystification, and original Marxism
> remained fundamentally on the ground of philosophical
> thought. At a decisive point in it, however, Marx made the
> transition to the mythic mode of thought. The subjective
> process of Entfremdungsgeschichte was embodied in an image
> of society.[4]

It should be noticed that this argument allows only two methods
of interpreting reality. The philosophical method, allegedly is to
explain outside events in terms of internal (mental) events.
Internal events are presumably understood through the method of
introspective or philosophical psychology. The procedure of myth

4. R. C. Tucker, PHILOSOPHY AND MYTH IN KARL MARX, p. 219.

is to conceive internal (mental) events in terms of outside events. Tucker seems to consider the status of the external world as essentially mind dependent. However, his use of the concept of myth indicates that the external world cannot be taken as a dumping ground for any and all contents of the mind or psyche. Yet, no criteria are offered for distinguishing which mental events are, in his words, 'by nature interior' and, consequently, not useful for interpreting external events. The view seems to be that reality, more particularly social reality, can be interpreted only in terms of the intentional concepts of individual psychology. The attempt to explain social and individual behavior in terms of sociological concepts is mistaken for the reason that such concepts can be shown through a nominalist analysis to be figments of the individual imagination, unreal entities projected onto the external world and vainly employed to explain individual behavior. In turn, the explanation of this sort of conceptual behavior is, quite simply, that it is pathological.

It is argued that Marx substituted for the Hegelian Absolute Spirit a collective, human species-self, 'alienated man writ large.' So long as Marx saw the world through the jaundiced eyes of alienated man, he had the merit of being a philosopher. He would, of course, have benefited from a little nominalist therapy. But, essentially, his subjective view of the world offered the chance of rehabilitation. Apparently, however, Marx regressed at a certain stage of his logical analysis. On the basis of a personal decomposition, Marx proceeded to polarize his concept of man into two antagonistic selves, 'the infinitely greedy, despotic, exploiting, vicious, werewolf-self of capital (Kapitalseele) on the one hand, and the exploited, enslaved, tormented, rebellious, productive self of labor on the other.'[5] Even at this stage, Marx might have patched up his philosophy with the admission of a more varied psychology of human motivation. But Marx turned away from the possibilities of philosophical psychology into myth--the projection onto the social scene of his own image of a divided, self-alienated man.

> This is Marx's myth of the warfare of labour and capital. It is through and through a moralistic myth, a tale of good and evil, a story of struggle between constructive and destructive forces for possession of the world. Its underlying moral theme is the theme of original Marxism: man's division against himself and dehumanization under the despotism of greed, and his final emancipation of himself and his productive activity from this despotism by the seizure of the alienated world of private property. The conflicting subjective forces of creativity and the will to infinite self-aggrandizement are seen and shown as class forces clashing

5. IBID., pp. 220-221.

across the battleground of society.[6]

Tucker argues that CAPITAL is based upon an entirely mytho-
logical psychology of the capitalist and his relation to labor,
documented by Marx in terms of a partial selection of economic
fact and detail. The question is whether the mythical personality
attributed to the capitalist is a figment of Marx's mind or of
Tucker's own mind. Marxian social science starts from the
premise that there is a legitimate level of sociological generalization and a nonfetishistic employment of group theoretical constructs. Max Weber, while remarking on the danger of assigning
causal efficacy to reified concepts, nevertheless concedes the
heuristic value of certain of the Marxian categories of sociological
analysis.[7] In his early writings, Marx criticized the errors of
conceptual reification in the Hegelian System.[8] Yet, it is
argued that Marx's mature theory is entirely dominated by a
fetishistic or, as Tucker would have it, an alienated con-
ceptualism.

The starting point of Marx's investigation of social phenomena is
that individual behavior, quite apart from the perceptions and
intentions of the individuals concerned, is part of a structured or
systematic order. It is the task of the social scientist to provide
a theoretical interpretation of the phenomenon of social order.
From this point of view Quesnay's TABLEAU ECONOMIQUE is the
great landmark of the social sciences.[9] As Marx acknowledged,
the basic analytic intuition of the circular flow of economic life--
the demonstration of how each economic period becomes the basis
of the next, not only technologically but as a stage in a process
of social reproduction solved by the exchanges between individual
acts of production and consumption--is the permanent achievement
of the physiocrats.

> Every child knows that if a country ceased to work, I will
> not say for a year, but for a few weeks, it would die.
> Every child knows too that the mass of products correspond-
> ing to the different and quantitatively determined masses of
> the total labour of society that this necessity of distributing
> social labour in definite proportions cannot be done away

6. IBID., p. 222.

7. Max Weber, THE METHODOLOGY OF THE SOCIAL SCIENCES, Glencoe,
Illinois: Free Press, 1949, p. 103.

8. P. Kahn, 'Société et état dans les oeuvres de jeunesse de Marx,' CAHIERS
INTERNATIONAUX DE SOCIOLOGIE, V (1949), 165-74; M. Rubel, 'Notes on Marx's
Conception of Democracy,' NEW POLITICS, I, No. 2 (Winter 1962), 78-90.

9. Joseph Schumpeter, ECONOMIC DOCTRINE AND METHOD, London: Allen
& Unwin, 1954, chap. II; Marx to Engels, London, 6 July 1863, SELECTED COR-
RESPONDENCE 1846-1895, New York: International Publishers, 1934.

with by the <u>particular</u> <u>form</u> of social production, but can only change the <u>form</u> <u>it</u> <u>assumes</u>, is self-evident. No natural laws can be done away with. What can change in changing historical circumstances, is the form in which these laws operate. And the form in which this proportional division of labour operates, in a state of society where the interconnection of social labour is manifested in the private exchange of the individual products of labour, is precisely the exchange value of these products.[10]

The Marxian labor theory of value expresses both the quantitative and the qualitative features of the laws determining the distribution of productive effort in a commodity-producing society.[11] In its quantitative or economic aspect, the labor theory of value is essentially general equilibrium theory which summarizes the forces integrating (a) the exchange ratios between commodities, (b) the quantity of each produced, and (c) the allocation of the labor force to the various branches of production. Qualitatively, the labor theory of value expresses the exchange relationships between commodities as a social relationship based upon the historical phenomena of the existence (i) of a developed social vision of labor, and (ii) private production.

Marx argues that it is not possible to express the workings of the law of value apart from the specification of a set of sociological middle principles. The procedure in CAPITAL is to construct a model of simple commodity production, that is, an economy of independent producers each owning his own means of production. The labor theory of value expresses the general equilibrium conditions for this special case.[12] Marx then varies the institutional features of his model of simple commodity production. The ownership of the means of production is concentrated into the hands of a class of capitalists, and labor itself becomes a commodity subject to the laws of exchange value. Marx's conclusion that exchange ratios in the case of capitalist production are ultimately determined according to the labor theory of value is, as is well known, the most controversial feature of Capital.[13] Whatever the case, Marx showed that the social order which classical economics took for granted was a violent order created

10.   Marx to Kugelmann, London, 11 July 1868, SELECTED CORRESPONDENCE.

11.   Paul M. Sweezy, THE THEORY OF CAPITALIST DEVELOPMENT, New York: Monthly Review Press, 1956, chaps. II and III; K. Marx, CAPITAL, Chicago: C. H. Kerr, 1909, Vol. III, chap. LI.

12.   Oscar Lange, 'Marxian Economics and Modern Economic Theory,' REVIEW OF ECONOMIC STUDIES II (1934-1935), 189-201.

13.   Ronald L. Meek, STUDIES IN THE LABOUR THEORY OF VALUE, London: Lawrence & Wishart, 1956.

by a process of radical social upheaval and enforced by 'iron laws.' Tucker's account of CAPITAL entirely ignores its nature as a piece of economic analysis. However, the economic content of CAPITAL cannot be passed over or simply attributed to Marx's casual empiricism.

Tucker deprives himself of an understanding of the analytic achievement of CAPITAL because the construct of an economic process or order is, by the standards of methodological individualism, an illusion. Marx's method is to show the operation of the laws of classical economic theory to be dependent upon a particular historical constellation definable in terms of a set of sociological and psychological middle principles.[14] It is in the transition from a simple-commodity-producing society to a capitalist mode of production that the psychology of the capitalist is engendered.

Let us consider Marx's general schema of the development of capital and capitalist psychology.

> The simple circulation of commodities--selling in order to buy--is a means of carrying out a purpose unconnected with circulation, namely, the appropriation of use-values, the satisfaction of wants. The circulation of money as capital is, on the contrary, an end in itself, for the expansion of value takes place only within this constantly renewed movement. The circulation of capital has therefore no limits. Thus the conscious representative of this movement, the possessor of money becomes a capitalist. His person, or rather his pocket, is the point from which the money starts and to which it returns. The expansion of value, which is the objective basis or main-spring of the circulation M-C-M, becomes his subjective aim, and it is only in so far as the appropriation of ever more and more wealth in the abstract becomes the sole motive of his operations, that he functions as a capitalist, that is, as capital personified and endowed with consciousness and a will. Use-values must therefore never be looked upon as the real aim of the capitalist; neither must the profit on any single transaction. The restless never-ending process of profit-making alone is what he aims at. This boundless greed after riches, the passionate chase after exchange-value, is common to the capitalist and the miser; but while the miser is merely a capitalist gone mad, the capitalist is a rational miser. The never-ending augmentation of exchange-value, which the

14. Adolph Löwe, ECONOMICS AND SOCIOLOGY, London: Allen & Unwin, 1935, pp. 138-139; K. Marx, Capital, Vol. III, 947-949, 966-968.

miser strives after, by seeking to save his money from circulation, is attained by the more acute capitalist, by constantly throwing it afresh into circulation.[15]

Under the sociological conditions of individual ownership of the means of production economic activity is motivated by the desire to satisfy wants. However, where the means of production are the property of a class of capitalists, economic activity is divided into the need of a laboring class to sell itself as a commodity in order to subsist and the imperious drive of the capitalist class to accumulate.

An economic system of some sort is a functional prerequisite of any society. The capitalist system is simply one historical variant of the economic order. According to Marx, capitalism is defined by specific property relations with respect to the ownership of the means of production. It is the socioeconomic system described by the term 'capitalism' which provides a structural focus for behavior oriented toward acquisition, accumulation, and profit-making. The so-called profit motive is not primarily a psychological disposition. It is a socially acquired goal which is given within the framework of a sociological situation, namely, commercial and industrial capitalism. 'We have to grasp the essential connection between private property, avarice, and the separation of labor, capital, and landed property; between exchange and competition, value and the devaluation of men, monopoly, and competition, etc.; the connection between this whole estrangement and the money system.'[16]

Marx's definition of the sociological situation (capitalism) which provides the matrix for the orientation toward profit concentrates attention upon the property relations or class positions with respect to the means of production. It may be that Marx's definition of capitalism is more relevant to historical rather than analytic features of a capitalist system.[17] Weber's analysis of the prerequisites of the capitalist system stresses the importance of the rationalization of accounting, technology, law, and the permanent enterprise. But neither Marx nor Weber considered the spirit of capitalism to be a basic feature of human nature.[18] The Protestant ethic, 'an unconsciously refined organization for

15. Karl Marx, CAPITAL, I, 169-171.

16. Karl Marx, ECONOMIC AND PHILOSOPHIC MANUSCRIPTS OF 1844, Moscow: Foreign Languages Press, 1959, p. 68.

17. Rally Dahrendorf, 'A Sociological Critique of Marx,' CLASS AND CLASS CONFLICT IN INDUSTRIAL SOCIETY, Stanford, California: Stanford University Press, 1959, chap IV.

18. Max Weber, GENERAL ECONOMIC HISTORY, trans. F. H. Knight, Glencoe, Illinois: Free Press, 1950, pp. 355-356.

the production of capitalist individuals' (Weber) provided the economic ethos at a particular juncture of the political and social history of industrial capitalism. The later stage of monopoly capitalism which has given rise to the phenomenon of the affluent society appears to have abandoned the Protestant ethic in favor of a consummatory ethic.[19]

In CAPITAL Marx provided a documented critique of the psychology and ethics of capitalism. Marx's method is to demonstrate that the psychological element which appears to be the driving force of capitalism, and is consequently rationalized in terms of the Judaeo-Protestant ethic, is in fact dependent upon a definite historical and sociological constellation defined by the class division of property relations.

> But in the course of historical evolution, and precisely through the inevitable fact that within the division of labour social relationships take on an independent existence, there appears a division within the life of each individual, in so far as it is personal and in so far as it is determined by some branch of labour and the conditions pertaining to it. (We do not mean it to be understood from this that, for example, the rentier, the capitalist, etc., cease to be persons, but their personality is conditioned and determined by quite definite class relationships, and the division appears only in their opposition to another class and, for themselves, only when they go bankrupt).[20]

Individual psychology is the dependent variable in the definition of a sociological situation, such as the nineteenth-century family, or capitalism. The functional design of these latter sociological systems acts selectively upon the motivation of the individual members so that their behavior, whatever its individual significance, though there will be considerable endemic convergence, contributes to the maintenance of these institutional systems as such. Thus Marx demonstrated, for example, that in a commodity-producing society, despite independent and uncoordinated decisions about production and sales, there results not a chaos but an order which is expressed in the operation of the law of value.

> Since these [individual capitalists] meet one another only as owners of commodities, and every one seeks to sell his

---

19. 'The Puritan ethos was not abandoned. It was merely overwhelmed by the massive power of modern merchandising,' J. K. Galbraith, THE AFFLUENT SOCIETY, Boston: Houghton Mifflin, 1958, p. 200.

20. Karl Marx, THE GERMAN IDEOLOGY, New York: International Publishers, 1947, Parts I and III, p. 76.

commodity as dearly as possible (being apparently guided in the regulation of his production by his own arbitrary will), the internal law enforces itself merely by means of their competition by their mutual pressure upon each other, by means of which the various deviations are balanced. Only as an internal law, and from the point of view of the individual agents as a blind law, does the law of value exert its influence here and maintain the social equilibrium of production in the turmoil of its accidental fluctuations.[21]

In any society there is an economic order. But under capitalism, the social equilibrium of production is maintained through the working of a 'blind' law. However, with certain changes in the relations of production and ownership of the means of production (the socioeconomic aspect of socialism) the 'blind' operation of the law of value would be replaced by the principles of rational economic planning.[22] The latter is a principal ingredient in the ethical formula of socialism. Thus, Marx is not saying that the functional autonomy of social institutions is an ethical imperative. Quite the contrary, the social framework of individual action should in fact be subject to the conscious control of its members. The difficulty for Marx was to express the ethical requirement that social institutions not obstruct the goal of achieving an authentic individual existence without falling into the errors of naive rationalism and the contractual formula of psychologistic individualism.[23] In practice, Marx often preferred to give greater stress to the institutional determinants of individual behavior rather than express himself in the psychologistic style of liberalism. He did so because his intuition of the ethical problem is deeper than that of bourgeois individualists.

The division between the personal and the class individual, the accidental nature of the conditions of life for the individual, appears only with the emergence of class, which is itself a product of the bourgeoisie. This accidental character is only engendered and developed by competition and the struggle of individuals among themselves. Thus, in imagination individuals seem freer under the dominance of the bourgeoisie than before, they are less free, because they are more subjected to the violence of things.[24]

21. Karl Marx, CAPITAL, III, 1026.

22. IBID., I, 90-91.

23. Karl Marx and Fredrich Engels, THE HOLY FAMILY OR CRITIQUE OF CRITICAL CRITIQUE, Moscow: Foreign Languages Publishing House, 1956, pp. 162-163.

24. Karl Marx, THE GERMAN IDEOLOGY, p. 77.

Tucker prefers to read CAPITAL as an allegorical tale of good and evil in which all the metaphors are drawn from economic theory and twisted into an insane theology.

> This [capital] is an economic concept in name only. The word comes from Adam Smith and the political economists; the idea, from Hegel and the world of German philosophy. Marx's KAPITAL is just as much a citizen of this world as, for example, Shopenhauer's WILLE or Nietzsche's WILLE ZUR MACHT, with which it has obvious affinities. But the immediate affiliation of the idea is Hegelian. The absolute Bereicherungstrieb is a translation in economic terms of the drive to infinite self-enrichment that Hegel ascribes to spirit, which is insatiably greedy to appropriate all things cognitively as 'property of the ego' and thus to assert its power over them. The Hegelian dialectic of aggrandizement, whereby spirit is driven to infinitize itself in terms of knowledge, reappears in Marx's mature thought as dialectic of the self-expansion of capital--a movement of self-infinitizing in terms of money.[25]

When one considers Tucker's interpretation of German idealist philosophy since Kant, one can only feel that he has fallen victim to his own mixture of myth and metaphor.[26] His summary of German idealism as a self-infinizing movement is meant to describe the phylogenesis of Marx's own neurotic conception that man is motivated by a drive for infinite self-aggrandizement in terms of wealth. German philosophy between Kant and Hegel is read in terms of the Faust theme. Now Marx considered that the romantic projections of the irreducible self concept of the Kantian epistemology are part of a neurotic literature not, as Tucker argues, because they conflict with the conceptions of biblical literature but because they lack an adequate sociological content.[27] Tucker seems to be willing to recognize that there is a certain moral advance in Feuerbach's view that man's business is not to deify himself but simply to reappropriate the full potential of his human nature, once the problem of God has become a dead issue. Tucker argues, further, that this is the position of original Marxism, with the difference that Marx considered Feuerbach's critical cognitive act an inadequate solution to the problem of alienation. But in the THESES ON FEUERBACH, Marx

---

25. Tucker, OP. CIT., pp. 213-214.

26. On the relation of German idealist philosophy to Protestant theology, see P. Asveld, LA PENSEE RELIGIEUSE DU JEUNE HEGEL: LIBERTE ET ALIENATION, Louvain: Publications Universitaires de Louvain, 1953; G. M. M. Cottier, L'ATHEISME DU JEUNE MARX: SES ORIGINES HEGELIENNES, Paris, J. Vrin, 1959.

27. Karl Marx, THE GERMAN IDEOLOGY, pp. 32, 50-51.

states his own argument that the problem of alienation is a sociological problem which requires practical political intervention for
its treatment.

Tucker's view is that Marx and Feuerbach were on the right
track so long as they considered the phenomenon of alienation
as a self problem. It was Marx who mythologized the psychological results when he projected the internal conflicts of his own
alienated self onto the social scene. What constitutes the shift
from original Marxism to mature Marxism is the sociological projection of an original intuition of psychological conflict. Moreover,
Marx himself suspected that the phenomenon of alienation might be
due more to man's 'own infamy' than to the complex of class and
property relationships in the production process. Apparently,
Marx later struggled to suppress the psychological interpretation
of capitalism by introducing as a principle of interpretation the
maxim that the individual psychic structure is patterned upon the
structure of external social relations. In the later writings, the
so-called profit motive or acquisitive instinct is to be considered
an element in the definition of a specific socioeconomic situation,
namely, competitive capitalist accumulation. But Tucker argues
that Marx in fact contradicted himself on this very point. In the
ECONOMIC AND PHILOSOPHIC MANUSCRIPTS OF 1844 Marx had
argued that the driving force, the ethic, of bourgeois political
economy is greed and the war between the greedy, namely,
competition. In his later writings, Marx's position changed to the
view that competition, as a market phenomenon, cannot be explained in terms of psychological motives. On the contrary the
existence of acquisitive behavior, which may be explained teleolo-
gically by a variety of ad hoc purposes, is structurally dependent
upon its function in maintaining the market situation. The fact of
the matter here is that Marx was well aware of the capitalist ethos
which Weber later described in his PROTESTANT ETHIC AND THE
SPIRIT OF CAPITALISM. Moreover, while they may have disagreed as to the short run, Marx and Weber agree that, in the
long run, the Protestant ethic is the dependent variable in the
relationship with capitalism. But Tucker's view is that Marx must
have been uncomfortably aware that the entire structure of
CAPITAL was dependent upon the postulate of infinite greed as
the driving force of capitalist production. Tucker then comments
upon what is in fact his own brain child as follows: 'To suggest
that this (the postulate of infinite greed) could be derived from
the competitive mechanism itself was a way of minimizing the total
dependence of the system upon a highly questionable postulate,
and at the same time of reinforcing the postulate.'[28] But this
rather doubtful psychological postulate of Marxism was deduced,
it should be remembered, from Tucker's analysis of German
idealism which we have discussed above.

28. Tucker, OP. CIT., p. 217.

We now consider the argument that the genuine philosophical element in Marxism is the moral concern with the phenomenon of self-alienation. Marx, we are to believe, located the source of self-alienation in a self-infinitizing movement, which he named KAPITAL but which in the Judeo-Christian tradition is ordinarily called the sin of pride. Marx's mistake was to believe that man's disease of the infinite is a fact either of religion or economics. The disintegration of the self as a result of taking either God or Henry Ford as one's ego ideal is certainly in individual cases a matter for the psychiatrist. Tucker argues that even where considerable numbers of people break down under similar illusions this never becomes more than a statistical phenomenon of individual psychology.[29] The evil lies within ourselves. It is never a social problem. To imagine otherwise, as Marx did, is to create a political myth.

It is frequently asserted that historical materialism lacks an adequate psychological theory.[30] It is argued, for example, that in order to escape psychologism Marx regressed to conceptual fetishism, using economic theory rather than philosophy or theology to foist a new alienated ideology upon the world.[31] Marx, however, was aware for critical purposes of the nominalist position that it is individuals who act and not institutions, social trends, or laws that 'act' upon individuals. Indeed, this was the principle Marx employed to attack the conceptual realism which characterized idealist historiography. "It is not 'history' which uses men as a means of achieving--as if it were an individual person--its own ends. History is nothing but the activity of men in pursuit of their ends."[32] At the same time, Marx did not advance a psychologistic explanation of social phenomena in terms of a contractual or rationalistic means--end model.

29. Tucker, OP. CIT., pp. 239-240.

30. 'The Marxist theory of motivation developed within this framework [historical materialism] has two components. The first emphasizes the role of purely external pressures on individuals: force, fraud and compulsion. The second begins with a concept of class interests,' N. Birnbaum, 'Conflicting Interpretations of the Rise of Capitalism: Marx and Weber,' BRITISH JOURNAL OF SOCIOLOGY, IV (June 1953), p. 130. Birnbaum's argument that Weber supplies the psychological analysis of the rationalization of economic life which Marx simply attributed to the 'immanent laws of capitalist development' overlooks that Marx in fact derived the Protestant or bourgeois ethic from the literature of the classical economists, as we have pointed out above.

31. L. D. Easton, 'Alienation and History in Early Marx,' PHILOSOPHY AND PHENOMENOLOGICAL RESEARCH XXII, no. 2 (December 1961), 193-205. Marx's critique of psychologism is recognized by one of his most hostile critics as Marx's major contribution to social science (see K. P. Popper, 'The Autonomy of Sociology,' THE OPEN SOCIETY AND ITS ENEMIES, New York: Harper and Row, 1963, Vol. II, chap. XIV).

32. Karl Marx, SELECTED WRITINGS IN SOCIOLOGY AND PHILOSOPHY, trans. and ed. T. B. Bottomore and M. Rubel, London: Watts & Co., 1956, p. 63.

It would be naïve, of course, to underestimate the difficulty raised for the social sciences, Marxian or not, by the question of the nature of the mechanism of interaction between the sociological and psychological aspects of behavior.[33]   Nevertheless, there are two notable attempts to account for individual psychology in Marxian terms.[34]   In his early writings, Erich Fromm attempted to explain the mechanism by which the individual introjects the sociological determinants of behavior.   The individual libidinal structure is shaped by influences in the family which is in turn located in the social class structure which shapes its economic life chances.[35]   In a complementary way, Herbert Marcuse has emphasized the nature of work as the medium through which the individual introjects the performance principle, that is, the dominant reality principle.[36]   Any form of society requires a modification of the instinctual expression of individuals in view of the basic necessity of work and the social division of labor involved in any working society.   However, according to Marcuse, the specific social institutions, laws, and property rights that embody the basic reality principle introduce additional controls which result in 'surplus repression' in order to preserve the interests of a class with a property right, so to speak, in the social structure.   Marxian psychology stresses the importance of the individual's psychological history and the changing institutional contexts within which the individual develops.   It is especially concerned with the defence of the argument that there are socially induced neuroses, largely described by the concept of alienation.

Now, if there are individual maladies whose source lies in the nature of the prevailing social institutions, for example, the nature of the work process, it follows that treatment of the condition will involve not only individual therapy but institutional reform.   While there is no logical connection between a given

33.   'So far no Marxist theoretician has yet detailed the crucial psychological and institutional nexuses which show how the "personifications" or masks of class role are donned by the individual as self-identity,' Daniel Bell, THE END OF IDEOLOGY, New York: Collier Books, 1961, p. 426.   For an attempt to treat these 'transmission belts,' se Paul A. Baran, MARXISM AND PSYCHOANALYSIS, 'Monthly Review Pamphlet series,' no. 13, New York: Monthly Review Press, 1960 pp. 50-52.

34.   More justly, one should include Sartre's attempts to add to Marxian anthropology the method of existential psychoanalysis (Jean-Paul Sartre, SEARCH FOR A METHOD, trans. Hazel E. Barnes, New York: Alfred A. Knopf, Inc., 1963).

35.   M. Birnbach, NEO-FREUDIAN SOCIAL PHILOSOPHY, Stanford: Stanford University Press, 1961, pp. 77-82.

36.   Herbert Marcuse, EROS AND CIVILIZATION, New York: Random House, 1962, p. 34.

methodological strategy and certain moral and political orientations, in practice the two do influence each other.[37] Tucker,
for example, rejects the view that there are sociological causes of
neurosis on the ground that to posit sociological entities is simply
to indulge in the projection of the components of an alienated
psyche. The alienated individual suffers from the myth-making
neurosis which induces him to believe that there are entities
outside his self-system which influence his behavior. As a
result, there arises the completely illusory view that the condition
of alienation can be treated by means of a political revolution.
The truth is, as Tucker will have it, that alienation is a personal
problem and its solution lies in an ethical conquest of the self.

> It is essentially a work of self-clarification and self-
> changing. Its tools are the power of understanding, the
> urge to be free, and the willingness to be merely human.
> Its dialectic is a Socratic dialectic of 'Know thyself'. The
> 'revolution' or real change of self that emerges in and
> through this movement of emancipation is, likewise, a moral
> revolution. The change of 'circumstances' with which it
> coincides is a change of the self's character, meaning the
> habitual circumstances within the self that have been shaped
> by alienated living and stand in the way of its freedom, the
> inner autocracy or coercive system. Such a revolution
> within the self cannot occur or start in a violent catastrophic
> episode. It is the outcome of a gradual process, and is this
> process taken as a whole. Alternatively, it is the merely
> theoretical point of culmination of the whole slow growth of
> inward freedom and repossession of the productive powers of
> the self which takes place in the movement and by the
> labour of self-liberation.[38]

The passage just quoted is remarkable for the way in which
Tucker introjects the external world by identifying 'circumstances'--why between quotes?--with 'habitual circumstances
within the self.' On this basis, Tucker then advances the view
that by revolution we may no longer mean a violent change[39]--
presumably, he disapproves of shock therapy--but only a
'theoretical point of culmination of the whole slow growth in
inward freedom.'

37. It has been suggested that Fromm's nominalist usage (THE SANE SOCIETY,
New York: Holt, Rinehart & Winston, 1955, pp. 72, 78, 273) provides support for
his theory of radical change (J. H. Schaar, ESCAPE FROM AUTHORITY, New York:
Basic Books, 1961, pp. 166-168.

38. Tucker, OP. CIT., pp. 240-241.

39. On Marx's use of the term 'revolution' see Lewis S. Feuer, John Stuart
Mill and Marxian Socialism,' JOURNAL OF THE HISTORY OF IDEAS, X, no. 2 (April
1949), 297-303.

Tucker's argument is that Marx's contribution to the social sciences is to be understood in the light of the dynamics of his neurosis. Marx's relatively valuable philosophical achievement derives from his early moral intuition of authentic individual existence. Marx's later investigations in the social sciences are simply a function of a myth-making neurosis engendered by his own circumstance of self-alienation. The manner in which Tucker's thesis fails to deal with the structure[40] of Marx's philosophical and sociological thought is illustrated in the para-doxical result it produces even when expanded somewhat. A. J. Gregor, for example, accepts Tucker's distinction between original and mature Marxism but attempts to salvage its over-all humanism by emphasizing its dependence upon Feuerbach's critique of idealism.[41] At the same timem Gregor argues that the year in which Marx wrote THE GERMAN IDEOLOGY, 1845, is precisely the year in which Marx settled with his philosophical conscience in an 'entirely empirical manner.'[42] According to Gregor, Marx, prior to THE GERMAN IDEOLOGY, at first argued that the pheno-menon of alienation is an ontological datum, a logical and causal condition of economic and political alienation. But Marx finally saw that this was simply an argument in the idealist mode. Thus he reversed it and got the empirical formula that it is the division of labor and private property which are the cause of alienation. But this argument carries us to the embarrassing conclusion that once private property and the social division of labor are abolished the phenomenon of alienation will disappear. Gregor sees that this 'almost romantic normative ideal' is a problem in the study of the mature Marx.

In the following chapter, we shall argue for the distinction be-tween the phenomenon of 'externalization' and that of 'estrange-ment' (or alienation), which in English are covered by the single term 'alienation.' Marx did not lament the necessity of creating socioeconomic institutions or objectifying human behavior (ex-ternalization). Here Gregor's reading of the ECONOMIC AND PHILOSOPHIC MANUSCRIPTS seems to be at fault, and even to

40. For a statement emphasizing the unity of Marx's thought in terms of the Hegelian frame of reference, see Raya Dunayevskaya, MARXISM AND FREEDOM, New York: Bookman Associates, 1957, Part III, and Jean Hyppolite, ETUDES SUR MARX ET HEGEL, Paris: Rivière, 1955, pp. 95-100.

41. A. J. Gregor, 'Philosophy and the Young Karl Marx,' STUDIES ON THE LEFT, II, no. 3 (1962), 95-102; cf. Lewis Feuer, 'What Is Alienation? The Career of a Concept,' NEW POLITICS, I, no. 3 (Spring 1962), 115-134.

42. A. J. Gregor, 'Erich Fromm and the Young Karl Marx,' STUDIES ON THE LEFT, III, no. 1 (1962), 85-92. The theory of the two Marxes is shared also by L. Kreiger, 'Marx and Engels as Historians,' JOURNAL OF THE HISTORY OF IDEAS, XIV, No. 3 (June 1953), 381-402; G. Gurvitch, 'La Sociologie du jeune Marx', LA VOCATION ACTUELLE DE LA SOCIOLOGIE, Paris: Presses Universitaires de France, 1950, pp. 568-602.

contradict his better understanding when discussing the relation
of Marx to Feuerbach. What Marx said in relation to Hegel is
that estrangement is not an epistemological problem, nor, as
Feuerbach thought, a theological product. Estrangement, but
not, of course, externalization, is a socioeconomic phenomenon.
Now Marx's stratagem of identifying the (undifferentiated)
phenomenon of alienation with economic exploitation and the class
structure of capitalism has suggested a definitional resolution of
the problem which the political history of socialism has yet to
provide. The significance of the contemporary discussion of the
philosophical structure of Marx's thought lies in the attempt to
recover its foundations in the phenomenology of the Western
mind. This is not an abstract endeavour, of course, any more
than the Hegelian legacy upon which Marx drew in the first
place. It is an essay in the clarification of the cultural presuppositions of the institutions and mentality of Western man.

Certainly, there is myth and drama in the Marxian heritage--not,
however, the guilt of Oedipus, as the Freudians would have it,
but the compassionate rebellion of Prometheus.

CHAPTER 4

MARX'S CONCEPT OF ALIENATION

In his article on 'Alienation and History in Early Marx' L. D. Easton has shown how Marx took over the concept of alienation which he found in Hegel's Phenomenology of the Spirit.[1] Apparently, however, when Marx formulated his mature theory of the social structure of capitalism and the laws of its development into socialism by means of a political revolution, Marx chose to neglect a number of critical points he had established in his early study of Hegel. But Mr. Easton does not specify any of the intervening mechanisms which are responsible for Marx's lapse of critical attention. It will be the purpose of this chapter to sketch two possible theorems by which Marx came to contradict himself. Some further comments will be made upon the need for awareness of the precise application of the attempts by Professors Propper and Hayek, for example, to dispose of Marxian social science on the ground that it is built upon the methodological fallacies of collectivism and historicism. These errors, though absent at first, are described as essential to the final state of Marxian social science in the following remarks of Mr. Easton:

> As Marx identified the end of man's alienation with the 'real movement' of history, he came to emphasize its independence from men's actions, likened its laws to those of nature which work with 'iron necessity towards inevitable results', and viewed it as a dialectical relation of classes and entities such as 'proletariat', 'civil society', and 'bourgeoisie'. Within this perspective, especially in terms of achieving class power, 'the State' as such becomes important.[2]

Marx's criticisms of Hegel's philosophical system exposed its strutural dependency upon the reification of concepts. Marx argued that Hegel had inverted the relation of logic to ontology. Earlier, Feuerbach had showed the concept of Divinity to be simply a projection of the ethical qualities of human individuals. Similarly, Hegel's dialectical law of the movement of History was exposed by Feuerbach as nothing else than the contradiction of philosophy with itself, namely, denying theology only to restore it later.[3]

1. PHILOSOPHY AND PHENOMENOLOGICAL RESEARCH, vol. XXII, no. 2 (December 1961), pp. 193-205; cf. Karl Löwith, "Man's Self-Alienation in the Early Writings of Marx" SOCIAL RESEARCH, vol. XXI, no. 2 (Summer 1954), pp. 204-230.

2. PHILOSOPHY AND PHENOMENOLOGICAL RESEARCH, vol. XXII, p. 203.

3. Karl Marx, ECONOMIC AND PHILOSOPHIC MANUSCRIPTS OF 1844, Moscow: Foreign Languages Publishing House. Critique of the Hegelian Dialectic and Philosophy as a whole.

In Marx's own words, there is a double error in Hegel:

> The first emerges most clearly in THE PHENOMENOLOGY,
> the Hegelian philosophy's place of origin. When, for
> instance, wealth, statepower, etc., are understood by Hegel
> as entities estranged from the <u>human</u> being, this only
> happens in their form as thoughts . . . They are thought-
> entities, and therefore merely an estrangement of <u>pure</u>, i.e.,
> abstract, philosophical thinking. The whole process there-
> fore ends with Absolute Knowledge.[4]

The second error is expressed more briefly within the discussion
of Hegel's first mistake:

> It is not the fact that the human being <u>objectifies</u> <u>himself</u>
> <u>inhumanly</u>, in opposition to himself, but the fact that he <u>ob-</u>
> <u>jectifies</u> <u>himself</u> in <u>distinction</u> from and in <u>opposition</u> to
> abstract thinking, that is the posited essence of the
> estrangement and the thing to be superseded.[5]

Hegel, according to Marx, had understood the problem of alienation solely in terms of the separation of the thinking subject from
its own experience which it can only express in terms of general
concepts. Hegel's PHENOMENOLOGY provides an analysis of
epistemological alienation in place of the sociopolitical alienation
which is the ontological source of the separation of man from his
essential nature. Hegel's philosophy is nothing else than the
philosophical expression of a disintegrated reality.

Are we then to believe that Marx merely substituted for Hegel's
PHENOMENOLOGY an economic theory which he then proceeded to
develop employing the same conceptual realism and dialectic which
he had critically exposed in Hegel?

It is in fact precisely this error which Marx criticized in Proudhon's LA PHILOSOPHIE DE LA MISÈRE[6] though he acknowledges
partial responsibility inasmuch as he was Proudhon's first tutor in
Hegelianism.[7]   Proudhon's half-assimilated Hegelianism, when
applied to economic phenomena, resulted in the description of
merely logical antagonisms between economic categories of rich and

4.   IBID., p. 149; THE HOLY FAMILY OR CRITIQUE OF CRITICAL
CRITIQUE, Moscow: Foreign Languages Publishing House, 1956, pp. 81-82.

5.   Karl Marx, ECONOMIC AND PHILOSOPHIC MANUSCRIPTS, p. 149.

6.   Marx to P. V. Annenkov, Brussels, 28 December 1846, in Karl Marx and
Fredrich Engels, SELECTED CORRESPONDENCE 1846-1895, New York: International
Publishers, 1934, pp. 5-18.

7.   Marx to Schweitzer, London, 24 January 1865, in SELECTED CORRESPON-
DENCE, pp. 169-176.

poor, monopoly and and competition, freedom and slavery. Proudhon, according to Marx, misunderstood the relation of economic theory to historical reality and provided a purely ideo- logical account of the basis of economic phenomena.

> Monsieur Proudhon has very well grasped the fact that men produce cloth, linen, silks, and it is a great merit on his part to have grasped this small amount. What he has not grasped is that these men, according to their powers, also produce the social relations amid which they prepare cloth and linen. Still less has he understood that men, who fashion their social relations in accordance with their material method of production, also fashion ideas and categories, that is to say the abstract, ideal expression of these same social relations. thus the categories are no more eternal than the relations they express. They are historic and transitory products. For M. Proudhon, on the contrary, abstractions and categories are the primordial cause. According to him they, and not men, make history. The abstraction, the category taken as such, i.e., apart from men and their material activities, is of course immortal, unmoved, un- changeable, it is only one form of the being of pure reason; which is only another way of saying that the abstraction as such is abstract. An admirable tautology!

> Thus, regarded as categories, economic relations for M. Proudhon are eternal formulae without origin or progress.[8]

In the course of his review of Proudon's work, Marx gives an extremely flexible formulation of the theory of historical materialism which provides the critique of ideological historio- graphy in the manner of Hegel and Proudhon. Marx raises the question: 'What is society, whatever its form may be?' He replies that it is 'the product of men's reciprocal activity'. This, how- ever, does not mean that individuals can choose this or that form of society. At a given stage of history men inherit from a previous generation a certain complement of material and cultural production possibilities. This phenomenon is the basis of a certain historical continuity and progression, since each succeed- ing generation can build upon the accumulated efforts of the past. 'Assume particular stages of development in production, commerce and consumption and you will have a corresponding social order, a corresponding organization of the family and of the ranks and classes, in a word, a corresponding civil society.'[9] Nevertheless, Marx does not at this time posit a

8. Marx to Annenkov, SELECTED CORRESPONDENCE, pp. 14-15.

9. IBID., p. 7.

one-to-one correlation between the economic substructure and the ideological superstructure. Although he considered the ideological factors dependent variables, Marx was aware that they tended to be lagged variables even possessing a reactive independence which gives to social change a revolutionary character.

It will be necessary to discover how Marx later allowed the theory of historical materialism to harden into the form of a theory of economic, perhaps technological epiphenomenalism. It will be suggested that this effect is in part due to epistemological polemics in which Marx sided with a realist, correspondence theory of knowledge in order to avoid excesses of subjective idealism and the historiography built upon it. The difficulties of the inflexible version of historical materialism are further compounded by the importation of the dialectical formula to express the development of the basic mechanism of social change. In the latter case, what is strictly a methodological decision, namely, the identification of the basic factor in social change, is confused with the political strategem of backing the proletariat as the ontological medium of social change. The effect of these latter moves in the development of Marx's social theory is to give it the very form of an alienated (estranged) ideology of which he himself had been an early critic.

Where Proudhon had failed, Marx believed himself to have succeeded. Moreover, Marx is ready to acknowledge his own success in terms of its original Hegelian inspiration. Even when criticizing Hegel, Marx distilled from the PHENOMENOLOGY an insight which provided a framework for all his later work and which is present even in CAPITAL. Marx summarizes his general criticism of Hegel with the recognition of the basic value of the Hegelian inquiry:

> The outstanding thing in Hegel's PHENOMENOLOGY and its final outcome--that is, the dialectic of negativity as the moving and generating principle--is thus first that Hegel conceives the self-genesis of man as a process, conceives objectification as loss of the object, as alienation and as transcendence of this alienation; that he thus grasps the essence of labour and comprehends objective man--true, because real man--as the outcome of man's own labour.

The perfectly sound intuition in Hegel is that man creates himself in the sense that he reproduces himself biologically and maintains himself through a process of socially organized labor. Just as theoretical concepts may be said to be mental constructs, so the social, political, and economic structure may be said to be the proper expression, product, or externalization of human beings considered as psycho-physical entities.

Man is directly a <u>natural being</u>. As a natural being and as a living natural being he is on the one hand furnished with <u>natural powers</u> <u>of</u> <u>life</u>--he is an <u>active</u> natural being. These forces exist in him as tendencies and abilities--as <u>impulses</u>. On the other hand, as a natural, corporeal, sensuous, objective being he is a <u>suffering</u>, conditioned and limited creature, like animals and plants. That is to say, the <u>objects</u> of his impulses exist outside him, as <u>objects</u> independent of him; yet these objects are <u>objects</u> of his <u>need</u>--essential <u>objects</u>, indispensable to the manifestation and confirmation of his essential powers. To say that man is a <u>corporeal</u>, living, sensuous, objective being full of natural vigour is to say that he has <u>real</u>, <u>sensuous</u>, <u>objects</u> as the objects of his being or of his life or that he can only <u>express</u> his life in real sensuous objects. To be objective, natural, and sensuous, and at the same time to have object, nature, and sense outside oneself, or oneself to be object, nature, and sense for a third party, is one and the same thing.[10]

As such Marx's formulation does not argue for the primacy of the socioeconomic substructure over the ideological superstructure. The very phrasing of this last remark is the result of a polemic which ignores the fact that both spheres involve ideational systems. The economic process is in fact a subculture within the total social culture. It may be that the economic system contains the engine of development which generates cultural possiblities of progress. Marx asks how it could be otherwise, unless one believes that history is made by kings and queens, saints and politicians.

There is nothing mysterious, says Marx, in the fact that man, as a psycho-physical entity, expresses himself through thought-constructs and cultural objects. The process of <u>externalization</u> (<u>Entäusserung</u>) is the natural expression of the <u>kind of being</u> man is. Marx does not lament the external world, for it is the precondition of all human effort, the means to human expression. It is when the products of man's mental and physical energy deny or despoil the integrity of man's nature that the phenomenon of <u>estrangement</u> (<u>Entfremdung</u>) is encountered.

Now the term alienation is frequently used to cover both the phenomenon of externalization and estrangement. This can only lead to a misunderstanding of Marx's use of the concept of alienation. It is clear that the externalization of human behavior into ideologies, social institutions, and material products is a necessary precondition of the phenomenon of estrangement, i.e.,

10.   Karl Marx, ECONOMIC AND PHILOSOPHIC MANUSCRIPTS, pp. 156-157.

man being treated, say, as a means to, rather than the end of, such cultural products. But the reverse is not true. It is not necessary that the phenonenon of externalization be accompanied by estrangement. In fact, if this were the case, then Marx's work becomes unintelligible.[11] Is not the whole purpose of Marx's critique of capitalism to show that capitalism, an historically progressive externalization (expression) of human energies attested to by the COMMUNIST MANIFESTO, is a necessary step toward the social organization of freedom under socialism or communism? Marx is not the critic of social structure as such. He is the analyst of historical social structures. His criticisms are ethical evaluations of the degree to which social structures realize an ideal of authentic being, i.e., nonestranged or unalienated existence.

Marx did not work out a complete ethical theory of authentic existence.[12] One might say that Marx was attempting to give a sociological interpretation of the regulative principle of Kantian epistemology and the categorical imperative Kantian ethics. Marx had absorbed through Hegel the Kantian critique of British and Continental empiricism.[13] When Marx objects to the idealist exaggeration of the contribution of consciousness to experience, it is not an anti-epistemological objection; it is a sociological restraint. However, it is the epistemological primacy of consciousness with respect to experience which provides the source of an ethical norm for the relation of individuals to social environment.

Marxian epistemology struggles with the basic postulate of all classical epistemology, namely, the supposition that the world precedes our consciousness of it.[14] Marx, particularly in the THESES ON FEUERBACH, understood that the objectivism of classical epistemology overlooks that man is a situated being, that

11. This may surprise those who try to give Marxism a face-lift by making just such an identification, i.e., revamping Marxism as a GENERAL critique of social organization and culture.

12. Vernon Venable, HUMAN NATURE: THE MARXIAN VIEW, New York: A. A. Knopf, 1945, pp. 203-213; Robert S. Cohen "Contemporary Marxism," THE REVIEW OF METAPHYSICS, vol. IV, no. 2 (December 1950), pp. 291-310. See also Chapter 5.

13. F. A. Hayek, THE COUNTER-REVOLUTION OF SCIENCE, Glencoe, Illinois: Free Press, 1952, attempts to dismiss Marxian social science along with the tradition of positivistic scientism since the French Revolution but overlooks that Hegel had in fact provided Marx with a critique of prerevolutionary positivism which has always been the basis of a critical relation between Marxism and Postivism. Cf. Herbert Marcuse, REASON AND REVOLUTION, New York: Humanities Press, 1954, p. 343; Frank E. Hartung, "The Social Function of Positivism," PHILOSOPHY OF SCIENCE, vol. IX, no. 4 (1944), pp. 328-341.

14. Leszek Kolakowski, "Karl Marx and the Classical Definition of Truth," L. Labedz, REVISIONISM, Essays on the History of Marxist Ideas, New York: Praeger, 1962, pp. 179-187.

knowledge is in terms of perspective and truth yielded by following out a given systematic orientation.[15]   Marx rejected the
epistemological solutions of both idealism and materialism.   However, he seems to have reacted most violently to the idealist
abuse of the constitutive element in thought.   The result is that
he fell back upon the objectivist view of classical epistemology in
its scientific materialist form.   The result of this equivocation is
very well summarized by E. Knight:

> The philosophy of Marx deviated into scientism because the
> first concern of most Marxists was to demonstrate how means
> of production had 'determined' the nature of all other mani-
> festations of social life throughout human history.   This was
> to forget that man can create value not only with his hands,
> but also with his mind.   The economic interpretation of
> history is proven not by consulting the records, but by
> turning this thought into matter.   The thinker, in other
> words, is a laborer, except that his product is an event or
> an institution rather than a commodity.   For the objective
> intellectual, at least in practice, ideas and things run
> parallel to one another; but the lines can be made to cross,
> and, indeed, the whole responsibility of the intellectual is to
> see that they do.[16]

Marx made two attempts to break through the world of alienation,
i.e., estrangement.   In the first, he rejected classical objectivist
epistemology and sketched a phenomenology of a world view based
upon the creativeness of authentic personality in the ECONOMIC
AND PHILOSOPHIC MANUSCRIPTS.   However, this move is submerged by the sociological restraints overemphasized in the
polemic with extreme subjective idealism.   This is otherwise the
only positive path to the formation of a nonestranged world view,
in which the cultural world is considered a human project and
human existence as an Ecstasis, as Heidegger for example, has
considered it.[17]

15.   Hannah Arendt, BETWEEN PAST AND FUTURE, New York: Viking Press,
1961, has criticized the arbitrary nature of certain postulates of political experience.
Given the hypothesis of the superiority of the Aryan race, the events at Dachau,
Belsen, and elsewhere are perfectly meaningful, necessary experiences.   Arendt
considers it the basic feature of the totalitarian society that it has the power to
establish "experience" in terms of arbitrary political postulates.   But Marx criticized
the nature of human experience yielded within the postulates of Classical political
economy in similar terms.   Arendt's criticism is in effect a natural law criticism of
arbitrary political conventions.   Marx's standard is humanist.   The problem is to
give an account of the standard of judgment which avoids the errors of transcen-
dentalism without falling into a form of political and sociological positivism.

16.   Everett Knight, THE OBJECTIVE SOCIETY New York: George Braziller
Inc., 1961, pp. 101-102; C. Wright Mills, THE, SOCIOLOGICAL IMAGINATION, New
York: Oxford University Press, 1961, chap. VI.

17.   Our interpretation of Marx's views in the PHILOSOPHIC AND ECONOMIC
MANUSCRIPTS is similar to the views of Heidegger on the nature of man: "Finding

The fact is, nonetheless, that Marx appears to have narrowed his broad sketch of a phenomenology of a nonalienated culture into a theory of economic alienation.

The methodological value of Marx's attempted reduction of the general problem of alienation to the specific form of economic exploitation will be examined in the following section of this essay. Critics of Marx's economic theory of history which emerged from his early interest in the phenomenon of alienation argue that Marx constructed a theory in terms of collective entities, 'proletariat', 'bourgeoisie', which evolve, independently of the behavior of their constituent members, along a historical path determined by successive developments and upheavals in the basic production process. Characterized in this way, Marxian social theory is thought to be clearly in contradiction with its original purpose of analyzing the preconditions of social and moral development.

Professors Popper and Hayek have advanced an influential nominalist criticism of Marxian essentialism or conceptual realism. Unfortunately, these critics do not distinguish methodological and normative questions. They argue that to posit theoretical entities of a collective or group nature is both an epistemological error and an indication of a normative devaluation of the individual. Professor Hayek argues that theoretical constructs, other than those of individual psychology, can be considered independent sociological variables only through the failure to distinguish 'those ideas which are <u>constitutive</u> of the phenomena we want to explain and the ideas which we ourselves or the very people whose actions we have to explain may have formed about these phenomena and which are not the cause of, but theories about, the social structures'. The analytic error is apparently coupled with a lack of moral courage. The representatives of scientism in the social sciences are 'afraid' to take the ideas of individuals as the data of their theories but instead substitute for them 'popular generalizations' about the reasons for individual behavior.[18]

himselt in the midst ot his possibilities, man as human-being is also one who projects (entwirft) them. Interpreting the verb to exist as to-go-out-of-the-self, implies that we are always making PROJECTS; some are more trivial than others, of course, but nevertheless we could not exist without making some sort of projects all the time. Man as human-being is thus a thrown-projecting being; he is thrown into his possibilities and he always projects them outward. Human-being is always anticipating itself (SICH VORWEG SEIN); it is never static, but always ECSTATIC." Edward A. Tiryakian, SOCIOLOGISM AND EXISTENTIALISM, New Jersy: Prentice-Hall, 1962, p. 109. However, it is not intended to argue for any general similarity between Marxism and Existentialism. The differences are set out briefly by Adam Schaff's two articles on "Marxism and Existentialism," MONTHLY REVIEW, vol. XIV, no. 1 (May 1962), pp. 12-18; and MONTHLY REVIEW, vol. XIV, no 2 (June 1962), pp. 100-111; and in my argument in Chapter 6 below.

    18.   Hayek confuses the participants' interpretations of their own behavior, which may provide relevant sociological hypotheses, with the independent legitimate theoretical constructions of the sociologist. Cf. John Rex, KEY PROBLEMS OF SOCIOLOGICAL THEORY, London, Routledge and Kegan Paul, 1961, p. 37.

Hayek is undoubtedly correct in arguing that theoretical constructs such as the 'whole', 'group', or 'class' cannot causally
affect individuals for the reason that the two phenomena are not
on the same level of existence.[19]   The truth in this argument,
however, when asserted together with the truism that the whole
is the sum of its parts and inseparable from them, is then
employed by Hayek to arrive at the more questionable proposition
that explanations of social phenomena must be in terms of
individual dispositions.[20]

Hayek's argument concerning the existence of group concepts and
laws generally confuses the logical question of descriptive
emergence in respect of concepts, which depends upon the
criterion of meaning, with the empirical question of the reduction
of the laws and theories of the social sciences.   Explanation
involves the deduction of the explanandum from true premises.
Only statements and not concepts can form the premises of a
deduction.

Reduction, which is a form of deduction, and thus of explanation,
is therefore a matter of laws and theories, not of concepts.[21]
So-called reduction of concepts is strictly a question of definition.
It is possible to define group concepts in terms of descriptive
relations between individuals.   But this does not permit the prediction of group behavior from that of its members without empirical composition laws which establish a connection between the
conduct of the individuals within the system and the resultant
behavior of the group.[22]

According to Professor Popper, the Marxian conception of history
is based upon the mistaken notion that social scientists can plot
the historical movements of society in the same way that a
physicist can predict planetary motion.[23]   The error in this

19.   Ernest Gellner, "Holism versus Individualism in History and Sociology,"
Patrick Gardiner, THEORIES OF HISTORY, Glencoe, Illinois: Free Press, 1959, pp.
488-503; S. Krupp, PATTERN IN ORGANIZATIONAL ANALYSIS, Philadelphia and
New York: Chilton Co., 1961, pp. 134-139; John O'Neill, Edited and with an introduction, MODES OF INDIVIDUALISM AND COLLECTIVISM, London: Heinemann, 1973
and New York: St. Martin's Press, 1976.

20.   For a critical discussion see T. Abel, "The Operation called VERSTEHEN,"
AMERICAN JOURNAL OF SOCIOLOGY, vol. LV, no. 3 (November 1948), pp. 211-218.

21.   Max Brodbeck, "Models, Meanings and Theories," L. Gross (ed.),
SYMPOSIUM ON SOCIOLOGICAL THEORY, White Plains, New York: Row Petersen
and Co., 1959, pp. 373-403; Ernest Nagel, THE STRUCTURE OF SCIENCE, New
York: Harcourt, Brace and World, 1961, chap. 2, The Reduction of Theories.

22.   Quentin Gibson, THE LOGIC OF SOCIAL INQUIRY, London: Routledge
Kegan and Paul, 1960, pp. 150-155.

23.   Karl R. Popper, THE POVERTY OF HISTORICISM, Boston: Beacon Press,
1957.

case consists of overlooking that the lawlike statements of natural science are stated together with a set of historical statements which indicate the occurrence of certain antecedent conditions.

Scientizing sociologists overlook the dependence of lawlike regularities upon the fulfilment of specific antecedent conditions. They more often than not mistake trends for laws. Furthermore, the practical interest which lies behind scientific prediction, also present in the transference of this goal to the social science, is said to be defeated by the very social laws on which practical political action might have been based. A kind of historical fatalism replaces the initial pragmatic interest in political action.

When Marx criticized the Hegelian system as an ideological system par excellence the substance of his argument was that theoretical constructs are not the sort of entities that can enter into causal relations on the level of historical existence.[24] Marx understood that the Hegelian 'state' is no more a causal factor in history than the concept of 'feudalism'. Moreover, he did not confuse that argument with the more questionable thesis that such theoretical entities as the 'state', 'society', 'capitalism', are spurious methodological constructs. It is the merit of Marxian social science not to have bogged down in the hyperfactualism and poverty of fruitful hypotheses which characterizes positivistic empiricism. Max Weber has pointed to this feature in some remarks which at the same time indicate the pitfalls not only of Marxian theory but of any theoretical structure;

> . . . all specifically Marxian 'Laws' and developmental constructs--in so far as they are theoretically sound--are ideal types. The eminent, indeed unique, heuristic significance of these ideal types when they are used for the assessment of reality is known to everyone who has ever employed Marxian concepts and hypotheses. Similarly their perniciousness, as soon as they are thought of as empirically rated or as real (i.e., truly metaphysical) 'effective forces', 'tendencies', etc., is likewise known to those who have used them.[25]

Just as Marx attacked the errors of methodological collectivism in its Hegelian form, so he criticized the conception of 'iron' social

    24.   There is a useful statement of Marx's views in his early writings on essentialism, conceptual realism, the nature of the state, history and the dialectical procedure of Marxian Sociology, in CAHIERS INTERNATIONAUX DE SOCIOLOGIE, vol. IV (1948), pp. 3-152; P. Kahn, "Société et état dans les oeuvres de jéunesse de Marx", CAHIERS INTERNATIONAUX DE SOCIOLOGIE, vol. V. (1949), pp. 165-175.

    25.   Max Weber, "Objectivity in Social Science and Social Policy," trans. E. A. Shils and H. A. Finch, THE METHODOLOGY OF THE SOCIAL SCIENCES, Glencoe, Illinois: Free Press, 1959, p. 103.

laws as it appeared in the analysis of the British classical economists. In this case Marx, in fact, made the very point which
Professor Popper accuses him of having ignored. Marx pointed
out that the laws of Classical economics only hold within a given
social constellation which provides a set of social and psychological middle principles which restrict the degree of variation in
social behavior, or, in other words, define regularities or
patterns of behavior for a given society. Marx's analysis of
social laws argues that so-called social laws are derivative from
the overall social orientation which defines a particular society.
A society which considers itself governed uniquely by natural
laws is alientated in a manner similar to the individual who sees
himself in the power of an institutional framework which he is not
free to modify. Marx's analysis is intended to show how social
institutions may be manipulated by individuals, modified by a
sociological realism which avoids the naive errors of liberal
rationalism.

Professor Popper misunderstands Marx by neglecting the
synthesis of economic deduction and sociological preconditions
which characterizes Marxian historical theory. Contrary to what
Popper gives us to understand, Marx in fact argued that there
are no absolute social laws of economics or politics apart from the
specification of a set of relevant sociological middle principles.[26]
It is a feature not only of Marxian economics but of all economics[27] that, in the words of A. Löwe, 'determinateness of
reasoning' is achieved only through the introduction of certain
sociological middle principles:

> Any realistic theory of the modern economic system must
> start from the general premise that it can no longer deal
> with a constant structure and with homogeneous processes,
> but that the economic order under consideration is subject to
> an evolutionary transformation. Therefore any deductive
> operation with invariable data is defective from the very
> outset. Long period analysis cannot dispense with a
> previous examination of the tendencies of the data them-
> selves. That is to say, the corresponding sociological con-
> stellation and its regular changes, and moreover with the
> examination of the mutual relations of the variations on both
> sides. Above all this dynamic chain of reciprocal causation
> between the economic process and its social environment calls
> for a theoretical system of coordinates which is on the one

26. Adolph Löwe, ECONOMICS AND SOCIOLOGY, London: George Allen and
Unwin, 1935; J. S. Mill, SYSTEM OF LOGIC, London, Longmans, Green and Co.,
1906, BK. VI, chap. 5.

27. S. Schoeffler, THE FAILURE OF ECONOMICS, Cambridge: Harvard University Press, 1955, applies Löwe's arguments in a critique of contemporary eco-
nometric process models.

hand determinate enough to define the course of individual movements, and on the other hand elastic enough to reproduce the regular transformation of the system as a whole. We need not expressly decide henceforth to insert sociological elements into our economic deduction--there was never any substantial statement which was not based on such premises. But we are to render manifest and open to continuous examination and revision those implications which formerly remained latent, and whose modifications were usually neglected.[28]

Oscar Lange has argued that the difference between the explanatory value of 'bourgeois' economics and Marxian economics lies in the ability of the latter to include institutional data which permit it to deal with the evolutionary problems that the static equilibrium systems are obliged to resign to economic history.[29] Bourgeois economics deal only with constant data. Changes in the data are considered exogeneous to the logical systems built upon them. The same criticism applies to the so-called dynamic theories which explain economic fluctuations in terms of time lags in the supply adjustments to price changes. The possibility of equilibrium is deduced from the nature of the adjustment mechanism. But changes in the underlying data upon which the adjustment mechanism works to produce fluctuations cannot be deduced from such theories. By contrast, through the specification of the institutional (class structure) date of the capitalist process changes in the basic data, i.e., the production function, can be deduced and certain laws of development of capitalism can be determined.

Lange also shows that some Marxists are mistaken in attributing the superiority of Marxian economics in dealing with the evolution of capitalism to the labor theory of value. The latter is a static equilibrium theory of value based upon even more restrictive institutional assumptions than the marginal utility theory of equilibrium. Provided only there be free competition, the formal principles of the theory of equilibrium apply equally to any exchange economy whether capitalistic or the case that Marx envisaged for the application of labor theory of value, namely, an economy of small independent producers each owning his own means of production (einfache Warenproduktion). The necessity of economic evolution, or, in other words, changes in the production-function, is dependent upon the introduction of specific institutional data which define the capitalist system and distinguish it from simple forms of exchange economy.

    28.   Adolph Löwe, ECONOMICS AND SOCIOLOGY, pp. 138-139; K. Marx, CAPITAL, Chicago: C. H. Kerr and Co., 1906, Vol. III, pp. 947-949; 966-968.

    29.   Oscar Lange, "Marxian Economics and Modern Economic Theory," REVIEW OF ECONOMIC STUDIES, Vol. 2 (1934-1935) pp. 189-201.

We have examined the argument that in his writings Marx fell into
the errors of conceptual realism and historical determinism. He
himself had criticized these faults in Hegel as the basic ingredients of an alienated ideology. We distinguished two rather
different phenomena, namely, estrangement (Entfremdung) and
externalization (Entäusserung), ordinarily covered by the term
alienation. Marx does not bewail the necessity of expressing or
externalizing experience in terms of general, objective concepts.
Thus it was necessary to show that, while Marx criticized
Hegelian theory as a form of epistemological alienation, he did not
confuse that argument with the legitimate employment of
theoretical constructs and generalizations as the basis of a social
science. The arguments of Professor Popper and Hayek are
simply a positivist and nominalist rejection of the possibility of
any social science.[30]

Marx does not shrink from the necessity of interaction with the
natural world in order to create medium for the expression of
human personality. To Marx the problem of alienation is not per
se either an epistemological or a technological problem. Alienation
is a phenomenon which arises when men are estranged from the
products of their mental, physical, and social activity with the
result that they fail to realize an ideal of authentic being.
According to Marx, conceptual realism, theological transcendental-
ism, etatism, and sociological theory oriented in terms of a framework of 'iron' social laws are merely manifestation of an existential
estrangement which arises within the organization of the means of
production.

The core of the problem of alienation (estrangement) as it appears
in Marx's more mature theory lies in the legitimacy of Marx's attempt to reduce the examination of all forms of estrangement to
the 'basic' phenomenon of economic exploitation or alienation.
Daniel Bell argues that by narrowing the general problem of
alienation to the specific question of economic alienation Marx
closed off a road to a more general and fruitful analysis of the

---

30.   The truly counter-revolutionists of science are the very critics of
"scientism," for example, E. Heimann, REASON AND FAITH IN MODERN SOCIETY,
LIBERALISM, MARXISM AND DEMOCRACY, Middletown, Conn.: Wesleyan University
Press, 1961, chap. III; Ludwig von Bertalanffy, "The Psychopathology of Scientism,"
H. Schoek and J. W. Higgins, SCIENTISM AND VALUES, New York: Van Nostrand
Co. Inc., 1960, pp. 202-218; Fritz Machlup, "The Inferiority Complex of the Social
Sciences," ed. M. Sennholz, ON FREEDOM AND FREE ENTERPRISE, Essays in Honor
of Ludwig von Mises, New York: Van Nostrand Co. Inc., 1956, pp. 161-172. Cf.
the criticisms of Popper's school of thought by E. Knight, THE OBJECTIVE
SOCIETY, New York: Geo. Braziller, Inc., 1962; E. H. Carr, WHAT IS HISTORY?,
New York: A. A. Knopf, 1962; Alisdair Macintyre, "Breaking the Chains of
Reason," OUT OF APATHY, London, New Left Books, 1960, pp. 216-222. I have
expressed my views on this problem in my introductory essay to MODES OF
INDIVIDUALISM AND COLLECTIVISM. This volume presents the whole of the
original argument raised by Hayek and Popper and their critics.

problems of social organization and personality structure. [31]

> The extraordinary thing was that Marx had taken a concept which German philosophy had seen as an ontological fact, and had given it a social content. As ontology, as an ultimate, man could only accept alienation. As a social fact, rooted in a specific system of historical relations, alienation could be overcome by changing the social system. But in narrowing the concept, Marx ran two risks; of falsely identifying the source of alienation only in the private property system; and of introducing a note of utopianism in the idea that once the private property system was abolished man would immediately be free. [32]

Bell's initial remark that Marx did not conceive alienation as an ontological fact is very well taken. If we accept the distinction between externalization and estrangement previously discussed, then Marx's position is quite clearly that the necessity of objectifying man's natural capacities is not at all problematic. Systematic thought, language, art, work, physical, and cultural objects are all natural expressions of the sort of being man is. This is the substance of Marx's critique of Hegel in THE ECONOMIC AND PHILOSOPHIC MANUSCRIPTS. What Marx did wish to argue is that both the process and the products of man's physical and mental activity may escape man's control and, far from being the natural means to the realization of an ethical ideal of authentic, creative being, result in an alienated, estranged condition of man. Marx believed that the basic source of the estrangement of man's freely creative energies lay in the nature of the sociological and technological organization of work or labor.

In Marx's later writings the theory of alienation is isomorphic with the theory of the class stratification of society. We may distinguish six postulates in Marx's theory of social class. [33]

    I.   All the cultural manifestations of civil society are ultimately functions of its class structure;

    II.   Class structure is determined by the structure of production;

    III.   The social process of production displays a capacity for evolution.

31. Daniel Bell, "The Rediscovery of Alienation," THE JOURNAL OF PHILOSOPHY, vol. LVI, no. 24 (November 1959), pp. 933-952.

32. THE JOURNAL OF PHILOSOPHY, vol. LVI, no. 24 (November 1959), p. 939.

33. Joseph Schumpeter, HISTORY OF ECONOMIC ANALYSIS, New York: Oxford University Press, 1954, p. 439.

It was part of the purpose of our earlier discussion to show that the above propositions are at least defensible working hypotheses, and as such, basic elements in Marxian social science. The difficulty is that these postulates cannot be separated, in Marxian theory, from the following three:

   IV. The class structure is composed of the owners and nonowners of the means of production;

    V. By virtue of their position relative to the means of production, the interests of the classes of owners and nonowners are antagonistic;

   VI. The class struggle which results from the antagonism of class interests provides the mechanism, political and economic, which implements the forces of immanent evolution.

Shumpeter remarks that is was an especially 'bold stroke of analytic strategy' to identify capitalism and the phenomenon of social class in terms of ownership in the means of production.[34] But the strategem is in fact perversely Hegelian. The attempt to schematize history in terms of the concept of class struggle between the owners and nonowners of the means of production has only a spurious generality.[35] Not all forms of social conflict are class conflicts. Not can every form of social change be accounted for in terms of changes in the basis of class power. Furthermore, Marx's assertion that there is a necessary tendency for class conflicts to become increasingly antagonistic until capitalist society is completely split asunder is quite obviously a nonsociological postulate derived from Hegel's dialectic. Finally, the kind of power which derives from legal ownership of the means of production is only a species of the general phenomenon of power and authority relations inherent in any social structure. The nature of the connections between specific forms of power arising from the industrial and political system and their interrelations with the social class and stratification patterns of a given society are a matter of empirical not logical connections.

Unfortunately, Marx's perception of the phenomenon of alienation is restricted to the forms of estrangement which appear in capitalist industrial society. According to Marx, such freedom as exists in capitalist society is enjoyed by the owners of the means

34.   Joseph Schumpeter, CAPITALISM, SOCIALISM AND DEMOCRACY, New York: Harper and Brothers, 1950, p. 19; B. Moore, Jr., POLITICAL POWER AND SOCIAL THEORY, Cambridge, Mass.:   Harvard University Press, 1958, chap. IV.

35.   Ralf Dahrendorf, CLASS AND CLASS CONFLICT IN INDUSTRIAL SOCIETY, Stanford, California: Stanford University Press, 1959, chap. IV; C. W. Mills, THE MARXISTS, New York. Dell Publishing Co., 1962, chap. 6.

of production and entails as its logical antithesis the slavery of
the proletariat. It is only when the proletariat acquires control
over the means of production and the conditions of its work that
freedom becomes general and alienation disappears. It should be
noticed that the collective ownership of the means of production
in socialist society is thought to put an end to two rather different elements in the phenomenon of economic alienation. In the
first place, collective ownership is considered a solution to the
problem of control over the _product_ of labor. In the second
place, it is thought to be a remedy for the dehumanization or
depersonalization which arises from specific role-concentrations
within the social and industrial division of labor.[36]

We shall not discuss here the various criticisms of the notion of
the worker's control of industry as a practical institution.[37] It
is quite clear that a planned economy involved decisions of
priority as to the relative expansion of capital-goods and con-
sumer-goods industries, decisions upon saving-investment ratios
and the relative growth and rationalization of industrial, agricultural, and service sectors. Such decisions require structured
relations of authority which, although perhaps initially related to
a technical or professional basis, tend to result in social stratification patterns which are the instrument of a system of dif-
ferential gratifications. In short, the performance principle of a
socialist society would necesarily involve patterns of deferred
gratification for the reason that this is a general existential
phenomenon.[38] So far from abolishing the asymmetry between
individual and social interests, the institutions of collective ownership of the means of production in fact depend upon an extremely
rationalized application of the principle of social authority and
control.

We have tried to defend the thesis that the externality of social
institutions and rule-governed behavior are not, as such, mani-
festations of human estrangement. We believe that it is consistent with Marx's own views that social institutions become
instruments of estrangement only when they fail to achieve purposes which the participants intended. Estrangement is primarily
a phenomenon of the idelogical superstructure. For example, the
practices required of a successful businessman may conflict with
the scruples of a person who wishes at the same time to be a

36. Karl Marx, ECONOMIC AND PHILOSOPHIC MANUSCRIPTS 1844, Estranged
Labour, pp. 67-83.

37. Daniel Bell, THE END OF IDEOLOGY, New York, Colliers Books, 1961,
chap. XV. "Two Roads from Marx: The Themes of Alienation and Exploitation and
Workers' Control in Socialist Thought"; A. L. Harris, "Utopian Elements in Marx's
Thought," ETHICS, vol. LV, no. 2 (January 1950), pp. 79-99.

38. Herbert Marcuse, EROS AND CIVILIZATION, New York: Vintage Books,
1962, chap. II.

businessman and a member of the Christian Church.[39]   In this
case, a person may feel estranged by the difficulty of harmoniz-
ing the economic means-value system with the end-value system
prescribed by his religion. He may in fact find that the ethos of
the economic subculture of which he disapproves pervades the
general value-system of the Christian life and its institutional
structure.   In this situation, the individual becomes the focus of
an institutional conflict and is burdened with the attempt to
rationalize conflicting value-systems.   We have in this example a
paradigm case of a socially-induced neurosis--the state of alienation or estrangement.[40]

This is a condition which has been described from various points
of view by Weber, Durkheim, Tönnies, and Mannheim and is a
pervasive concern of much sociological journal-literature.[41]   Max
Weber focused his analysis upon the tension between the charismatic potential of the individual and the necessity of compulsive
conformity within role-bound areas, lacking any overall normative
structure.   Mannheim also called attention to the phenomenon of
functional rationalization which induces a flight from responsibility
due to the 'expropriation of understanding and intellectual
activity'.   Durkheim described the state of anomie as a 'disease of
the infinite' that is to say, the confinement of man's impulsive
nature within a normative social structure which routinizes and
conventionalizes man's needs.   Marcuse has analyzed the conflict
between the freedom of the libidinal subject-object which the
human organism desires and the conscription of mind and body as
the tools of alienated labor required by the historically conditioned forms of the reality principle. i.e., ἀνάγχη the existential
fact of scarcity relationships.[42]

Marx's diagnosis and his prescription for the condition of alienation (estrangement) appears to be less general than the investigations of later writers and his remedy rather more sanguine.[43]

39.   Karen Horney, THE NEUROTIC PERSONALITY OF OUR TIME, New York,
W. W. Norton and Company, 1937; M. Birnbach, NEO-FREUDIAN SOCIAL
PHILOSOPHY, Stanford, California: Stanford University Press, 1961.

40.   M. Seeman, "On the Meaning of Alienation," AMERICAN SOCIOLOGICAL
REVIEW, vol. XXIV, no. 6 (December 1959), pp. 783-791; J. P. Clark, "Measuring
Alienation within a Social System," AMERICAN SOCIOLOGICAL REVIEW, vol. XXIV,
no. 6 (December 1959), pp. 849-852; R. C. Tucker, PHILOSOPHY AND MYTH IN
KARL MARX, Cambridge: Cambridge University Press, 1961, pp. 148-149, considers
that it was Marx's personal neurosis to have considered social institutions as the
predisposing factor in the condition of alienation.

41.   S. C. Harris, A CONCEPTUAL ANALYSIS OF ALIENATION, M. A. Thesis,
Columbia University, (1956).

42.   Herbert Marcuse, EROS AND CIVILIZATION, chap. II.

43.   David Braybrooke, "Diagnosis and Remedy in Marx's Doctrine of Alienation," SOCIAL RESEARCH, vol. XXV. no. 3 (Autumn 1958). pp. 325-345.

These two faults are due, on the one hand, to a defect of analysis and, on the other, to an excess of ethical prescription. Ultimately, Marx appears to have fallen into a form of sociological anarchism. This is the dangerous possibility which derives from understanding alienation as a phenomenon resulting purely and simply from the institutional organization (externalization) of human behavior. The positive element in Marx's theory of alienation is the ethical ideal of a nonestranged relation between the individual and the artifacts and institutions of his cultural environment.

Mr. Braybrooke has observed that the nature of alienation (estrangement) is bound up with the concept of purpose. Marx complained that under capitalism a great number of jobs cannot be identified with any purpose of the worker in any sense beyond being a mere means to survival. Thsat is to say, specific tasks have no intrinsic interest for the laborer nor can they be rationalized as elements of a framework which the worker generally feels to be realizing interests and purposes of his own. Now, we ordinarily speak of a person having a purpose in doing X, or doing X for a purpose, when he performs X in the belief that it is a causal condition of something further, Y, which he values. It is not absolutely necessary that the person can give more than an elliptical account of the causal connection between X and Y. Furthermore, a person may be held responsible for the connections between actions, for example, the result Y of X, if X was done by him on purpose. Though, of course, X may have a number of unforseeable results. In that case it will be a matter of legal or ethical decision as to how far, if at all, an act which at first sight may be said to be 'his' in a descriptive sense is also to be ascribed to him as a matter of personal responsibility. Having a 'sense of purpose' in one's work may then be understood as some feeling of responsibility for the causal connection between one's actions within a broadly defined area, for example, working at a plant or teaching in a school rationalized as total activities. A number of other ethical values will contribute to what we call a 'sense of purpose', e.g., to a voluntarily self-sacrificing interest, a willingness to balance short-run and long-run gains, a sense of personal identification with the ultimate values realized by the task or occupation.

Marx appears to have argued that a worker is alienated when he neither understands nor feels any connection between his specific task and the job of which it is part, or the relations between his task, plant, industry, and the overall economy.

> We presuppose labor in a form that stamps it as exclusively human. A spider conducts operations that resemble those of a weaver, and the bee puts to shame many an architect in the construction of her cells. But what distinguishes the

worst architect from the best of bees is this, that the
architect raises his structure in imagination before he erects
it in reality. At the end of every labor process, we get a
result that already existed in the imagination of the laborer
at its commencement. He not only effects a change of form
in the material on which he works, but he also realizes a
purpose of his own that gives the law to his modus
operandi, and to which he must subordinate his will. And
this subordination is no mere momentary act. Besides the
exertion of the bodily organs, the process demands that,
during the whole operation the workmen's will be steadily in
consonance with his purpose. This means close attention.
The less he is attracted by the nature of the work, and the
mode in which it is carried on, and the less, therefore, he
enjoys it as something which gives play to his bodily and
mental powers, the more close his attention is forced to
be. [44]

The expropriation of worker understanding is due to the exclu-
sion of labor from industry control and decision making. Under
such conditions, according to Marx, a worker can have no sense
of purpose in his labor. The purpose of labor under these
conditions is subordinate to physical survival and avoidance of
the misery of unemployment. Marx's solution to the problem of
alienation or estrangement is based upon a projected abolition of
the division of labor and the control of industry by workers as
the ingredients of a planned economy which would replace the
capitalist production system and competitive market. Marx
believed that the tendency of the technological processes of
industry to become increasingly complex and consequently to
demand more highly skilled, intelligent labor had been dimly
recognized by the Factory Act, provisions for workers' education,
technical and agricultural schools, écoles d'enseignement pro-
fessionnel. However, the full implications of this phenomenon
would, Marx believed, overthrow capitalism in so far as it was
tied to an ossified division of labor.

But if, on the one hand, variation of work at present
imposes itself after the manner of an overpowering natural
law, and with the blindly destructive action of a natural law
that meets with resistance at all points, Modern Industry, on
the other hand, through its catastrophes imposes the
necessity of recognizing, as a fundamental law of production,
variation of work, consequently fitness of the labourer for
varied work, consequently the greatest possible development
of his varied aptitudes. It· becomes a question of life and
death for society to adapt the mode of production to the
normal functioning of this law. Modern Industry, indeed,

44. Karl Marx, CAPITAL, Chicago: C. H. Kerr Co., 1906, vol. I, p. 198.

compels society, under penalty of death, to replace the detail-worker of to-day, crippled by lifelong repetition of one and the same trivial operation, and thus reduced to the mere fragment of a man, by the fully developed individual, fit for a variety of labours, ready to face any change of production, and to whom the different social functions he performs, are but so many modes of giving free scope to his own natural and acquired powers.

The existence of classes originated in the division of labour, and the division of labour as it has been known up to the present will completely disappear. For mechanical and chemical processes are not enought to bring industrial and agricultural production up to the level we have described; the capacities of the men who make use of these processes must undergo a corresponding development. Just as the peasants and manufacturing workers of the last century changed their whole way of life and became quite different people when they were impressed into big industry, in the same way communal control over production by society as a whole and the resulting new development will both require an entirely different kind of human material. People will no longer be, as they are today, subordinated to a single branch of production, bound to it, exploited by it; they will no longer develop one of their faculties at the expense of all others; they will no longer know only one branch, or one branch of a single branch, of production as a whole. Even industry as it is today is finding such people less and less useful. Industry controlled by society as a whole and operated according to a plan presupposes well-rounded human beings, their faculties developed in balanced fashion, able to see the system of production in its entirety. The form of the division of labour which makes one a peasant, another a cobbler, a third a factory worker, a fourth a stock-market operator has already been undermined by machinery and will completely disappear. Education will enable young people quickly to familiarize themselves with the whole system of production and to pass from one branch of production to another in response to the needs of society or their own inclinations. It will therefore free them from the one-sided character which the present-day division of labour impresses upon every individual. Communist society will in this way make it possible for its members to put their comprehensively developed faculties to full use. But when this happens classes will necessarily disappear. [45]

45. Karl Marx, CAPITAL, vol. I, pp. 533-534; THE GERMAN IDEOLOGY, edited and Introduction by R. Pascal, New York: International Publishers, 1947, Pts I and II, pp. 21-23, 75; Fredrich Engels, PRINCIPLES OF COMMUNISM, translated by Paul M. Sweezy, New York: Monthly Review Pamphlet Series, No. 4, 1952, Question 20. "What will be the consequences of the ultimate disappearance of private property?"

While one can sympathize with Marx's criticisms of the debilitating and stupifying effect of the more microscopic phases of work processes and the caste features of the social division of labor, any social reform movement predicated on the basis of the abolition of all forms of the division of labor is fantastic. Certainly, the realization of an ideal of authentic personality would require, at the very least, that men be liberated from the most banausic tasks and that they have some sense of choice and worth in their daily work. In addition to the intellectual, moral, and craft abilities demanded by work of a certain level, one might expect from the worker a general understanding of the relation of his occupation to the overall economy and its general welfare implications.

Marx's interest in the phenomenon of estrangement is primarily an ethical interest. Although he attempted an analysis of the structure of alienation (estrangement) in its epistemological, theological, and economic-political forms, Marx did not sufficiently stress the basic structural features of any society. Indeed, Engels was forced to remind the anarchists that social life is impossible without structural principles of authority and control.

> . . . a certain authority, no matter how delegated, and, on the other hand, a certain subordination are things which, independent of all social organization, are imposed upon us together with the material conditions under which we produce and make products circulate.

> We have seen, besides, that the material conditions of production and circulation inevitably develop with large-scale industry and large-scale agriculture, and increasingly tend to enlarge the scope of this authority. Hence it is absurd to speak of the principle of authority as being absolutely evil and of the principle of autonomy as being absolutely good. Authority and autonomy are relative things, whose spheres vary with the various phases of the development of society.[46]

The historical urgency of Marx's ethical concept of nonalienated personality fails to transcend his analysis of capitalist society. But man is constantly subject to new forms of historical necessity (ἀνάγκη) which create new dimensions of the moral problem. The test of the vigour of Marxian social science and its ethics is its ability to furnish techniques for dealing with the next stages of capitalism, as well as the problems of socialist societies on the path of industrialization.

    46.   Karl Marx and Fredrich Engels, BASIC WRITINGS ON POLITICS AND PHILOSOPHY, edited by Lewis S. Feuer, New York: Anchor Books, Doubleday and Co. Inc., 1959, p. 484.

CHAPTER 5

ON THE HISTORY OF THE HUMAN SENSES
IN VICO AND MARX

I propose to think together Vico and Marx as historians and poets of the human senses--despite an earlier report which failed to find any real family between Vico and Marx.[1] This is an essay, then, which challenges the patented determination of history to reassemble first and last things in the uninhabited orders of science. If today we can think together Vico and Marx it is because we are open to a more self-conscious practice of science, less inclined now to forget its ties with our vulgar wisdom of origins and ends. Thus we can think together Vico and Marx because each reverberates in the other "in deeseperation of deispiration at the diasporation of his diesparation."[2] For neither Marx nor Vico ever thought history outside of time's body,[3] which is the institution of those fantastic universals "found of the round of the sound of the lound" of the age of men, gathering thunder, acorns, animals, and speech in order to clothe man's bodily beginnings in civil beauty and divine piety.

> Here we may reflect how much it took for the men of the gentile world to be tamed from their feral native liberty through a long period of cyclopean family discipline to the point of obeying naturally the laws in the civil states which were to come later. Hence there remained the eternal property that happier than the commonwealth conceived by Plato are those where the fathers teach only religion and where they are admired by their sons as sages, revered as their priests, and feared as their kings. Such and so much divine force was needed to reduce these giants, as savage as they were crude, to human deities. Since they were unable to express this force abstractly, they represented it in concrete physical form as a cord, called chorda in Greek and in Latin at first fides, whose original and proper meaning appears in the phrase fides deorum, force of the gods. From this cord (for the lyre must have begun with the monochord) they fashioned the lyre of Orpheus, to the accompaniment of which, singing to them the force of the gods in the auspices, he tamed the beasts of Greece to

1. Eugene Kamenka, "Vico and Marxism," in Giorgio Tagliacozzo and Hayden V. White, Eds., GIAMBATTISTA VICO: AN INTERNATIONAL SYMPOSIUM, Baltimore: Johns Hopkins Press, 1969, pp. 137-143.

2. James Joyce, FINNEGANS WAKE, New York: Viking Press, 1939, p. 257.

3. John O'Neill, "Times Body," in his MAKING SENSE TOGETHER: AN INTRODUCTION TO WILD SOCIOLOGY, New York: Harper & Row, 1974, pp. 28-38.

humanity. And Amphion raised the walls of Thebes with stones that moved themselves. These were the stones which Deucalion and Pyrrha, standing before the temple of Themis (that is, in fear of divine justice) with veiled heads (the modesty of marriage), found lying before their feet (for men were at first stupid, and lapis, stone, remained Latin for a stupid person) and threw over their shoulders (introducing family institutions by means of household discipline), thus making men of them. . . . [4]

Vico and Marx are the twice-born scientists of man. This is not because our history survives through sheer repetition or dizzy spells. It is because human history is never displayed before itself and rather folds upon us in our living and dying so that Vico is no more before Marx than we are after Marx. Thus in thinking together Vico and Marx it is also ourselves that we recollect. "Teems of times and happy returns. The seim anew. Ordovico or viricordo. Anna was, Livia is, Plurabelle's to be. Northmen's thing made southfolk's place but howmulty plurators made eachone in person? Latin me that my trinity scholard, out of eure sanscreed into oure eryan." [5] For it is in the spirit of man to remember man in his spirits, and kindly to discover man's history like the beat of his own heart. All history is therefore the history of our species-being (Gattungswesen), of the genera-tion of men whose hearts and minds are schooled in that house-hold of being which we have not to assemble through science because it arises above all from our living together whose vulgar wisdom is the limit of all our sciences.

As for the other part of household discipline, the education of bodies, the fathers with their frightful religions, their cyclopean authority, and their sacred ablutions began to educe, or bring forth, from the giant bodies of their sons the proper human form. . . . And herein is providence above all to be admired, for it is ordained that until such times as domestic education should supervene, the lost men should become giants in order that in their feral wanderings they might endure with their robust constitutions the in-clemency of the heavens and the seasons, and that they might with their disproportionate strength penetrate the great forest of the earth (which must have been very dense as a result of the recent flood), so that, fleeing from wild beasts and pursuing reluctant women and thus becoming lost from each other, they might be scattered through it in search of food and water until it should be found in due

4.   THE NEW SCIENCE OF GIAMBATTISTA VICO, translated by Thomas G. Bergin and Max H. Fisch, Ithaca: Cornell University Press, 1968, par. 523.

5.   James Joyce, FINNEGANS WAKE, p. 215.

time fully populated; while after they began to remain in one place with their women, first in caves, then in huts near perennial springs and in the fields which, brought under cultivation, gave them sustenance, providence ordained that, from the causes we are now setting forth, they should shrink to the present stature of mankind.[6]

It is not because Vico and Marx were economists that we must think them together. It is because we cannot think economic life itself apart from its poetry first grasped by Vico and made by Marx the incarnate principle of all human labor, joy, and suffering. The fundamental thesis of poetic economics is that man is a work of his own senses and intellect and that these are never so alien to him, even in their remote beginnings, as not to build upon them our very humanity. Thus the human body is the ground of all those institutions of sense and intellect which enter into the gradual making of the history through which we hold together mankind in the face of all its sufferings and losses.

Private property is only the sensuous expression of the fact that man is both objective to himself and even more becomes a hostile and inhuman object to himself, that the expression of his life entails its externalization, its realization becomes the loss of its reality, an alien reality. Similarly the positive supersession of private property, that is, the sensuous appropriation by and for man of human essence and human life, of objective man and his works, should not be conceived of only as direct and exclusive enjoyment, as possession and having. Man appropriates his universal being in a universal manner, as a whole man. Each of his relationships to the world--seeing, hearing, smell, tasting, feeling, thinking, contemplating, willing, acting, loving--in short all the organs whose form is a communal one, are in their objective action, or their relation to the object, the appropriation of human reality, their relation to the object, is the confirmation of human reality. It is therefore as manifold as the determinations and activities of human nature. It is human effectiveness and suffering, for suffering, understood in the human sense, is an enjoyment of the self for man.[7]

Poetic economics is therefore never a simple science of needs and utilities but rather belongs to a general theory of human education. Poetic economics is a general science of those divine and human artifacts that men have made in order to make themselves human. Utilitarian economics is merely a science of our first

6. THE NEW SCIENCE, par. 524.

7. Karl Marx, "Economic and Philosophic Manuscripts," in his EARLY TEXTS, translated and edited by David McLellan, Oxford: Basil Blackwell, 1971, p. 151.

body, our organic body whose emblem is nature. But nature is not outside of man any more than man is outside of nature. Marxist economics is therefore not merely a science of domination, since it cannot be blind to the human costs of man's lordship of nature.[8]   Nature is our own doing, neither more hostile nor less kindly than we make it appear in our own institutions.

> The human significance of nature is only available to social man; for only to social man is nature available as a bond with other men, as the basis for his own existence for others and theirs for him, and as the vital element in human reality; only to social man is nature the foundation of his own human existence.   Only as such has his natural existence become a human existence and nature itself become human.   Thus society completes the essential unity of man and nature, it is the genuine resurrection of nature, the accomplished naturalism of man and the accomplished human- ism of nature.[9]

Poetic economics is not hasty with science's separation of man from his elemental needs; it is properly a science of expression which preserves the metaphysical resonance of human religion, politics, economics, and art.   Poetic economics therefore does not regard religion as an illusion, as an uncertain way of seeing what science can teach us for sure.   Indeed, religion, myth and magic are not the simple expression of man's failure to see things. Rather, they are man's vision of the failure of things where men are set against themselves in oppression and exploitation.   Thus poetic economics is inspired by the dream of man's wholeness, the dream of love's body, that is, the incarnate union of all men in Marx's day around a round day:

> For as soon as the distribution of labour comes into being, each man has a particular, exclusive sphere of activity, which is forced upon him and from which he cannot escape. He is a hunter, a fisherman, a shepherd, or a critical critic, and must remain so if he does not want to lose his means of livelihood; while in communist society, where nobody has one exclusive sphere of activity, but each can become ac- complished in any branch he wishes, society regulates the general production and thus makes it possible for me to do one thing today and another tomorrow, to hunt in the morn- ing, fish in the afternoon, rear cattle in the evening,

8.   Ch. 6, "History as Human History in Hegel and Marx."

9.   Marx, ECONOMIC AND PHILOSOPHIC MANUSCRIPTS, p. 150.

criticize after dinner, just as I have a mind, without ever becoming hunter, fisherman, shepherd or critic.[10]

Poetic economics rejects the mathematical division of sense and intellect, of nature and society and of town and countryside which have separated the men of the forests from the dark men of today's factories who labor in the unseasonable accumulation of science and capital. As Vico appealed to our wild and savage nature in order to renew science, so Marx in turn called upon a heroic class of men in whom human nature has been brutalized in order to save our very humanity.

Marxist economics, like Vico's poetic economics is a general science of the institutions of the human senses as the instruments of a general reality or a universal field of synergy whereby each of us contributes to all of mankind and none of us begins without that anonymous legacy of the human body and the vulgar wisdom of civic life. Therefore socialist society cannot be the product of Marxist economics insofar as Marxism remains a science of domination, forgetful of the poetic foundations of economics[11] Mathematical economics is merely a science of man's first body which rules inorganic nature and men's exploitative relationships. Thus in industrial societies the productive process tends to integrate man's _organic body_ within industry's higher mechanical and physico-chemical processes. At this level the _productive body_ is separated from our first organic body through the superfoetation of its needs and its expanding alienation from _love's body_ is accomplished by the rationalization of its sensory and intellect processes in the service of commercial life.[12] Poetic economics is therefore not a science of the productive body simply because in the modern world production intensifies labor in pursuit of levels of consumption beyond the sensible and libidinal limits of man's integral body. By the same process the industrial system integrates the world's body into its economy of desires which destroy those elemental times and places that are not simply the dwelling places of unhistorical men but the very sources of our humanity.

Vico's poetic economics renews science by calling to mind the question underlying all science, namely how it is men have made themselves human. It is with the same underlying question that

10. Karl Marx and Frederick Engels, THE GERMAN IDEOLOGY, Parts I and III, edited and with an introduction by R. Pascal, New York: International Publishers, 1969, p. 22.

11. Ch. 1, "For Marx against Althusser."

12. John O'Neill, "Authority, Knowledge and the Body Politic," in his SOCIOLOGY AS A SKIN TRADE: ESSAYS TOWARDS A REFLEXIVE SOCIOLOGY New York: Harper & Row, 1972, pp. 68-80.

Marx recalls the vast alienation of man's labor and intellect which supplies the engines of production and consumption in the modern world. Marx's call for revolution reverberates the memory of a prehistorical unity of sense and society.[13] It resurrects the world's body in the reawakening of history's dream of a time before the separation of sense and intellect, of a place where man's promise and potentiality had not been broken and betrayed.

> Communism as completed naturalism is humanism and as completed humanism is naturalism. It is the genuine solution of the antagonism between man and nature and between man and man. It is the true solution of the stuggle between essence and existence, between objectification and self-affirmation, between freedom and necessity, between individual and species. It is the solution to the riddle of history and knows itself to be this solution.[14]

Poetic economics brings forth the education of man's body and spirit. Vico's philological method loves man in his speech and gathers his humanity from poetry. In the same way Marx's method is materialist or sensuous and invokes the unity of man and nature in the history of social development. Now Vico reminds us that the new science of man is not to be practiced without piety, which is the love men of today owe to what their ancestors have yielded to them through the sense and nonsense of history's suffering. Therefore piety must likewise rule Marxist humanism in order that its new men not live in forgetfulness of those whose labor and intellect were wasted before and during the revolution. For surely a great sadness weighs upon communist society mindful of the past's injustice and its unrewarded suffering. Marxist humanism therefore is only truly secular in the remembrance per omnia saecula saeculorum of the generations of human labor and suffering that have made possible the very vision of socialist revolution.

> A Klee painting named "Angelus Novus" shows an angel looking as though he is about to move away from something he is fixedly contemplating. His eyes are staring, his mouth is open, his wings are spread. This is how one pictures the angel of history. His face is turned towards the past. Where we perceive a chain of events, he sees one single catastrophe which keeps piling wreckage upon wreckage and hurls it in front of his feet. The angel would like to stay,

---

13. I am not, of course, arguing that there is no need for an analytic element in Marxist thought. My argument is that Marxism becomes a science because it is first of all a humanist project in the light of which it must critically evaluate its specific praxes. Cf. ch. 2, "Habermas and Althusser On Theory and Criticism in Marx."

14. Karl Marx, ECONOMIC AND PHILOSOPHIC MANUSCRIPTS, p. 148.

awaken the dead, and make whole what has been smashed. But a storm is blowing from Paradise; it has got caught in his wings with such violence that the angel can no longer close them. This storm irresistibly propels him into the future to which his back is turned while the pile of debris before him grows skyward. This storm is what we call progress. [15]

In thinking together Vico and Marx, we make of the world's body a reminder that we are never our own creature and are always in flight from ourselves. We are no closer to self-knowledge for living today than our fellow men who once lived in forests and caves calling down upon themselves their own gods. Like time's body we separate from ourselves from moment to moment in thought and speech, in labor and in prayer. The unity of mankind is therefore at any time and in any place a monument we raise in our own honor to record the history of the world's labor still struggling to bring forth the poetry of man. [16]

15.   Walter Benjamin, "Theses on the Philosophy of History," in his ILLUMINA-TIONS, edited and with an introduction by Hannah Arendt, New York: Harcourt, Brace & World, 1968, pp. 259-260.

16.   John O'Neill, "Critique and Remembrance," in John O'Neill, ed., ON CRITICAL THEORY, New York: Seabury Press, 1976, pp. 1-12.

CHAPTER 6

HISTORY AS HUMAN HISTORY

IN HEGEL AND MARX

The rediscovery of the concept of alienation by Marxists in search of a framework for the interpretation and critique of socialist reality has been challenged as an attempt to refurbish a speculative Hegelian notion which Marx abandoned for the more precise concept of exploitation. The 'historical Marx,' that is to say, Marx of the COMMUNIST MANIFESTO and CAPITAL, whom Marxists themselves have given to history, is now to be forsaken for a history made out of the revolutionary event of Marx's discovery of alienation in the property system and the utopian suggestion that the collectivization of property would end alienation and the prehistory of man.[1] These events might be taken to indicate that here at any rate Marx's critique of Hegel appears to have backfired and that Hegel's original concept of alienation as an ontological experience is the more general concept that Marxists now need for the understanding of the unhappy socialist consciousness.

I think it can be argued that what is usually set forth as Marx's redefinition of the Hegelian concept of alienation is nothing else than a progression to be found in THE PHENOMENOLOGY OF MIND. If this is indeed so, then the 'existentialist' version of Hegel's concept of alienation is not wholly true to Hegel's account of the relation between the individual and society and cannot be employed to revise Marx. The attempt to correct late Marx with early Marx appears to be a correction in favor of Hegel only if Hegel himself is corrected in terms of a reading of the early phenomenological description of the 'Unhappy Consciousness.' But if this discussion is followed through to the historical description of self-estrangement and culture then it becomes clear that in Hegel the experience of alienation is neither individual nor social in origin but the historical mediation of society and the individual through the process of work as self-expression or culture (<u>Bildung</u>) in which alienation is ultimately suspended. Now I admit that this more complete account of Hegel's concept of alienation is closer to that of Marx than perhaps Marx himself understood in the ECONOMIC AND PHILOSOPHIC MANUSCRIPTS 1844. But if we must consider Marx's philosophical and economic thought as a unity,[2] as I think we must, then our Hegelian

---

1.　John O'Neill, "Alienation, Class Struggle and Marxian Anti-Politics," REVIEW OF METAPHYSICS, XVII, No. 3, (March 1964), 462-471.

2.　See Chapter 4, "Marx's Concept of Alienation."

friends must do the same for Hegel. We may then proceed in agreement, as Marx was fond of saying to Engels.

I am dealing with the convergence between Hegel and Marx and I want to show that the 'existentialist' version of this phenomenon is not properly grounded in either Hegel or Marx. The consequences of this may be seen in Sartre's struggle in the CRITIQUE DE LA RAISON DIALECTIQUE to unite the ontological alienation involved in the dialectic of recognition of the other with a concept of intersubjectivity as the necessary ground of political action and organization.

The ultimate goal of self-consciousness is to recover the unity of the self and the world which it discovers abstractly in the unity of the mind and its objects. The recovery of the world is mediated by desire which reveals the world as my praxis. But this is still only abstractly a world until my interests are recognized by the other. The dialectic of recognition appears as a life and death struggle because of desire which binds consciousness to the world of things and simultaneously reveals its transcendence as the negation of things and the Other. But the categories of subject and object, negation, self, other and recognition are not a priori categories of experience. They arise in the course of the self-interpretation by consciousness of its modes of lived experience which involve consciousness in a dialectic between intentionality and an irreducible ontological difference which generates the world and the recognition of the Other. For if consciousness did not encounter the resistance of things and others, it could only know things perceptually and others by analogy and it would have no organic or social life. But this means that consciousness can never be satisfied in a desire for objects and the Other. For in this it would only consume itself whereas it needs a common world in which things and others reflect consciousness back upon itself. 'Self-consciousness, which is absolutely _for itself_, and characterizes its object directly as negative, or is primarily desire, will really, therefore, find through experience this object's independence.'[3] Desire then is not the actuality of self-consciousness but only its potentiality for actualizing itself in a common world and inter-subjectivity. Hence the struggle to the death which originates in desire is exteriorized in the relation to objects established between the Master and the Slave which preserves their independence in the form of a living dependency. 'In this experience self-consciousness becomes aware that life is as essential to it as pure self-consciousness.'[4]

    3.   THE PHENOMENOLOGY OF MIND, translated by J. B. Baillie, London: Allen & Unwin, 1910, p. 221.

    4.   IBID., p. 234.

With respect (fear) for life that is born from the struggle to the
death there is initiated a further dialectic in which the Slave's
apprenticeship to things makes possible the practical observation
of the laws of their operation. Though he works for another, the
Slave learns to work with objects whose independence now submits
to his production though not to his consumption. By the same
token the Master's independence of things mediated by the Slave
becomes his dependence upon the Slave's cultivation.

> Labour, on the other hand, is desire restrained and
> checked, evanescence delayed and postponed; in other
> words, labour shapes and fashions the thing. The negative
> relation to the object passes into the form of the object, into
> something that is permanent and remains; because it is just
> for the labourer that the object has independence.[5]

Thus from the recognition of the value of life and the fear of
death, expressed in submission to things for the sake of life, the
experience of domination and servitude opens up the cycle of
culture as the objective mediation of self-expression and the
world. It is through work that the world is revealed as conscious praxis, as a field of individual interests which are in turn
opened to the interests of others and hence to a common measure
of good and evil. As a field of practical intentions the world is
the element of consciousness, its 'original nature' which the
activity of consciousness molds to its purposes. Hegel is quite
explicit that there is no room for the experience of estrangement
in the act whereby the self externalizes itself in the world of
objects. It is the very nature of consciousness to act to
externalize itself in the deed, or work.

> The act is something simply determinate, universal to be
> grasped as an abstract, distinctive whole; it is murder,
> theft, a benefit, a deed of bravery, and so on, and what it
> is can be said of it. It is such and such, and its being is
> not merely a symbol, it is the fact itself. It is this, and
> the individual human being is what the act is. In the simple
> fact that the act is the individual is for others what he
> really is and with a certain general nature, and ceases to be
> merely something that is 'meant' or 'presumed' to be this or
> that. No doubt he is not put there in the form of mind; but
> when it is a question of his being qua being, and the two-
> fold being of bodily shape and act are pitted against one
> another, each claiming to be his true reality, the deed alone
> is to be affirmed as his genuine being--not his figure or
> shape, which would express what he 'means' to convey by
> his acts, or what any one might 'conjecture' he merely could

5.   IBID., p. 238

do. In the same way, on the other hand, when his performance and his inner possibility, capacity, or intention are
opposed, the former alone is to be regarded as his true
reality, even if he deceives himself on the point, and, after
he has turned from his action into himself, means to be
something else in his 'inner mind' than what he is in the
act. Individuality, which commits itself to the objective
element, when it passes over into a deed no doubt puts
itself to the risk of being altered and perverted. But what
settles the character of the act is just this--whether the
deed is a real thing that holds together, or whether it is
merely a pretended or 'supposed' performance, which is in
itself null and void and passes away. Objectification does
not alter the act itself; it merely shows what the deed is,
i.e., whether it is or whether it is nothing.[6]

Only if we abstract the moments of purpose, means, and object
can we speak of the transcendence of consciousness over its
accomplished deeds or works. But apart from the process of
work, consciousness would remain an empty project and its
freedom a pure negativity without a world. It is in the process
of work that consciousness experiences the identity of freedom
and nature. The externalization of consciousness is a natural
experience through which an objective culture and history is
created which in turn gives shape to the individual who acquires
through it his essential or generic humanity.

It is often remarked that Hegel spiritualized action where Marx
materialized it. Marx himself believed this to be the substance of
his critique of Hegel. But I think there is some evidence for the
argument that Hegel and Marx are engaged in a similar critique of
alienation as estrangement from action as expression; and thus
there is a continuity between Hegel's THE PHENOMENOLOGY OF
MIND and Marx's ECONOMIC AND PHILOSOPHIC MANUSCRIPTS.

In his remarKs on physiognomy Hegel argues that the externalization of consciousness is not contingently related to its purpose
but is essential to consciousness as embodied being. Thus the
human hand and human speech are essential organs of conscious
expression and it is by means of them that we establish a common
world of artifacts and meanings. It is through the body that we
give to our immediate surroundings 'a general human shape and
form, or at least the general character of a climate, of a portion
of the world,' just as we find regions of the world characterized
by different customs and culture. It is through the expressive
organs of the hand and speech that we realize a unity of purpose
and object which conveys our presence in the world and to

6.   IBID., pp. 349-350.

others. The human body is thus the expressive instrument of spirit and not its simple objective alienation; it is the instrument whereby there can be culture and history which in turn shape human sensibility, thought, and perception.

> For if the organs in general proved to be incapable of being taken as expression of the inner for the reason that in them the action is present as a process, while the action as a deed or (finished) act is merely external, and inner and outer in this way fall apart are or can be alien to one another, the organ must, in view of the peculiarity now considered, be again taken as also a middle term for both. . . .[7]

Thus self-consciousness is not estranged by its natural being, for the human body is an expressive organ through which meaning is embodied in speech and the work of human hands which together articulate the nature of man.

> That the hand, however, must exhibit and reveal the inherent nature of individuality as regards its fate, is easily seen from the fact that after the organ of speech it is the hand most of all by which a man actualizes and manifests himself. It is the animated artificer of his fortune; we may say of the hand it is what a man does, for in it as the effective organ of his fulfilment he is there present as the animating soul; and since he is ultimately and originally his own fate, the hand will thus express this innate inherent nature.[8]

The expression of the human spirit is not the abstract confrontation of a pure interiority with a simple exteriority but the reciprocation of intentionality, gesture, and the deed through which joy, sorrow, and nobility delineate their own meaning in the eyes, the voice, and the hands of man.

The growth of human culture is the growth of human sensibility. So long as culture is dependent upon the class domination of Resources or Wealth, then the judgment of Good is identified with the Power to command wealth and Bad with the wealth that always threatens to be lacking but for power over it. But the universalization of culture implicit in the expressive activity of work is progressively made explicit in the power of the spoken word to express the intellectual, political, and economic ideal of action as self-expression, of which the supreme prerevolutionary expression is Diderot's NEVEU DE RAMEAU. The liberal identification of

7.   IBID., p. 343.

8.   IBID., p. 343.

self-expression with the organization of society as a system of needs results in a hybrid political economy. And it is the critique of political economy begun in Hegel which provides the bridge to Marx. The nub of Hegel's critique of liberal society is that it rests upon a confusion of a law discovered in the workings of the passions, the invisible law of the market, with law in the ethical sense of a law embraced by rational self-consciousness. This distinction is the basis for Hegel's transition to his philosophy of the State which Karl Löwith, for example, considers as an apparent dialectical transition within liberal society, or rather only its 'suspension through the ideal of the polis.'[9] We might then understand Hegel's critique of liberal society not as a recommendation that the 'State' supersede 'Society,' but that the liberal subordination of law to an empirical law of the passions as a criterion for the organization of society be superseded in favor of a society organized about a conception of law based on the sublime need of self-consciousness to achieve self-expression in its objects and activities.

Whatever the nature of the differences between THE PHENOMEN- OLOGY OF MIND and the PHILOSOPHY OF RIGHT, it is perhaps fateful that Marx began his critique of Hegel with an attack on the Hegelian conception of the State. Marx attacks the Hegelian State as a cultural universal on the ground that it only abstractly mediates the separation between the private interests of the bourgeoisie, summarized in the doctrine of Natural Rights, and the nature of Man supposedly outlined in the doctrine of Rights. 'Here man is far from being conceived as a member of a general class; rather the life of this class itself, society, is conceived as a framework external to the individuals, a restriction upon their original independence. The only bond holding them together is . . . need and private interest.'[10] Marx concludes that bourgeois society cannot be transcended politically for the state rests upon and is nothing else than the legitimation of an in- dividualistic society. The critique of bourgeois society can only be grounded in a reexamination of the process through which the totality of human life and expression is reduced to a set of needs defined by the impoverishment of labor.

It is not necessary to trace Marx's economic and historical analysis of the institutional preconditions of alienation.[11] This is the aspect of Marx's work which, though not lacking in Hegel, separates Marx from Hegel. The differences, however, seem smaller once attention is given to Marx's conception of the

---

9.   Karl Löwith, FROM HEGEL TO NIETZSCHE, translated by David E. Green, New York: Holt, Rinehart, and Winston, 1964, p. 242.

10.   IBID., p. 245.

11.   See Chapter 3, "Marxism and Mythology."

universal nature of work and the human world and sensibility which is its product. I have tried to show earlier that Hegel did not regard man as pure self-consciousness. His treatment of consciousness as embodied being in which the organs of hand and speech are the naturally expressive and creative agencies of a human world should at least modify the criticism that Hegel's concept of alienation confused the two processes of externalization and estrangement. Insofar as Hegel's conception of Man is that of an embodied consciousness, then I think Hegel could well have concurred with the anthropological concept that Marx thought he was opposing to Hegel in the following remark.

> To say that man is a corporeal, living, real, sensuous, objective being full of natural vigour is to say that he has real, sensuous objects as the objects of his being or of his life, or that he can only express his life in real, sensuous objects. To be objective, natural, and sensuous, and at the same time to have object, nature, and sense outside oneself, or oneself to be object, nature, and sense for a third part, is one and the same thing.[12]

Finally, there are several aspects of Marx's concept of alienation among which there is, I think, a central notion where again Marx and Hegel share a common conception of action as self-expression. For Marx alienation is a fact of political economy not of phenomenology. That is to say, in the first place, under capitalism man is estranged from the product of his work which in turn estranges him from his own nature as a sensuous and social being. Under such conditions the meaning of work becomes merely a means of subsistence for the satisfaction of purely animal needs and loses its nature as a human need which is to work creatively even in the absence of physical needs. Man and Nature are thus involved in a cultural matrix in which the natural history of man is interwoven with the humanization of natural history.

> Only through the objectivity unfolded richness of man's essential being is the richness of subjective human sensibility (a musical ear, an eye for beauty of form--in short, senses capable of human gratifications, senses confirming themselves as essential powers of man) either cultivated or brought into being. For not only the five senses but also the so-called mental senses--the practical senses (will, love, etc.)--in a word, human sense--the humanness of the senses--comes to be by virtue of its object, by virtue of humanized nature. The forming of the five senses is a labour of the entire history of the world down to the present.[13]

12.   ECONOMIC AND PHILOSOPHIC MANUSCRIPTS OF 1844, Moscow: Foreign Languages Publishing House, 1956, p. 156.

13.   IBID., p. 108.

The evolution of human nature proceeds in terms of the interaction between man and nature and the technology and social
relations of production which mediate that process. In this sense
the potentiality of human nature may be regarded as a function of
the means and relations of production.

> Because of this simple fact that every succeeding generation
> finds itself in possession of the productive forces won by
> the previous generation which serve it as the raw material
> for new production, a connection arises in human history, a
> history of humanity takes shape which has become all the
> more a history of humanity since the productive forces of
> man and therefore his social relations have been extended.
> Hence it necessarily follows: the social history of men is
> never anything but the history of their individual develop-
> ment, whether they are conscious of it or not. [14]

Thus, I think, it is possible to conclude that neither Hegel nor
Marx separated Nature from History and that both regarded world
history as a history of culture in which human needs furnish a
primary structure open to a multiplicity of cultural forms which in
turn shape the existential character of need but directed toward
the truly human needs of creativity and sociality. I have tried to
show the sense of this in the previous chapter.

I shall now return to Marx and Vico to develop that connection
further and to rejoin my argument with related themes in contemporary critical theory.

14.   Marx to Annenkov, Brussels, 28 December 1846, SELECTED CORRESPON-
DENCE, 1846-1895, translated by Dora Torr, London: Lawrence and Wishart Ltd.,
1934. p. 7.

CHAPTER 7

NATURALISM IN VICO AND MARX:

A DISCOURSE THEORY OF THE BODY POLITIC

> The human mind is naturally inclined by the senses to see itself externally in the body, and only with great difficulty does it come to understand itself by means of reflection. This axiom gives us the universal principle of etymology in all languages: words are carried over from bodies and from the properties of bodies to signify the contributions of the mind and spirit.[1]

Vico and Marx are two of the greatest naturalists. They are, by the same token, two of the great humanists. Today, such a claim would seem paradoxical inasmuch as nothing threatens humanism so much as the naturalist methods of the human and social sciences in their embrace of a universal scientism. Yet Vico and Marx rejected both materialism and idealism because of their inadequate conception of man's embodied mind and sensuous history. In the words of Marx:

> But man is not only a natural being, he is a human natural being. This means that he is a being that exists for himself, thus a species-being that must confirm and exercise himself as such in his being and knowledge. Thus human objects are not natural objects as they immediately present themselves nor is human sense, in its purely objective existence, human sensitivity and human objectivity. Neither nature in its objective aspect nor in its subjective aspect is immediately adequate to the human being. And as everything natural must have an origin, so man too has his process of origin, history, which can, however, be known by him and thus is a conscious process of origin that transcends itself. <u>History is the true natural history of man</u>.[2]

The echo of Vico's NEW SCIENCE is easily heard in this passage, and we have shown in Chapter 6 how Marx is indebted to Vico for his conception of 'natural man' and a radically historicized account of the development of the human senses. Here we propose to accept Habermas's argument[3] that Marx's naturalism fails to

1. Vico, NEW SCIENCE, Paras. 236-237.

2. Karl Marx, "Economic and Philosophical Manuscripts," p. 169 in KARL MARX EARLY TEXTS, translated and edited by David McLellan, Oxford: Basil Blackwell, 1971.

3. Jürgen Habermas, KNOWLEDGE AND HUMAN INTERESTS, translated by Jeremy J. Shapiro, Boston: Beacon Press, 1971, pp. 62-63.

achieve the historical transcendence implicit in it because Marx
did not sufficiently distinguish the level of language and communicative praxis from the level of economy. He thereby failed to
ground the convertability of historical experience and historical
reflection-- verum et factum convertuntur--falling into an economistic naturalism alien to his own humanism.[4] But whereas
Habermas also considers Vico's naturalism to be wholly under-
written by Providence, and thereby deprived of any emancipatory
reflection, we shall try to show how Vico's philology may be
developed so that we gain a subversive conception of poetic
economy, that is, of the body politic.

For Marx, the integral body politic is a pre-and-posthistorical
phenomenon. Thus, in the historical period, Marx's natural man
serves rather as a critical principle for thinking and rethinking
the foundations of society and political economy. Insofar as
Marx's naturalistic methodology focused upon the analysis of the
economic process and tended, as Habermas argues, to ignore the
level of communicative process, we think that Vico's philological
naturalism supplied a corrective. We shall then argue that Vico's
philological naturalism avoids the linguistic degeneration that
characterizes all scientistic political economy. It thereby
preserves the radically subversive language of the body politic as
an essential force in the contemporary struggle between humanism
and scientism.

Vico grounds the human sciences in the history of the world's
body, as we have seen earlier.[5] We cannot sufficiently stress
the originality of Vico's giants (grossi bestioni). It is upon their
shoulders   that   the   philosophers   stand--whether   Plato   or
Descartes. That is the core of the NEW SCIENCE as fundamental
anthropology. It is, of course, inseparable from Vico's philological method, his literary archaeology, whereby he removed the
philosophical accumulations of rationalism to reveal an originary
materialism as the only possible ground of our civil humanity.
Whatever the ingenuity of later thinkers, they stand in a
necessary, historical line with the founding ingenuity of that
corporeal imagination exercised by the first men whose bodies
ruled them as the generative source of all relationships, concepts,
and generalizations. This is the historical ground of common
sense considered as an achievement that is fundamental to any
higher unity of mankind pursued as a reflective enterprise of
reason and morals. By the same token, this embodied logic furnishes the scientific ground of the NEW SCIENCE itself, of its

    4. For Habermas's views on the relation between Vico and Marx see especially
his THEORY AND PRACTICE, translated by John Viertel, Boston: Beacon Press,
1973, pp. 242-252.

    5. See Chapter 5.

axioms and hypotheses, of its comparative method, of every test of the truths of its postulated ideal eternal history. Therefore our giants are not allegorical creatures. They gave to the thundering sky a great body like their own and made Jove their god, ruler of all men, source of all things. United under Jove's saving rule, they thereby established the first human communities--under vulgar law, religiously and without the conceits of philosophy. The body politic, therefore, owes itself to these first awkward bodies who scared themselves into being ruled by their own fantastic ideas of frightful religions, terrible paternal powers and sacred ablutions. To these awkward ancestors we owe the foundation of harmony

(a) in ourselves, our minds and bodies,

(b) in our households

The heroes apprehended with human senses those two truths which make up the whole of economic doctrine, and which were preserved in the two Latin verbs <u>educere</u> and <u>educare</u>. In the prevailing best usage the first of these applies to the education of the spirit and the second to that of the body. The first, by a learned metaphor, was transferred by the natural philosophers to the bringing forth of forms from matter. For heroic education began to bring forth in a certain way the form of the human soul which had been completely submerged in the huge bodies of the giants, and began likewise to bring forth the form of the human body itself in its just dimensions from the disproportionate giant bodies.[6]

All politics are beholden to the corporeal grounds of poetic economy. In the first case, our giants set the mind and imagination above the heart and the base passions, and being without writing, they founded the arts of humanity upon invention and judgement in accordance with the particulars of their experience. Thus all later humanity is indebted to the vulgar metaphysics of the first incorporation whereby our giants proportioned themselves to the human frame educating their bodies to suit them to the basic institutions of civil humanity--religion, marriage and burial.

But these first men, who later became the princes of the gentile nations, must have done their thinking under the strong impulsion of violent passions, as beasts do. We must therefore proceed from vulgar metaphysics, such as we will find the theology of the poets to have been, and seek by its

6. Vico, NEW SCIENCE, para. 520.

aid that frightful thought of some divinity which imposed form and measure on the bestial passions of these lost men and thus transformed them into human passions. From this thought must have sprung the impulse proper to the human will, to hold in check the emotions impressed on the mind by the body, so as either to quiet them altogether, as becomes the wise man, or at least to direct them to better use, as becomes the civil man. This control over the motions of their bodies is certainly an effect of the freedom of human choice, and thus of free will, which is the home and seal of all the virtues, and among the others of justice.[7]

Vico preserves the poetic principle whereby man's nature is shaped and in turn shapes God's nature in so far as man can know anything of it. Vico's man sings nature from the very beginning. He therefore listens to being in nature and in himself. This, moreover, is a social necessity. The sounds of nature are the inspiration for the sounds and songs of the first men in human society. Language, music and society are co-eval elements of man's incarnation:

> Whence the Roman custom mentioned by Cicero whereby children learned the law of the Twelve Tables by singing it tamquam necessarium carmen, 'as a required song'.[8]

And earlier, the rhapsodes travelled from city to city in Greece singing the books of Homer; for in the Odyssey it is said of a good storyteller that he has told the tale like a singer amid the circle of men. Homeric poetry, therefore, gathered a community of men who delighted in sonorous buildings shaped to the human ear and voice as well as to the human eye. For men are truly gathered where other men speak and sing.

Vico rightly gathers the first men under Jove's thunderbolts. Without language or ideas, without priests or philosophers, the first men, "stupid, insensate, and horrible beasts", could only picture thunder and lightning in terms of their own rumbling and shouting. And so they walked the earth--the surest discovery of the NEW SCIENCE as a science, and not as its mere poetry. The discovery of the poetic origins of mankind is the surest discovery of a renewed science whose incorporate humanity defends it from rationalist anachronisms. The critical, analytic procedures of Vico's philological method separate poetry and science in order to preserve the real history of their unity and distinction as modification's of embodied mind:

7. IBID. , para. 340.

8. IBID., para. 469.

From these first men, stupid, insensate, and horrible beasts, are the philosophers and philologians should have begun their investigations of the wisdom of the ancient gentiles; that is, from the giants in the proper sense in which we have just taken them . . . And they should have begun with metaphysics, which seeks its proofs not in the external world but within the modifications of the mind of him who meditates it. For since this world of nations has certainly been made by men, it is within these modifications that its principles should have been sought.[9]

The scientific power of the NEW SCIENCE lies in the calm with which it measures and recovers the distance between science and poetry as fundamental modifications of the human mind and senses. For this reason Vico's giants are neither figments of a sentimentalized imagination nor fictions of an objective science for which history is nothing but its own artifact. Rather, they are the natural agents of a history that is intelligible through our effort to read and hear it as our own and that is thereby part of that continuous tradition of eloquence which marks the best of humanism. Thus Vichian history is itself a civil institution inseparable from men's modifications of his own mind and body that are the history of man making himself. For the same reason, we can only recover the corpse of history through the critical-- philological method of the NEW SCIENCE in which we apprentice ourselves to decoding the "three languages" of man, together with their respective forms of political, legal and national life:

To sum up, a man is properly only mind, body and speech, and speech stands as it were midway between mind and body. Hence with regard to what is just, the certain began in mute times with the body. Then when the so-called articulate languages were invented, it advanced to ideas made certain by spoken formulae. And finally, when our human reason was fully developed, it reached its end in the true in the ideas themselves with regard to what is just, as determined by reason from the detailed circumstances of the facts.[10]

Men speak differently in different ages. But those who speak well speak to all ages where there are still men who love eloquence and despise the solitude of soul that inhabits empty rhetoric and mass propaganda. So far from locking us up in a linguistic relativism, Vico's "Roman" rhetoric is the sounding affirmation of collective life, made reasonable and continuous

9. IBID., para. 347.

10. IBID., para. 1045.

under law.[11] Eloquence, is indispensable to true polity and it
is therefore inconceivable that human society could have emerged
from the mute fear of Hobbesian individualism or of Cartesian
discourse abstracted from civil concerns. Indeed, the modern
philosophy of language lives off the very moral capital of
rhetorical language which it suppresses yet presumes upon for
community. In short, Vico understood that the integrity of civil
society rests in the hearts of men and not only in their minds.
Therefore language and eloquence are essential to law and politics
and these can never be reduced to sciences. Lacking in adequate
philological method, Descartes and Hobbes failed to ground
philosophy and law as properly universal sciences of public
welfare that are nevertheless not completely transcendent with
respect to the contexts and particulars of their own local and
natural history. True polity is preserved through the piety of
its origins and in a constant retrieval and translation of the past
in order to achieve an inhabitable future. In this sense, then,
Vico's method is grounded in a situated and embodied naturalism
that is thoroughly opposed to the reductive and anachronistic
employment of naturalism in the utilitarian and rationalist tradition
of law and the social sciences.

Vico's men learn to seek truth before they seek utility. The circulation of truth according to Cartesian rules of clarity is, however, not the same thing as the social and historical acquisition of
the arts of learning the truth. Knowledge cannot be reduced to
the professional practices of science and logic; it must include all
commonsense, legal and historical modes of reasoning, evidence,
conjecture and refutation. All men are endowed with an ability to
learn the truth. This is an historical, legal and pedogogical task
that cannot, without enormously negative civil consequences be
abrogated in favor of the rationalist procedures of philosophy and
science--or similarly based social sciences. Thus Vico anticipates
a later distinction in the Marxist theory of production, namely,
the distinction between:

(a) the social production of utility

(b) the social production of truth

Like Habermas and Apel,[12] Vico much earlier insisted upon the
priority of the society of truth (<u>societas</u> <u>veri</u>) over the society of
use (<u>societas</u> <u>aequi</u> <u>boni</u>). Habermas and Apel have each argued

11. Michael Mooney, "The Primacy of Language in Vico," in VICO AND CON-
TEMPORARY THOUGHT, Pt. I, pp. 191-210.

12. Karl-Otto Apel, "The Communication community as the transcendental
presupposition for the social sciences," pp. 136-179 in his TOWARDS A TRANSFOR-
MATION OF PHILOSOPHY, translated by Glyn Adey and David Frisby, London and
Boston: Routledge and Kegan Paul, 1980.

for the communicative a priori as a corrective to Marx's economistic naturalism. Like Vico, they now see that the grounds of reason and morals are properly linguistic or rhetorical achievements of the human community and, as such, not reducible to the same allocative principles of instrumental rationality which may govern the economy and its applied science.[13] In short, Vico anticipates the contemporary shift of attention to language and practical reasoning as basic human institutions whose analytic reconstruction may provide the grounds of reasonable society. It should not be forgotten that the NEW SCIENCE is intended to have a practical or emancipatory effect. First of all, inasmuch as it is the science of the modifications of our own minds, it enters into the wisdom of these practices. But not simply as a speculative philosophy of history. That would neglect Vico's 'republican' concerns. In other words, the NEW SCIENCE is not intended to remain a piece of abstract reasoning divorced from the prudential and moral contexts of civil action and community. Modern science owes its peculiar force to its contravention of common sense.[14] But the human sciences cannot be similarly abstracted from common sense without ruin to the community. Rather, we need to differentiate the communities of human knowledge and to integrate them within a single polity in which the wisdom of the rulers is rooted in the common sense of the people it fosters and relies upon, as the mind and the imagination are rooted in the human body. Today's rulers, however, will not deprive themselves of the technical arm of the instrumentally and national sciences. This is to be granted. Therefore we can neither separate nor subordinate in any simple way the human and the natural sciences as discursive achievements of modern polity. What is to be resisted is the ideology or false rhetoric of the scientization of political and socioeconomic life. In short, we need to preserve the classical arts of rhetoric inasmuch as these fostered the capacity for situated judgements with respect to the particulars and generalities of communal experience. The practical side of the NEW SCIENCE is therefore the call for a political pedagogy that would foster the fruitful union of reason and common sense across the divisions of expertise and public knowledge.[15] This is the subversive intent of the NEW SCIENCE with respect to the modernism of Descartes and Hobbes; it is the basis of Vico's alliance with the grossi bestioni against the conceits (boria) of the new

13.   John O'Neill, MAKING SENSE TOGETHER, An Introduction to Wild Sociology, New York: Harper and Row, 1974.

14.   Edmund Husserl, THE CRISIS OF THE EUROPEAN SCIENCES AND TRANSCENDENTAL PHENOMENOLOGY, An introduction to phenomenological philosophy, translated by David Carr, Evanston: Northwestern University Press, 1970.

15.   John O'Neill, "The Mutuality of Accounts: An Essay on Trust", pp. 369-380 in THEORETICAL PERSPECTIVES IN SOCIOLOGY, edited by Scott G. NcNall, New York: St. Martin's Press, 1979.

giants of modern science.

Vico's dynamics of the sociolinguistic transformations of human consciousness have been briefly formulated as follows:

> Put most simply, the analogy states the following generic similarities between transitions in societies and the topological transformations of speech:
>
> 1.   The transition from metaphorical idientification by naming external reality in terms taken from the most particular and most sensible ideas of the parts of the body and the emotional states to metonymic reductions is analogous to the transition from the rule of the gods to the rule of aristocracies;
>
> 2.   The transition from metonymic reductions to synecdochic constructions of wholes from parts, genera from species, and so on is analogous to the transition from aristocratic rule to democratic rule; and
>
> 3.   The transition from synecdochic constructions to ironic statement is analogous to the transition from democracies ruled by law to the decadent societies whose members have no respect for law.[16]

The potentially subversive practice in Vico's socio-philological method may be seen if we treat it as critical and reconstructive technique for coming to terms with the dominant formulations of the administration and interpretation of modern society as a science-based community. Thus it is common to all forms of scientism to recollect human history as the growth of scientific, experimental knowledge whose principles of universalism, ability to learn from errors, and essential scepticism are regarded as normative and constitutive features of a liberal and open society. Consistent with this overall scientistic metaphor, it is possible to speak of social reforms as 'experiments' and to regard the scientific administration of social reform as an ongoing experiment conducted without any intrusion of values or ideology. Thus the philosophy of science, regardless of any concern with the way it glosses the actual practices of the community of science, is employed to generate a master metaphor of the liberal, open and experimental society whose health is in its eschewal of all ideological values and misconceptions of knowledge that otherwise

---

16. Hayden White, "The Tropics of History: The Deep Structure of the NEW SCIENCE," p. 78, in GIAMBATTISTA VICO'S SCIENCE OF HUMANITY, edited by Giorgio Tagliacozzo and Donald Phillip Verene, Baltimore and London: The Johns Hopkins University Press, 1976.

drive societies into totalitarianism.[17] In short, critical rationalism may claim for itself an evolutionary status recapitulated in its own narrative history of the subordination of the senses to mind, of homeopathy to allopathy, and the rejection of all particularistic value and knowledge procedures in favor of universalistic, rationally instrumental community of achievement. Extended in this way, the metaphoric and synecdochic employment of the logic of scientific inquiry as a sociologic of the very community it presupposes turns into a reflexive irony. Social problems are not definable in the same way as scientific problems; social change is not reducible to the history of science, anymore than the latter can be abstracted from the social changes that have accompanied the growth of science. As Vico might put it, there is a barbarism of scientistic reflection that is greater than the first barbarism of our giant ancestors. We need, then, to listen again, to revise our separatisms, to mind our dualisms and to rethink the body politic in terms of that very bodily metaphor of the union of the members of society and the integrity of all its members regardless of their varying capacity for intellect, sensibility, labor, and common sense.

We consider that our extended mataphor of the body politic provides an initial specification of Vico's two basic axioms regarding the critical hermeneutic of political institutions:

I. Common sense is judgment without reflection, shared by an entire class, an entire people, an entire nation, or the entire human race.

II. Uniform ideas originating among entire peoples unknown to each other must have a common ground of truth.[18]

Viewed in this fashion, the body politic requires that we construct scenarios for the mutual accountability of the communities of natural and social science within the larger democratic community of commonsense political and legal practice. The metaphor of body-politics, in keeping with Vico's own views, would therefore replace the scientistic metaphor in the dominant imagery of the polity. In this way, we might restore the public functions of rhetoric in the rational advocacy of knowledge and values that address the three basic domains of the body politic, which we differentiate as follows:

---

17. H. T. Wilson, THE AMERICAN IDEOLOGY, Science, technology and organization as modes of rationality in advanced industrial societies, London and Boston: Routledge and Kegan Paul, 1977.

18. Vico, NEW SCIENCE, Paras. 142-144.

	Levels	Institutions	Discourse
(I)	the bio-body	family	well-being
Body (II)	the productive body	work	expression
Politic (III)	the libidinal body	personality	happiness

Each of the three levels of the body politic is represented in a characteristic institution which is in turn allocated its proper domain of discourse. Although the various institutional and discourse realms of the body politic are only analytically differentiated, they may be said to constitute an evolutionary process in which the congruency of the three discursive orders maximizes the commonwealth.[19]   Every society needs to reproduce itself biologically and materially.   These needs are articulated at the institutional levels of work and the family where discourse focuses upon the translation of notions of well-being, health, suffering, estrangement and self-expression.   Here we cannot deal with the variety of social science knowledge and alternative socioeconomic institutions that are generated at these two levels of the body politic.   In the later evolutionary stages, the articulation of the libidinal body generates discourse demands that impinge differentially upon the institutions of family and work.   To date, the institutionalization of these 'revolutionary' demands represents a challenge to all modes of scientistic social and political knowledge. Meantime, we can envisage an extension of Habermas's program for the rational justification of the ideal speech community in terms of the specific discursive contexts of the tri-level body politic.[20]   It would be necessary to generate a typology of knowledge and evaluation claims with regard to the bio-body, the productive body, and the libidinal body at each appropriate institutional level, with further criteria for urgency, democratic force, and the like.

The bio-body politic represents a way of collecting the interest men have in their well-being, their bodily health and their reproduction.   The welfare of the family is iconic of the satisfaction of these demands.   The productive body politic represents the complex organization of labor and intellect expended in the social reproduction of the body politic.   Here, too, we speak of a healthy family.   The libidinal body politic represents the complex organization of labor and intellect expended in the social reproduction of the body politic.   Here, we speak of a healthy person.

19.   Jürgen Habermas, "What is Universal Pragmatics?" pp. 1-68, in his COMMUNICATION AND THE EVOLUTION OF SOCIETY, translated by Thomas McCarthy, Boston: Beacon Press, 1979.

20.   John O'Neill, "Language and the Legitimation Problem," SOCIOLOGY 11:2, 1977:   351-358.

The libidinal body politic represents a level of desire that fulfils the order of personality insofar as it transcends the goods of family and economy. So long as men continue to be birthed and familied of one another, then the bodily, social, and libidinial orders of living will not be separable pursuits. By the same token, the body politic cannot be reduced to purely economistic satisfactions any more than to the dream of love's body. A dinstinctive feature of the metaphor of the body politic is that it allows us to stand away from the system, i.e., machine, cybernetic, and organization metaphors that reduce the problem of political legitimacy to sheerly cognitivist sciences. This shift in turn recovers the plain rationalities of everyday living, family survival, health, self-respect, love, and communion. Members are aware of the necessary interrelationships between their family, economic, and personal commitments. They judge the benefits of their labors in the productive sector of the body politic in terms of the returns to their familial and personal lives. They are willing to make trade-offs between the demands of family life and the ambitions of their personal and libidinal life. In short, members have a fairly complex understanding of their corporate life which is not reducible to the single pattern of utilitarian or decisionistic reasoning that governs calculations in the productive sector.

By differentiating these three levels of the body politic, we further separate ourselves from naturalistic accounts of the political legitimacy problem by introducing a logic of ethical development as the fundamental myth of political life. The three levels of family, economic, and personal life represent an historical-ethical development and also permit it to identify con-tradictions or constraints and regressions in the body politic. Thus, we can identify alienation as a complex phenomenon that affects not only the productive body but also the bio-body and libidinal body. Conversely, alienation is not solved merely by satisfying organic needs, nor by the smooth engineering of pro-ductive relations since these do not meet the demands of the libidinal body. By the same token, we cannot abstract the dreams of libidinal life from our commitments to familial and eco-nomic life. Thus a critical theory of the legitimacy problems of the body politic is simultaneously a constitutive theory of social development and of members' recognition of the places in their lives where this development is blocked and even deteriorating. Members' expression of their experience with the underlying logic of development that sustains political legitimacy will not be limited to official electoral conduct. It will include such subversive practices as strikes, family breakdown, crime, protest, lampoons, neighborhood and street gatherings, music, song, poster and wall art. A critical theory of political legitimacy does not discount the rationality of members' ordinary accounts of their political ex-perience in terms of the vocabularies of family, work, and

person.   Moreover, it does not presume upon either the found
rationality or irrationality of such accounts.

Every political community has to find a symbolic expression of its
beliefs concerning the sources, sustenance and potential threats
to the orderly conduct of its members.[21]   Thus the language of
the body-politic, as Vico would have recognized, is a recurring
expression of reflection upon the nature of order and disorder in
the human community.   From the plebeian secession in Rome to
contemporary street politics, the human body has provided the
language and the very text of political protest and confrontation
with the agencies that administer our inhumanity: This rhetorical
conception of the body politic, for which I have argued in keeping with Vico's vision, differs from the administrative science of
politics in that it remains continuous with ancient political life.
That is to say, we argue that the business of politics is to foster
citizens capable of the good life.   Therefore, political legitimacy
must be grounded in prudential judgments excercised in practical
contexts of belief and action that regenerate political education
without subordinating it to a political science outside the life of
the polity.   As such, our theory of the body politic constitutes a
small step towards a possibility within the NEW SCIENCE that
Habermas himself has remarked upon.[22]

    21.   John O'Neill, "Authority, Knowledge and the Body Politic," pp. 68-80 in
his SOCIOLOGY AS A SKIN TRADE, Essays towards a reflexive sociology, New
York: Harper and Row, 1972.

    22.   Habermas, OP. CIT: pp. 43-46.

CHAPTER 8

CAN PHENOMENOLOGY BE CRITICAL?

What is asked when we ask whether phenomenology can be critical? The question is whether we can be authentically aware of the reflexive limits of the corpus of social science knowledge due to its implicit ties with the order of history and politics. The very question is evidence of a certain uneasiness, but also of a determination to dwell within its circle at least as much as to drive for a solution. How shall we proceed then? For to begin, I cannot settle for you the nature of phenomenology. Of course, I am aware that I might attempt to set out some of the principal features of Husserlian phenomenology. But the nature of the auspices for such an exposition should not be confused with its method of historiography and reference whose very intention of making its appeal public invites criticism and reappraisal, and is ultimately the same thing as philosophical argument. The question of the authoritative procedures for introducing phenomenology is made even more problematic by the developments in phenomenology from Husserl to Heidegger, Scheler, and Jaspers; or through Sartre and Merleau-Ponty; not to mention Schutz and the ethnomethodology of Garfinkel and Cicourel. Faced with a similar problem, Merleau-Ponty has remarked that 'we shall find in ourselves, and nowhere else, the unity and true meaning of phenomenology.' In other words, we must take our own context, namely, our gathering out of mutual concern with the contemporary issues in the social sciences, as the topic for phenomenological theorizing.

I want to develop a phenomenological conception of critique and argument under a rule of limit and cosmic order which is simultaneously the ground of political order and rebellion. Habermas has argued[1] that Husserl's critique of positivist science does not go far enough in simply denying the separation between knowledge and the life-world. In so far as science and philosophy, including the social sciences, separate the activity of theorizing from the world of human interests, both rest upon a positivist ontology. The prescriptions for this separation constitute the rule of methodological objectivity or segregation of subjective interests and values. The unfortunate practical consequences of the separation of science and values can only be corrected through an understanding of the true relation between knowledge and interest, in other words, of <u>praxis</u>. Husserl's critique of the objectivism of science and the natural attitude which is its prescientific ground, may be taken as an obvious

---

1. Jürgen Habermas, "Knowledge and Interests: a general perspective," appendix to his KNOWLEDGE AND HUMAN INTERESTS, translated by Jeremy J. Shapiro, London: Heinemann Educational Books, 1971.

sense in which phenomenology is critical. But it does not go far enough to free transcendental phenomenology itself from practical interest. Habermas invokes the etymology of θεωρια in order to trace a development in the concept of theory from the original activity of the representative sent by a <u>polis</u> to witness the sacred festival of another city to the philosopher's μιμησισ or representation in the order of his soul of the natural κοσμοσ.

> Husserl rightly criticizes the objectivist illusion that deludes the sciences with the image of a reality-in-itself, consisting of facts structured in a lawlike manner; it conceals the constitution of these facts, and thereby prevents consciousness of the interlocking of knowledge with interests from the life-world. Because phenomenology brings this to consciousness, it is itself, in Husserl's view, free of such interests. It thus earns the title of pure theory unjustly claimed by the sciences. It is to this freeing of knowledge from interest that Husserl attaches the expectation of practical efficacy. But the error is clear. Theory in the sense of the classical tradition only had an impact on life because it was thought to have discovered in the cosmic order an ideal world structure, including the prototype for the order of the human world. Only as <u>cosmology</u> was <u>theoria</u> also capable of orienting human action. Thus Husserl cannot expect self-formative processes to originate in a phenomenology that, as transcendental philosophy, purifies the classical theory of its cosmological contents, conserving something like the theoretical attitude only in an abstract manner. Theory had educational and cultural implications not because it had freed knowledge from interest. To the contrary, it did so because it derived <u>pseudo-normative power</u> from <u>the concealment of its actual interest</u>. While criticizing the objectivist self-understanding of the sciences, Husserl succumbs to another objectivism, which was always attached to the traditional concept of theory.[2]

Whether or not Husserl neglected the original connection between θεωρια and its consequences for the philosophical way of life, as Habermas argues, it is important to stress the ambivalence in classical philosophical knowledge with respect to the idea of Beauty and Goodness. Habermas tends to overlook this tension. Miss Hannah Arendt, however, has argued that the subordination of life in the pursuit of human affairs (βιοσ πολιτικοσ) to the 'theoretical way of life' (βιοσ θεωρητικοσ) is a result of the Platonic subordination of the contemplative love of the true essence of Being, under the idea of the Beautiful, to the idea of Good, or an art of measurement which provides a rule to the

2. IBID., pp. 305-306.

philosopher's potential disorientation in everyday political life.[3] In other words, there is an essential ambivalence in western knowledge between the values of the recognition and domination of Being which has been consequential for its political tradition, particularly when the pattern of domination is based upon modern scientific knowledge which breaks once and for all the connection between κοσμοσ and θεωρια.

Modern social science knowledge has reduced its independence as a form of theoretical life to a rule of methodology founded upon the auspices of technical rationality. This results in a dis- enchanted objectivism or rationalization of the interest and values which guide technological domination as a form or 'conduct of life,' to use Max Weber's phase. However, Weber's formal rationality, so far from resting upon 'value-free' auspices, is in fact an historical constellation whose precondition is the separa- tion of the orders of knowledge, work, and politics. In the period of the bourgeois ascendency, the value-free conception of rationality furnishes a critical concept of the development of human potential locked in the feudal world of 'traditional' values. Weber makes a fatality of technical rationality, thereby identifying its historical role with political domination as such,[4] whereas Marx's critique of class political economy showed the critical limits of economic rationality. Social science knowledge needs to be grounded in a limited but authentic reflexivity through which it recognizes its ties to individual values and community interests, notwithstanding its attempts to avoid bias and ideology. Habermas himself furnishes five theses which I shall interpret as the auspices of a limited reflexivity responsible to the project of homo faber:

(i)   The achievements of the transcendental subject have their basis in the natural history of the human species.

(ii) Knowledge equally serves as an instrument and transcends mere self-preservation.

(iii) Knowledge-constitutive interests take form in the medium of work, language, and power.

(iv) In the power of self-reflection, knowledge and interest are one.

(v)   The unity of knowledge and interest proves itself in a dialectic that takes the historical traces of suppressed dialogue and reconstructs what has been suppressed.

3.   Hannah Arendt, BETWEEN PAST AND FUTURE, Six Exercises in Political Thought, Cleveland and New York: Meridian Books, 1963, pp. 112-115.

4.   Herbert Marcuse, "Industrialization and Capitalism in Max Weber," NEGA- TIONS, Essays in Critical Theory, Boston: Beacon Press, 1968.

Together these five theses reveal the axiological basis of human
knowledge as a pattern of communication, control, and decision,
predicated upon man's self-made and thus largely symbolic project
of creation and freedom. The human project is a structure of
biological, social and, I would add, libidinal values, which are
institutionalized through the media of language, work, and
politics. The vehicle of the human project is a common tradition
and identity tied to speech, creation, and citizenship which relate
individual expressions to everyday social life and culture. In
each of these realms there is practical metaphysics of the relation
of particulars to universals, within the limits of common speech,
the exchange of labor, and the pursuit of the common good.
Moreover, there is, as Habermas argues, an essential relation
between the orders of language, works, and politics. The man
who is not free in his labor is not free to speak and thus freedom
of speech presupposes an end of economic exploitation as well as
of political repression. Dialogue and poetry are therefore the
primary expressions of the bond between speech and politics; it
is through them that knowledge achieves reflexive awareness of
the values of the human community to which it belongs and is
thus able to play its role in the constitution of the body politic.
I have mentioned the work of the poet in the politics of freedom
because he, as well as the novelist and musician, is the guardian
of tradition and creativity. I think it is necessary to relate the
knowledge-constitutive interests to the expressive, libidinal
interests of the body politic in order to extend political dialogue
into the street, the songs and everyday confrontations within the
body politic. For these are the life-world understandings of the
traditions of need and rebellion.

Modern consciousness is tied to the standpoints of anthropology
and historicism which reveal that all knowledge about man, including scientific knowledge, presupposes some metaphysical
position on the relation between human facticity, knowledge, and
values.[5] Thus we can only speak of the reflective ties between
subjectivity and the regional ontologies of the worlds of science,
economics, politics, and everyday life, and not of a naïve realist,
subject/object dichotomy.

It may help to clarify the conception of limited reflexivity which I
am proposing for political theorizing if I contrast it with the
consequences of a total reflexivity of absolute knowledge. There
is, for example, a conception of reflexivity which is very close to
the limited notion I am fostering, but which is quite alien to it in
its consequences for the orders of language, thought, and
politics. I have in mind the sociological conception of reflexivity

    5. Ludwig Landgrebe, MAJOR PROBLEMS IN CONTEMPORARY EUROPEAN
PHILOSOPHY, From Dilthey to Heidegger, translated by Kurt. F. Reinhardt, New
York: Frederick Ungar Publishing Co., 1966, p. II.

as the awareness of the infrastructures of knowledge in culture, class, and biography. At first sight, the consequences of the sociology of knowledge and ideology might appear to make for a moderation of political argument through an understanding of the intervening circumstances of class and history. But in practice it has brutalized political awareness and obscured the science of politics for which Mannheim had hoped. It was to these issues that both Husserl and Weber addressed themselves in their reflections on the vocations of science and politics. Both were concerned with the nihilism that was a potential conclusion from historicism and the sociology of knowledge. Husserl and Weber approached these problems in terms of an inquiry into the very foundations of western knowledge or science. Let us recall briefly Weber's reflections, which are perhaps better known to sociologists and political scientists, and then turn to Husserl's struggles with these problems in THE CRISIS OF EUROPEAN SCIENCES.[6]

At first sight, the connection between Weber's reflections on the vocations of science, politics, and capitalism are not evident. Superficially, modern economics, politics, and science present us with an exotic competition of goods and values without a rational standard of choice. We accumulate knowledge much as we do money, and the result is a vast obsolescence of commonsense knowledge and values. Any attempt to introduce order into this process is as disturbing to it as the occasions for these very attempts, so that our politics is snared in a polytheism of value. 'And with this,' says Weber, 'we come to inquire into the meaning of science. For, after all, it is not self-evident that something subordinate to such a law is sensible and meaningful in itself. Why does one engage in doing something that in reality never comes, and never can come to an end.'[7] Weber's question about the auspices of modern science is simultaneously a question about the grounds of modern community and personality in a world from which God is absent and order thereby an enigma to a disenchanted world of value accumulation. Weber compares his own questioning of the meaning of science with Tolstoi's question about the meaning of death in the modern world, where man is pitted against himself in a self-infinitude of want and desire. 'And because death is meaningless, civilized life as such is meaningless; by its very "progressiveness" it gives death the imprint of meaninglessness.'[8] In this way Weber made sociology aware of its own reflexive need to embed in a community of purpose

6. Edmund Husserl, THE CRISIS OF EUROPEAN SCIENCES AND TRANSCEN-
DENTAL PHENOMENOLOGY, An Introduction to Phenomenological Philosophy,
translated by David Carr, Evanston: Northwestern University Press, 1970.

7. Max Weber, "Science as a Vocation," FROM MAX WEBER, Essays in
Sociology, translated, edited, and with an introduction by H. Gerth and C. Wright
Mills, New York: Oxford University Press, 1958, p. 138.

8. IBID., p. 140.

whose institution is as much a charismatic hope as a goal of rationality.

Weber's conclusions though they do not satisfy Marcuse's conception of critical theory, are in striking contrast with the Parsonian interpretation of Weber which serves to make sociological knowledge an irony of functionalist practice. That is to say, the Parsonian version of sociological knowledge invents a utupia of social system and pattern variable action congruence in order to embed its own instrumentalist rationality as a precipitate of utilitarian culture. Whether it starts from Hobbes's nasty vision or from Luther's excremental vision, Parsonian sociology reduces the problem of its own reflexivity to the anodyne of instrumental knowledge, hoping thereby to substitute affluence for the glory of love's risen body. While we cannot dwell upon Parsonian sociology in any detail, it may not be amiss, in view of its adoption into political science, to comment that Parsons' latest generalization of the instrumentalist vision based upon the master metaphor of money as the most generalized means of exchange and efficacy, only serves to further mystify the grounds of political order by neglecting the ways in which the behavior of money is nothing else than the algebra of the system of stratification and exploitation for which Parsons pretends to account. In short, and in contrast with the critics of Parsonian ideology, I would argue, that it is Parsons' conception of theorizing as an activity grounded in the means-end schema which generates his intrinsic notions of social structure and personality as a functionalist utopia of congruent orders of individuals and collective reality. Yet the unconscious merit of Parsons' classical study of the corpus of utilitarian social science knowledge[9] is to have focused on the ambivalence of the instrumental and ritual values of human knowledge, subordinated to the a priori of individual interest.

I have turned my argument towards the topic of sociological reflexivity not for the purpose of engaging in criticism as it is conventionally understood, but for the purpose of coming to terms with the very phenomenon of sociological reflexivity, namely, how it is that we can show the limits of sociology and still be engaged in authentic sociological theorizing. This is the question that I began with when I set myself the task of asking whether phenomenology could be critically aware of its own limits and its implicit ties with history and politics. I shall now pursue this topic in Husserl's later writings, acknowledging that my reading of them is a continuation of an earlier reading by Merleau-Ponty. More concretely, my reading of Husserl and Merleau-Ponty is

9. Talcott Parsons, THE STRUCTURE OF SOCIAL ACTION. A Study in Social Theory with Special Reference to a Group of Recent European Writers, New York: The Free Press of Glencoe, 1964.

essentially a borrowing from them both, continuous with everything else we borrow in life. For, indeed, as Merleau-Ponty
remarks, "I borrow myself from others; I create others from my
own thoughts. This is no failure to perceive others; it is the
perception of others."

We need a conception of the reflexive grounds of social science
knowledge which will be grounded in the facts of institutional life
and yet remain equally true to the claims of science and poetry,
or to what is general as well as what is unique in our experience.
Reflecting upon the crisis of the European sciences, Husserl
remarked that 'the dream is over' of there ever being an apodictic
or rigorous science of philosophy. Some have thought that it is
only those who set such goals for philosophy who are likely to
turn to philosophical disbelief and despair. In such circumstances, it is the task of phenomenological philosophy to take its
historical bearings, to acknowledge its debts to the life-world
which it presupposes so long as there is no total threat to civilization, but which must then concern it.

The philosopher, says Husserl, 'takes something from history.'
But history is not a warehouse, or a rummage heap from which
we can take 'things,' because facts, documents, philosophical,
and literary works, are not palpably before us, apart from our
own undwelling and interpretations. Furthermore, we do not,
strictly speaking, transmit or hand down a scientific, literary, or
historical tradition. We may be Renaissance historians without
having read or researched every aspect of the Renaissance, just
as we may be Platonists without a concern for every word of
Plato, so that we might as well speak of a 'poetic transmission'
which owes as much to us as to fact. And yet none of this need
imperil the teleology of knowledge, of science, history, or
philosophy:

> Let us be more precise. I know, of course, what I am
> striving for under the title of philosophy, as the goal and
> field of my work. And yet I do not know. What autonomous
> thinker has ever been satisfied with this, his 'knowledge'?
> For what autonomous thinker, in his philosophizing life, has
> 'philosophy' ever ceased to be an enigma? Everyone has the
> sense of philosophy's end, to whose realization his life is
> devoted; everyone has certain formulae, expressed in defini-
> tions; but only secondary thinkers who in truth should not
> be called philosophers, are consoled by their definitions,
> beating to death with their word-concepts the problematic
> telos of philosophizing. In that obscure 'knowledge,' and in
> the word-concepts of the formulae, the historical is con-
> cealed; it is, according to its own proper sense, the
> spiritual inheritance of him who philosophizes; and in the
> same way, obviously, he understands the others in whose

company, in critical friendship and enmity, he philosophizes.
And in philosophizing he is also in company with himself as
he earlier understood and did philosophy; and he knows
that, in the process, historical tradition, as he understood it
and used it, entered into him in a motivating way and as a
spiritual sediment. His historical picture, in part made by
himself and in part taken over, his 'poetic invention of the
history of philosophy,' has not and does not remain fixed--
that he knows; and yet every 'invention' serves him, and
can serve him in understanding himself and his aim, and his
own aim in relation to that of other and their 'inventions,'
their aims, and finally what it is that is common to all,
which makes philosophy 'as such' as a unitary telos and
makes the systems attempts at its fulfilment for us all, for
us (who are) at the same time in company with the
philosophers of the past (in the various ways we have been
able to invent them for ourselves).[10]

Merleau-Ponty remarks how well Husserl's term Stiftung, foundation or establishment, captures the fecundity of cultural creations
by which they endure into our present and open a field of
inquiry to which they are continuously relevant.

It is thus that the world as soon as he has seen it, his first
attempts at painting, and the whole past of painting all
deliver up a tradition to the painter-- that is, Husserl
remarks the power to forget origins and to give to the past
not a survival, which is the hypocritical form of forgetfulness, but a new life, which is the noble form of memory.[11]

Through language, art and writing, what was only an ideal meaning in the mind of an individual, achieves an objective and public
status, enters a community of thinkers, which is the presupposition of truth. Thus we witness the event of that circuit of
reflection in which what was first recognized as neither local nor
temporal 'according to the meaning of its being,' comes to rest
upon the locality and temporality of speech, which belongs neither
to the objective world nor the world of ideas.

Ideal existence is based upon the document, not, of course,
as a physical object, or even as the vehicle of one-to-one
significations assigned to it by the language in which it is
written, but upon the document in so far as, again by an
'intentional transgression,' it solicits and brings together all

10. THE CRISIS OF EUROPEAN SCIENCES AND TRANSCENDENTAL PHENO-
MENOLOGY, pp. 394-395.

11. M. Merleau-Ponty, SIGNS, translated by Richard C. McCleary, Evanston:
Northwestern University Press, 1964, p. 59.

lives in pursuit of knowledge--and as such establishes and re-establishes a 'Logos' of the cultural world.[12]

We need, then, a conception of the auspices of philosophical reflexivity that is consistent with 'poetic invention' (Dichtung), as well as with the community in which we philosophize. Such a notion may be present to us in the concept of reflexivity as institution rather than as transcendental constitution. By means of the notion of institution we may furnish a conception of reflexivity which, instead of resting upon a transcendental subjectivity, is given in a field of presence and coexistence which situates reflexivity and truth as sedimentation and search. We must think of reflexivity as tied to the textual structures of temporality and situation through which subjectivity and objectivity are constituted as the intentional unity and style of the world. 'Thus what we understand by the concept of institution are those events in an experience which endow it with durable dimensions, in relation to which a whole series of other experiences will acquire meaning, will form an intelligible series or a history--or again those events which sediment in me a meaning, not just as survivals or residus, but as the invitation to a sequel, the necessity of a future.'[13]

The institution of reflexivity is founded upon a series of exchanges between subjectivity and situation in which the polarities of means and ends or question and answer are continuously established and renewed, no less than the institution of idea, truth, and culture. Reflexivity, therefore, is not an a priori, but a a task which we take up in order to achieve self-improvization, as well as the acquisition of a tradition or style of thought which is the recovery of an original auspice opened in the past. To this we bring a living expression or the inauguration of a world and the outline of a future, which is nothing else than ourselves, 'borne only by the caryatid of our efforts, which converge by the sole fact that they are efforts to express.'[14]

The notion of critique which we may derive from the concept of reflexivity as institution is one which is grounded in a contextual environment which lies open horizontally to the corpus of social science knowledge rather than through any transcendental reflection. This notion of critique is the result of abandoning Husserl's attempt to construct an eidetic of any possible corpus of

12.   IBID., pp. 96-97.

13.   M. Merleau-Ponty, THEMES FROM THE LECTURES AT THE COLLEGE DE FRANCE 1952-1960, translated by John O'Neill, Evanston: Northwestern University Press, 1970, pp. 40-41.

14.   SIGNS, p. 69.

knowledge as the correlative of a universal and timeless con-
stituting reflexivity and the problems it raises for intersubjectivity, rationality, and philosophy itself. The corpus of the
historical and social sciences is not, properly speaking, constituted through any object or any act of reflection. It arises
from a continual production or verification (reprise) which each
individual undertakes according to his situation and times. Thus
each one's work must be continually reviewed to unearth its own
auspices sedimented in the archaeology of human science. This is
not a simplistic argument for eternal starts, any more than a
crude rejection of the accumulation of human knowledge. It is
rather an attempt to interpret the rhetorical nature of the appeal
of knowledge and criticism through which tradition and rebellion
are made.

'Reading' a text is inevitably an essay in rhetoric, that is to say,
if we follow Aristotle, leaving aside Plato's insistence on the
mastery of truth, it requires a profound knowledge or care for
the souls one seeks to persuade. This concern to suit one's
speech or argument to the other person's soul is the anthropological ground of all talk, argument, and criticism. It is at the
heart of what is serious in our concern to discuss with one
another, to correct and to persuade. It is for this reason that
we elaborate upon one another's speech and thought. And we
never argue so fiercely as between ourselves, because what is at
stake is the utopian connection between truth, justice, and
beauty. We sense implicitly the style of the world from a manner
of speaking and thinking, so that we are drawn by its resonance,
or else confused and repulsed. The error in modern communication and information theory is that it overlooks the rhetorical
vehicle of speech, reading, and writing. It does this because in
turn it lacks any conception of the intention to institute solidarity
and a just social order in the relations between the partners to
human speech.

What emerges from these examples is that the universality and
truth aimed at by theoretical consciousness is not an intrinsic
property of the idea. It is an acquisition continuously
established and re-established in a community and tradition of
knowledge called for and responded to by individuals in specific
historical situations. Understood in this way, history is the call
of one thought to another, because each individual's work or
action is created across the path of self and others towards a
public which it elicits rather than serves.[15] That is to say,
history is the field which individual effort requires in order to
become one with the community it seeks to build so that, where it

15. "Materials for a Theory of History," in THEMES FROM THE LECTURES AT
THE COLLEGE DE FRANCE, pp. 27-38.

is successful, its invention appears always to have been necessary. Individual action, then, is the invention of history, because it is shaped in a present which previously was not just a
void waiting to be determined by the word or deed, but a tissue
of calling and response which is the life of no one and everyone.
Every one of life's actions, insofar as it invokes its truth, lives
in the expectation of an historical inscription a judgment not of
its intention or consequences but of its fecundity, which is the
relevance of its 'story' to the present.

> True history thus gets its life entirely from us. It is in our
> present that it gets the force to refer everything else to the
> present. The other whom I respect gets his life from me as
> I get mine from him. A philosophy of history does not take
> away any of my rights or initiatives. It simply adds to my
> obligations as a solitary person the obligation to understand
> situations other than my own and to create a path between
> my life and that of others, that is, express myself. [16]

The object of human knowledge is not, strictly speaking, an
object; it is the institution within human space and historical time
of artefacts, tools, services, institutions which are depositaries of
what men before us have thought, needed, and valued. Cultural
objects in this sense are the vestiges of embodied beings who live
in society and communicate with one another as embodied
minds. [17]   It is such human beings who have opened up for us
the hearth of culture and institutions, which it is our first duty
to tender. And this we do, not as mere drudgery, but as the
cultivation of our own growth, the basis for our departures and
the source to which we return for fresh inspiration. Human
institutions are the ground of our common and individual achievements, enriching us and impoverishing us with a legacy which
was never quite intended for us and is yet never totally rejected
by us, even when we refuse it. This human legacy is never fully
ours until we learn to alter it through our own inventions, our
personal style.

Human experience and vision accumulates only in the circle of
social relations and institutions, which enlarge and deepen the
sense of our sentiments, deeds, and works through the symbiosis
of solidarity and personality. Human action is essentially the
unfolding of a cultural space and its historical dimensions, so that
in a strict sense we never accomplish anything except as a collective and historial project. For the individual action involves,

16.   SIGNS, p. 75.

17.   John O'Neill, PERCEPTION, EXPRESSION AND HISTORY; The Social
Phenomenology of Maurice Merleau-Ponty, Evanston: Northwestern University Press,
1970.

therefore, a constant dialogue with others, a recovery of the past and the projection of breaks which are never entirely successful. But this is not a source of irremediable alienation; it is the feature of our experience which calls for its completion through a collective, with a history that knows a tradition as well as a future. Such a collectivity or institution is never wholly reified; it is made and unmade, with a particular grain in each of us who lives and alters what he draws upon for his life. And this is a feature not only of human institutions, but of our thoughts, our sentiments and, above all, of human talk. Understood in this way, human institutions are the sole means that we have of keeping faith with one another, while being true to ourselves.

The ultimate feature of the phenomenological institutions of reflexivity is that it grounds critique in membership and tradition. Thus the critic's auspices are the same as those of anyone working in a community of language, work, and politics. In the critical act there is a simultaneity of authorship and authenticity which is the declaration of membership in a continuing philosophical, literary, or scientific community. The critic does not alienate himself from his community, which would be the consequence of an absolute knowledge and ultimate nihilism. This is not to say that the critic is not rebellious; it is to remark upon the consequences of solitude and solidarity as the starting points of criticism.

Criticism in our sense is very close to Camus' conception of rebellion and order under the sun. Criticism reflects an aspiration to order under the auspices of the things that are present and of our fellow men, under a limit which is reflexively the recognition of solidarity and a rule of memory as an antidote to revolutionary absurdity:

> At this meridian of thought, the rebel thus rejects divinity in order to share in the struggles and destiny of all men. We shall choose Ithaca, the faithful land, frugal and audacious thought, lucid action, and the generosity of the man who understands. In the light, the earth remains our first and our last love. Our brothers are breathing under the same sky as we; justice is a living thing. Now is born that strange joy which helps one live and die, and which we shall never again postpone to a later time. On the sorrowing earth it is the unresting thorn, the bitter brew, the harsh wind off the sea, the old and the new dawn. With this joy, through long struggle, we small remake the soul of our time, and a Europe which will exclude nothing. Not even that phantom Nietzsche, who for twelve years after his downfall was continually invoked by the West as the blasted image of its loftiest knowledge and its nihilism; nor the prophet of justice without mercy who lies, by mistake, in the

unbelievers' pit at Highgate Cemetery; nor the deified
mummy of the man of action in his glass coffin; nor any part
of what the intelligence and energy of Europe have cease-
lessly furnished to the pride of a contemptible period. All
may indeed live again, side by side with the martyrs of 1905,
but on condition that it is understood that they correct one
another, and that a limit, under the sun, shall curb them
all. Each tells the other that he is not God; this is the end
of romanticism. At this moment, when each of us must fit
an arrow to his bow and enter the lists anew, to reconquer,
within history and in spite of it, that which he owns
already, the thin yield of his fields, the brief love of this
earth, at this moment when at last a man is born, it is time
to forsake our age and its adolescent furies. The bow
bends, the wood complains. At the moment of supreme
tension, there will leap into flight an unswerving arrow, a
shaft that is inflexible and free.[18]

I have tried, then, to outline a notion of criticism as a mode of
theoretical life which is reflexively tied to the institutions of
philosophy, art, and the sciences. The heart of this conception
is its adherence to the presence of the things around as and of
our fellow men in recognition of the institutional life which they
share through the work of language, labor, and politics. It is a
notion of critical theorizing whose auspices lie nowhere else than
in the community of knowledge and value which are its claim to
any contribution. The voice of such criticism is neither fanatical
nor cynical, although it is in no way a simple affirmation of the
claims of the community and tradition in which it belongs. What I
have in mind is a conception of criticism which does not exploit
the differences between the way things are and how they might
be but rather leaves itself open to the experience of their
reversal, to the care for what is sublime as well as of what is
desperate in the human condition and the times through which it
passes.

For the reasons outlined above we cannot accept the paradigmatic
value of the psychoanalytic conversation, at least insofar as the
passive objectivity of the analyst is false to the dialogic search in
which no member of the language community is absolutely
privileged, and is therefore necessarily historical rather than
clinical.[19] Moreover, we need to remember that human speech

18. Albert Camus, THE REBEL, An Essay on Man in Revolt, translated by
Anthony Bower, New York: Vintage Books, 1956, p. 306.

19. Habermas has himself provided for this conclusion in his essay "Toward a
Theory of Communicative Competence," in RECENT SOCIOLOGY NO. 2, Patterns of
Communicative Behaviour, edited by Hans Peter Dreitzel, New York: Macmillan,
1970.

has no absolute goal of rational clarification, of disbelief, and rejection of prejudice.   Human speech, dialogue, and conversation seeks just as well acceptance, or the understanding of what was already our belief, our native prejudice.   This is the circle of language in which we dwell--the hermeneutic circle--which is not broken even when all come to understand our motives, our past experience.   For there is nothing beyond death which alters what we have lived, although our understanding may return it to the silence of our being.   There is, in other words, a naïve dogmatism underlying the liberal social science conception of understanding which still draws upon the rationalist tradition of Enlightenment unmasking.   But there is nothing behind the face of the man who speaks, beyond what else he has to say or how he keeps his silence.   We find meaning between words and sentences and between men; there is nothing either in the back of this or beyond it.

CHAPTER 9

MERLEAU-PONTY'S CRITIQUE OF MARXIST SCIENTISM

In the immediate postwar period of hardening East-West relations, Merleau-Ponty began to rethink Marxism from the phenomenological perspective. In HUMANISM AND TERROR, he studied the Soviet Trials, in order to understand from the standpoint of the revolutionaries their notions of individual and collective responsibility. He also opened up the larger study followed in ADVENTURES OF THE DIALECTIC in which Marxist scientism is criticized in terms of a Leninist and Weberian conception of the philosophy of history. In the following essay, these arguments are set out descriptively, or as nearly as possible in Merleau-Ponty's own terms. I have, of course, organized the arguments and made explanatory comments where necessary. Merleau-Ponty did not write in the discursive style favored by the social sciences. This reflects the difference between hermeneutical and causal analysis. Rather than reduce Merleau-Ponty's thought to a mode of discourse of which he was extremely critical, not only on epistemological grounds, but also because of its attempt to reduce the autonomy of language and style, I have chosen to preface the argument with some analytic reading rules that I believe underlie its construction. I believe that a discussion over the responsibility of reading and writing would not be alien to Merleau-Ponty's thought and would also contribute to the critique of literary scientism.

ANALYTIC RECONSTRUCTION OF THE FOLLOWING ARGUMENT

Merleau-Ponty's argument relies upon the history of Marxism, while at the same time claiming that Marxism confers upon history a meaning without which history would be sheer violence. HUMANISM AND TERROR announces in its very title the twin birth of man and violence. In THE REBEL Camus has argued that the birth of man is the beginning of endless violence. When Merleau-Ponty makes the ADVENTURES OF THE DIALECTIC his topic, he has again to find a thread to history, avoiding the extremes of premature closure or of senseless ups and downs. It may be said that, after all, both HUMANISM AND TERROR and ADVENTURES OF THE DIALECTIC are topical works outside of the interests of political philosophy. But then we have surrendered the world to violence in order to preserve the harmony of history. Alternatively, we may risk the face of philosophy in search of truths that will be found to be partial, and possibly even destructive, when held in competition with other values and beliefs. Merleau-Ponty is a valuable thinker because he refused to separate politics and philosophy. He could do this because as a philosopher he was not wedded to the ideal of absolute knowledge, and because in politics he was just as opposed to historical fatalism as to senseless violence. Merleau-Ponty struggled to comprehend his times. He was not withdrawn. Nor did he surrender himself to aesthetic revulsion. He claimed no privileged theory of action, and so he avoided sloganizing the issues of rethinking Marxism at a time when positions were hardening in the East and West.

I want now to formulate the narrative that follows in the form of a number of rules of procedure which I believe furnish an analytic reconstruction of the arguments of Marxist humanism. These are the rules that I believe can be abstracted from the history of rethinking Marx in terms of Hegel, in order to provide a critique of Marxist scientism. By the same token, these rules may be interpreted as rules for anyone participating in the community of argument since Lenin read Marx in the light of Hegel. We may then think of the Marxist tradition as a set of rival reading practices that have to be understood as the very issues of Marxist politics, and not simply as glosses upon events intelligible apart from such practices. I consider this the basic postulate of Marxist humanism. It is challenged by Marxist scientism, such as that of Althusser, inasmuch as the latter espouses a conception of historical events whose life would be independent of the hermeneutical continuity of rival interpretations.

I   Thus, in the first place, we must subject our own discussion of Marxism to the <u>humanist</u> <u>rule</u> that the nature of Marxism is not given to Marxists as the simple negation of bourgeois liberalism and capitalism. This is the Marxism of Commissars. It lacks its own voice. In other words, Marxism has no monopoly over criticism. Humanist Marxism must keep itself in question and it can only do this by means of a lively recognition of the limitations facing both socialist and liberal discourse.

II   We may then treat the first rule as a procedure for reconstructing the history of Marxist thought since Marx himself read Hegel, through Lenin, into the Hegelian Marxism of Lukács and Kojève (we should also include Korsch who is closer to Kant) as the work of eliciting the Hegelian dialectic of recognition as:

   (a) an ideal telos of history

   (b) a method of hermeneutical analysis

III   The test of these rules is offered in Merleau-Ponty's treatment of violence. We cannot consider violence as limited to either communism or capitalism, nor can we be sure that proletarian violence is only a temporary revolutionary expedient. For where the Party intervenes to bring the protetariat into history, there is always the risk that the Party will subject the proletariat to its own rule.

(a1) history and politics are made by men;

(a2) men themselves must be made human in the objective course of history and politics;

(a3) let us call the Party the action of bringing together (a1) and (a2) and the tension between (a1) and (a2) the field of justice and violence.

Thus, a phenomenological approach to the Soviet Trials will proceed hermeneutically, so as to avoid false antitheses in the construction of the member's praxis in trying to resolve the double commitment to historical inevitability and political responsibility.

(b1) The Trials are not to be treated a priori as illegal or corrupt justice;

(b2) nor can we justify collectivization ex post facto;

(b3) we must let stand member's rival readings of the primacy of economic and political decisions.

IV   In light of the preceding rules we are necessarily engaged in a double task.

(a)   the critique of Marxist scientism

(b)   a hermeneutic of history and politics

V   We may treat both tasks as the elicitation of an historical and political norm of intersubjectivity, specifically, the question is, How are free men to be led to freedom? Marxist humanism is thus (broadly conceived) a pedagogical problem. Consequently, all future Marxist discussion should contribute to the development of socialist education and to an understanding of the relationship between truth and justice.

WAITING FOR MARX

It is impossible to think of modern political history apart from the Russian revolution. At the same time, it is hard not to be ambivalent towards the history and politics of Marxism itself. In the days before Communism ruled a major part of the world, one could believe that Communism would shunt all forms of political and economic exploitation into the siding of prehistory. In those days Marxism was emancipatory knowledge wonderfully scornful of the iron laws of history and economics. This is not to say that

Marxist critique failed to recognize the weight of historical structures. Indeed, we owe Marx much of the credit for a structuralist analysis of historical development. By the same token,
there has always been an uncertain relation between Marxist
analysis of the determinism of historical structures and its
prophecy of a proletarian fulfillment of historical law. Prior to
the actual experience of the Revolution, it was easy enough to
think of it as a temporary, albeit violent, intervention on the side
of justice against a moribund but destructive ruling class. But
the revolution is itself an institution and it soon acquires a
history of its own, leaders and enemies, priorities and policies
that could not be foreseen. In view of these complexities, Communist practice inevitably hardened and Marxism soon became the
intellectual property of the Party abandoning the education of the
proletariat in favor of slogans and dogma. This is the context of
what we call Marxist scientism[1]. That is to say, once Marxism
became Party knowledge and a tool for the industrialization of
Soviet society, Marxism indentified with economic determinism and
the values of scientific naturalism at the expense of its own
radical humanism. This is variously described as the difference
between Communism and Marxism, the difference between theory
and practice, or the difference between the early, Hegelianized
Marx and the later, scientific Marx.[2]

Today socialism and capitalism are equally in question insofar as
the same ideology of technological domination underlies their apparently opposed political and ideological systems. We can no
longer assume that Marxism challenges capitalism and justifies the
sufferings of revolution unless we can be sure that Marxism
possesses the philosophical resources for rethinking the logic of
technical rationality and the Party practices that have forced this
logic upon the proletariat in the name of the Revolution. The
task we are faced with is a reflection upon the very logos of
western rationality. It is only against this broad background
that we can understand the historically specific goals and ambitions of western Marxism. In particular, it is in this way that we
can best understand the phenomenon of recent attempts to rethink
Marxism in terms of Hegelian phenomenology in order to liberate
Marxist praxis from the limitations of positivist knowledge.[3] To

1.   The critique of Marxist scientism was first advanced for English readers
(if we leave aside the earlier and then untranslated work of Karl Korsch, MARXISM
AND PHILOSOPHY and Georg Lukács, HISTORY AND CLASS CONSCIOUSNESS) by
Karl Popper in his THE OPEN SOCIETY AND ITS ENEMIES and THE POVERTY OF
HISTORICISM. I have examined this debate in John O'Neill (ed.), MODES OF IN-
DIVIDUALISM AND COLLECTIVISM, London: Heinemann and New York, St. Martin's
Press, 1973.

2.   For the unity of Marxist humanism and science, see Chapters 1, 3, 4.

3.   George Lichtheim, FROM MARX TO HEGEL, and other Essays. London:
Orbach and Chambers, 1971.

rethink Marxism, however, means that we put it in abeyance as the only 'other' answer that we have to the uncertainties of our times. In other words, it means that we need to examine the categories of Marxist thought such as man, nature, history, party and revolution, in order to recover a proper sense of their dialectical relations so that they are not organized around a simple logic of domination. What this will involve is a recovery of the relation between the already meaningful world of everyday life and the specific practices of science, economics and politics through which we attempt to construct a socialist society mindful of the historical risks and responsibilities of such a project. In short, by placing Marxism in abeyance while we rethink the meaning of socialism we educate ourselves into a permanently critical attitude towards the Party and History as guarantors of socialist rationality and freedom.

Merleau-Ponty's critique of Marxist scientism cannot be well understood unless we situate it in the intellectual history of France and the post World War II rejection of Communism by Leftist intellectuals who at the same time turned to the revival of Marxism.[4] This renaissance of Marxist thinking in part reflected the task of catching up with Central European thought--Korsch and Lukács-- as well as with German phenomenology--Hegel, Husserl, Heidegger, not to mention Weber and Freud. The task was to separate the radical humanist philosophy of Marx from the Engels-Lenin orthodoxy of positivism and scientism.[5] In practice this meant reading Hegel anew and on this basis interpreting Marx's early writings. Merleau-Ponty was among many like Sartre and Hyppolite[6] who listened to Alexandre Kojève's lectures[7] on Hegel's PHENOMENOLOGY OF MIND. It was not until the mid-1950's that the rift between Communism and Marxism--a difficult distinction for outsiders, let alone insiders--became wide open. Apart from other broken friendships, the friendships of Merleau-Ponty and Sartre and of Sartre and Camus were destroyed in the wake of HUMANISM AND TERROR, ADVENTURES OF THE DIALECTIC and Camus's THE REBEL.[8] Later, in his CRITIQUE DE LA RAISON DIALECTIQUE, Sartre attempted to learn from this

4. George Lichtheim, MARXISM IN MODERN FRANCE, New York and London: Columbia University Press, 1966 and his FROM MARX TO HEGEL, 1971.

5. Alfred Schmidt, THE CONCEPT OF NATURE IN MARX, London: NLB, 1971.

6. Jean Hyppolite, STUDIES ON MARX AND HEGEL, Edited and Translated by John O'Neill, New York: Basic Books and London, Heinemann, 1969.

7. Alexandre Kojève, INTRODUCTION TO THE READING OF HEGEL, New York: Basic Books, 1969.

8. Richard Crossman (ed.), THE GOD THAT FAILED, New York: Harper and Row, 1949; Michel-Antoine Burnier, CHOICE OF ACTION, Translated by Bernard Murchland, New York: Random House, 1968.

the 'lesson of history', as he himself put it, in a massive effort to construct an adequate Marxist history and sociology.

It is much easier for us long after World War II to consider capitalism and socialism as subcultures of industrialism rather than as mortal antagonists. But in 1945 it was possible to hope that Communism was the solution to the capitalist syndrome of war and depression. For Leftist intellectuals in Europe the Soviet war effort and the Communist resistance promised a renewal of life once peace came. But peace never came, except as what we call the Cold War. In such an atmosphere, intellectual attitudes were forced to harden. Capitalists and socialists increasingly blamed each other for all the violence and oppression in world. The price of loyalty either to socialism or capitalism became a blind and uncritical faith.

The argument of HUMANISM AND TERROR is especially difficult to understand if the radical alternative forced upon French politics by the Cold War split between America and the Soviet Union is accepted without question. In 1947 there was still a chance, at least in the mind of a non-Communist Leftist intellectual like Merleau-Ponty, that France and Europe would not have to become a satellite either to America or the Soviet Union. The hopes of the Resistance for immediate revolutionary change after the war had withered away in the tripartist tangles of the Communists, Socialists, and Christian Democrats. In March 1947, the Truman doctrine was initiated and in April the Big Four dis- cussions on Germany failed. The introduction of the Marshall Plan in June of the same year, condemned by Molotov's walkout on the Paris Conference in July, hastened the breakdown of tripartism. Suspicion of the anti-Soviet implications of the Marshall Plan caused many of the Left to look towards a neutralist position for Europe, but made them uncertain whether to build this position around the Socialist Party which had failed so far to take any independent line, or the Communist Party, which could be expected to follow a Soviet line. But the drift was towards a pro-Western, anti-Soviet European integration led by the center and right elements of the French Third Force, including the Gaullists. Within two years, the formation of the Brussels Treaty Organization, the North Atlantic Treaty Organization, and the Soviet Cominform brought down the iron curtain of which Winston Churchill had spoken in his Fulton Speech in March of 1946.

The intellectual French Left was in an impossible situation which no combination of Marxism or existenialism seemed capable of remedying. French capitalism was bad, but American capitalism was even more anathema to the Left, if only because it was in the rudest of health internationally, though perhaps not at home. At the same time French socialism was anything but independent and its chances looked no better with Communist help. In such a situation it was impossible to be an anti-Communist if this meant being pro-American, witnessing the Americanization of Europe, and foreswearing the Communists who had fought bravely in the Resistance. On the other hand, it was not possible to be a Communist if this meant being blind to the hardening of the Soviet regime and becoming a witness to the Communist brand of imperialism which broke so many Marxist minds. It is not surprising that many on the Left as well as the Right were unable to bear such ambiguity and therefore welcomed any sign to show clearly which side to support, even if it meant a 'conversion' to the most extreme left and right positions.

I want to argue that in HUMANISM AND TERROR[9] Merleau-Ponty does more than illustrate the fateful connection between revolution and responsibility as it appears in the drama of the Moscow Trials. I think it can be shown that Merleau-Ponty develops a theory of the relations between political action, truth and responsibility which is the proper basis for understanding his approach to the problem of the relation between socialist humanism and revolutionary terror. HUMANISM AND TERROR was prompted by Koestler's dramatization of the Moscow Trials in DARKNESS AT NOON. Merleau-Ponty's reply to Koestler's novel takes the form of an essay in which he develops a phenomenology of revolutionary action and responsibility in order to transcend Koestler's confrontation of the Yogi and the Commissar. The argument depends upon a philosophy of history and truth which draws upon Merleau-Ponty's phenomenology of perception, embodiment and intersubjectivity. Here I shall restrict myself to the political arguments without entering into the structure of Merleau-Ponty's philosophical thought which in any case is better revealed in a certain style of argument rather than through any system.[10]

> Politics, whether of understanding or of reason, oscillates between the world of reality and that of values, between individual judgment and common action, between the present and the future. Even if one thinks, as Marx did, that these poles are united in a historical factor--the proletariat--which is at one and the same time power and value, yet as there may well be disagreement on the manner of making the proletariat enter history and take possession of it, Marxist politics is, just like all the others, undemonstrable. The difference is that Marxist politics understands this and that

9. Maurice Merleau-Ponty, HUMANISM AND TERROR, An Essay on the Communist Problem, Translated and with an Introduction by John O'Neill, Boston: Beacon Press, 1969.

10. John O'Neill, PERCEPTION, EXPRESSION AND HISTORY: The Social Phenomenology of Maurice Merleau-Ponty, Evanston: Northwestern University Press, 1970 and Maurice Merleau-Ponty, PHENOMENOLOGY, LANGUAGE AND SOCIOLOGY, Selected Essays, Edited by John O'Neill, London: Heinemann, 1974.

it has, more than any other politics, explored the labyrinth.[11]

It is typical of Merleau-Ponty to speak factually whereas he is addressing an ideal that his own work brings to reality. It needed Merleau-Ponty among others to take Marxist thinkers through the labyrinth of politics for them to understand the true nature of political trial and error. The philosopher of ambiguity,[12] as Merleau-Ponty has been called, prefers to raise questions rather than offer answers. This is not because he is nerveless but precisely because he wishes to bring to life the historical presumptions of Marxist thought. It is not literally the case that Marxists consider their knowledge undemonstrable. From the COMMUNIST MANIFESTO to the Russian Revolution there is a fairly straight line--at least doctrinally. But in fact such a line represents a colossal abstraction from the doctrinal debates and historical contingencies that shaped these debates and in turn were interpreted through them. Merleau-Ponty believed it was possible to discern in the terrible reality of the Moscow Trials the places where the life of Marxist thought was larger than the simplistic moral antithesis of the Yogi and the Commissar. Of course, Merleau-Ponty's purpose is easily misunderstood. Koestler's DARKNESS AT NOON is certainly true to Soviet practice from the time of the Trials to the later revelations in the Cominform Campaign against Tito, the Rajk-Kosov trials, the Soviet labor camps and mental hospitals. Like many on the Left, Merleau-Ponty himself had to open his eyes to Communist practice. Yet at the same time he begins to rethink Marxist philosophy of history and politics along the lines that have led to a renaissance of Marxist-Hegelian thought while only the most blind could have held on to the romance with Soviet institutions.

In HUMANISM AND TERROR Merleau-Ponty is concerned with revolution as the genesis of political community and with the dilemma of violence which in the name of fraternity becomes self-consumptive. This is the moral dilemma to which the Yogi responds by spiritualizing political action and which the Commissar handles by objectivizing his conduct in the name of historical forces. These alternatives, as posed by Koestler, are rejected by Merleau-Ponty on the grounds that they lose the essential ambivalence of political action and revolutionary responsibility. The science and practice of history never coincide. Because of this contingency, political action is always the decision

11.   Maurice Merleau-Ponty, ADVENTURES OF THE DIALECTIC, Translated by Joseph Bien, Evanston: Northwestern University Press, 1973, p. 6.   My emphasis.

12.   Alphonse de Waelhens, UNE PHILOSOPHIE DE L'AMBIGUITE, L'existential-isme de Maurice Merleau-Ponty, Louvain: Publications Universitaires de Louvain, 1967.

of a future which is not determined uniquely by the facts of the
situation. Thus there enters into political conduct the need to
acknowledge responsibility and the fundamental terror we experience for the consequences of our own decisions as well as for
the effects of other men's actions upon ourselves.

> We do not have a choice between purity and violence but
> between different kinds of violence. Inasmuch as we are
> incarnate beings, violence is our lot. There is no per-
> suasion even without seduction, or in the final analysis,
> contempt. Violence is the common origin of all regimes.
> Life, discussion and political choice occur only against a
> background of violence. What matters and what we have to
> discuss is not violence but its sense or its future. It is a
> law of human action that the present encroaches upon the
> future, the self upon other people. Thus intrusion is not
> only a fact of political life, it also happens in private life.
> In love, in affection, or in friendship we do not encounter
> face to face "consciousness" whose absolute individuality we
> could respect at every moment, but beings qualified as "my
> son", "my wife", "my friend" whom we carry along with us
> into common projects where they receive (like ourselves) a
> definite role with specific rights and duties. So, in collec-
> tive history the spiritual atoms trail their historical role and
> are tied to one another by the threads of their actions.
> What is more, they are blended with the totality of actions,
> whether or not deliberate, which they exert upon others and
> the world so that there does not exist a plurality of subjects
> but an intersubjectivity and that is why there exists a
> common measure of the evil inflicted upon certain people and
> of the good gotten out of it by others.[13]

Yet Merleau-Ponty refuses to draw the sceptical conclusion that
violence and conflict derive from the essentially antisocial nature
of the human passions. In his essay on Montaigne[14] which
allows us to anticipate here his differences with Sartre, he interprets Montaigne's scepticism in terms of the paradox of embodied
consciousness, namely, to be constantly involved in the world
through perception, politics or love and yet always at a distance
from it, without which we could know nothing of it. The sceptic
only withdraws from the world, its passions and follies, in order
to find himself at grips with the world having, as it were merely
slackened the intentional ties between himself and the world in

13. HUMANISM AND TERROR, pp. 109-110. My emphasis.

14. Maurice Merleau-Ponty, "Reading Montaigne", SIGNS, Translated by
Richard C. McLeary, Evanston: Northwestern University Press, 1964; John O'Neill,
"Between Montaigne and Machiavelli", in SOCIOLOGY AS A SKIN TRADE, pp. 96-
110.

order to comprehend the paradox of his being-in-the-world.
Scepticism with regard to the passions only deprives them of
value if we assume a total, Sartrean self-possession, whereas, we
are never wholly ouselves, Merleau-Ponty would say, but always
interested in the world through the passions which we are.
Scepticism and misanthropy, whatever the appearance, have no
place in Marxist politics for the reason that the essential ambivalence of politics is that its violence derives from what is most
valuable in men--the ideas of truth and justice which each intends
for all because men do not live side by side like pebbles but each
in all.

Marxism does not invent the problem of violence, as Koestler
would suggest, except in the sense that it assumes and attempts
to control the violence which bourgeois society tolerates in the
fatalities of race, war, domestic and colonial poverty. The
Marxist revolutionary is faced only with a choice between different kinds of violence and not with the choice to forego violence.
The question which the revolutionary poses is not whether any
one will be hurt but whether the act of violence leads to a future
state of society in which humanist values have been translated
into a common style of life expressed as much in low levels of
infant mortality as in solipsistic, philosophical and literary specu-
lation. If consciousness were a lonely and isolated phenomenon,
as it is pictured in the individualist tradition of philosophy and
the social sciences, and above all in Sartre, then the Yogi's
horror at a single death is enough to condemn a whole regime
regardless of its humanist or socialist aims. But this is an assumption which Marxist-Hegelianism challenges. We never exist
even in splendid philosophical isolation let alone social isolation.
We exist through one another, in specific situations mediated by
specific social relations in which we encroach upon others and are
committed by others so that our intentions are rarely entirely our
own any more than their results. In these exchanges we necessarily prevail upon one another and one generation necessarily
commits the future.[15]

The Marxist revolutionary starts from the evident truth of the
embodied values of men and of the evil of human suffering. Only
later does he learn that in the course of building the economic
foundations of a socialist society he has to make decisions which
subject individuals to forms of violence upon which the future of
the revolution may depend. Marxism does not create this
dilemma; it merely expresses it. Koestler, on the other hand,
poses the problem in such a way as to miss the essential ambivalence of the subjective and objective options of the Yogi and
the Commissar. The values of the Yogi are not simply the

15. John O'Neill, "Situation, Action and Language", in SOCIOLOGY AS A SKIN
TRADE, pp. 81-93.

reverse of those of the Commissar because each experiences an internal reversal of the subjective and objective values whenever either is assumed as an absolute end. It is for this reason that Commissar Rubashov once imprisoned experiences the value of the self in the depths of its inner life where it opens up to the White Guard in the next cell as someone to whom one can speak. The tapping on the prison walls is the primordial institution of human communication for whose sake Rubashov had set out on his revolutionary career.

In the debate over the alternatives of industrialization and collectivization there were facts to support the various arguments of Stalin, Bukharin, and Trotsky. But their divergences arose within the very Marxian conception of history which they all shared. Each regarded history as a reality made through action in line with yet altering the shape of social forces, just as a landscape is progressively revealed with each step we take through it.

> History is terror because we have to move into it not by any straight line that is always easy to trace but by taking our bearings at every moment in a general situation which is changing, like a traveller who pushes into a changing countryside continuously altered by his own advance, where what looked like an obstacle becomes an opening and where the shortest path turns out the longest.[16]

But the leaders of a revolution are not on a casual stroll. They walk on the wild side and must accept responsibility for the path they choose and to be judged by it as soon as they open it up. For this reason Merleau-Ponty argued that the Moscow Trials have to be understood in terms of the Marxist philosophy of history in which history is a drama open towards the future in such a way that the significance of the action at any point of time is never unequivocal and can only be established from the futurist orientation of those in power. The Trials therefore never go beyond the level of a 'ceremony of language' in which the meaning of 'terrorism', 'wrecking', 'espionage', 'defeatism', 'responsbility' and 'confession' has to be sensed entirely in the verbal exhanges and not through reference to an external ground of verification.

The Trials reveal the form and style of the Marxist revolutionary. The revolutionary judges what exists in terms of what is to come; he regards the future as more vital than the present to which it owes its birth. From this perspective there can be no purely subjective honor; we are what we are for others and our relation to them. So often in the Court Proceedings the 'capitulators' while presenting themselves in the light of enemies of the Party

16. HUMANISM AND TERROR, pp. 100-101.

and the masses at the same time hint at the discrepancies between the subjective and objective aspects of their careers. Their statements are to be understood not as formulations of the facts alleged in them except reflectively and by means of certain rules of translation. Consider the following exchange between Vyshinsky and Bukharin:

Vyshinsky: Tell me, did Tomsky link up the perpetration of a hostile act against Gorky with the question of the overthrow of the Soviet government?
Bukharin: In essence he did.
Vyshinsky: In essence he did?
Bukharin: Yes, I have answered.
Vyshinsky; I am interested in the essence.
Bukharin: But you are asking concretely . . .
Vyshinsky: Did your talk with Tomsky provide reason to believe that the question of a hostile act against Alexei Maximovich Gorky was being linked up with the task of overthrowing the Stalin leadership?
Bukharin: Yes, in essence this could be said.
Vyshinsky: Consequently, you knew that some hostile act against Gorky was under consideration?
Bukharin: Yes.
Vyshinsky: And what hostile act in your opinion was referred to?
Bukharin: I gave no thought to the matter at all at that time and I had no idea . . .
Vyshinsky: Tell us what you did think.
Bukharin: I hardly thought at all.
Vyshinsky: But was it not a serious matter? The conversation was about what?
Bukharin: Permit me to explain in a few words. Now, post factum, now, during the investigation, I can say . . .
Vyshinsky: Not during the investigation but during your conversation with Tomsky.
Bukharin: But this was only a fleeting conversation, a conversation with took place during a meeting of the Political Bureau and lasted only a few seconds.
Vyshinsky: I am not interested in how long this conversation lasted; you could have spoken to Tomsky for a whole hour somewhere in a corner, therefore your arguments are of no importance to me. What is important to me are the facts, and these I want to establish. [17]

It is not possible to understand these verbal plays apart from the Hegelian-Marxist expressions of the hypostases through which the

17. REPORT OF COURT PROCEEDINGS IN THE CASE OF THE ANTI-SOVIET "BLOC OF RIGHTS AND TROTSKYITES", Moscow, March 2-13, 1938. Published by the People's Commissariat of Justice of the U.S.S.R., Moscow: 1938.

logic of social forces reveals the essence of a situation or fact
and its relevance for revolutionary action.[18]   They will otherwise only seem to be the result of a corrupt legal process and as
such the pure expression of Soviet terror.   If HUMANISM AND
TERROR were merely engaged in an ex post facto justification of
Stalinism then Merleau-Ponty would simply have been doing bad
historiography.   But he understood himself to be involved in
trying to comprehend Stalinism ex ante or from the political
agent's standpoint, in other words, in the subjective terms of a
Marxist philosophy of history and not just a Stalinist rewrite.

RESPONSIBLE HISTORY

It is, then, Merleau-Ponty's interpretation of the Marxist philosophy of history that must concern us.   His method of presentation
in this case, as elsewhere, involves the familiar alternatives of
determinism and voluntarism.   As a complete alternative, determinism is incompatible with the need for political action, though it
may be extremely effective in the rhetoric of politics to be able to
reassure one's comrades that history is on their side; and similarly, a voluntarism that does not take into account the social preconditions of revolution is likely to waste itself in abortive action.
Political reflection and political action occur in a milieu or inter-
world which is essentially ambiguous because the facts of the
situation can never be totalized and yet we are obliged to act
upon our estimation of them.   Because of the double contingency
of the openness of the future and the partiality of human decision, political divergences, deception and violence are irreducible
historical phenomena, accepted as such by all revolutionaries.

> There is no history where the course of events is a series of
> episodes without unity, or where it is a struggle already
> decided in the heaven of ideas.   History is where there is a
> logic within contingence, a reason within unreason, where
> there is a historical perception which, like perception in
> general, leaves in the background what cannot enter the
> foreground but seizes the lines of force as they are
> generated and actively leads their traces to a conclusion.
> This analogy should not be interpreted as a shameful
> organicism or finalism, but as a reference to the fact that all
> symbolic systems--perception, language, history--only be-
> come what they were although in order to do so they need to
> be taken up into human initiative.[19]

    18.   Nathan Leites and Elsa Bernaut, RITUAL OF LIQUIDATION, The Case of
the Moscow Trials, Glencoe: The Free Press, 1954.

    19.   Maurice Merleau-Ponty, THEMES FROM THE LECTURES AT THE COLLEGE
DE FRANCE, '1952-1960, Translated by John O'Neill, Evanston: Northwestern
University Press, 1970, pp. 29-30.

136

FOR MARX AGAINST ALTHUSSER

Marxism is not a spectacle secure from its own intervention in our
common history. Marxists need a philosophy of history because
human history is neither open in an arbitrary way not so closed
that we are relieved of the responsibility of reading its signs and
implementing our own chances. The future is not stillborn in the
present nor does the past lie unalterably upon the present.
Between the past and the future there is the presence of ourselves which is the chance we have of testing our limits. In the
human world men cannot be the object of their own practice
except where oppression rules--that is to say, where some men
subject others to the rule of things. Yet men need leaders as
much as leaders need men. Thus there arises for Marxism the
dreadful problem, once men are determined to be free, of how it
is free men are to be led along the path of freedom. For freedom
is not the absence of limits which would make knowledge and
leadership unnecessary. Freedom is only possible in the real
world of limits and situated possibilities which require the institution of thoughtful and responsible leadership.[20]

In confronting the problematic of freedom and truth, Merleau-
Ponty reflected upon man's options in terms of Max Weber's
response to the historical task of understanding. He saw in
Weber one who tried to live responsibly in the face of conflicting
demands of knowledge and action. This was possible, in the first
place, because Weber understood that history is not the passive
material of historiography any more than the practice of historiography is itself free of historical interests and values.
There is no neutral material of history. History is not a
spectacle for us because it is our own living, our own violence
and our own beliefs. Why then are revolutionary politics not an
utterly cynical resort to violence and nothing but a sceptical
appeal to justice and truth? For the very reason, says Merleau-
Ponty, that no ones lives history from a purely pragmatic standpoint, not even he who claims to do so. Scepticism is a conclusion which could only be reached if one were to draw--as does
Sartre--a radical distinction between political knowledge and
political action. But allowing that we only experience things and
the future according to a probable connection does not mean that
the world lacks a certain style or physiognomy for us. We live in
terms of subjective certainties which we intend as practical and
universal typifications that are in no way illusory unless we posit
some apodictic certainty outside the grounds of human experience.
We do not experience uncertainty at the core of our being. The
center of our experience is a common world in which we make
appraisals, enlist support and seek to convince sceptics and

20. Jonn O'Neill, "Le Langage et la décolonisation: Fanon et Freire",
SOCIOLOGIE ET SOCIETES, Vol. VI, No. 2, Novembre 1974, pp. 53-65.

opponents, never doubting the fundamental permutation of subjective and objective evidence.[21]

If we accept the Marxist view that there is meaning in history as
in the rest of our lives, then it follows that Marxist politics are
based upon an objective analysis of the main trends in history
and not simply on the will of the Communist Party. In other
words there is a materialist foundation to Marxist politics. At the
same time, the trends in history do not lead necessarily to a
socialist society.   History is made through human action and
political choices which are never perfectly informed and thus
there is always a contingent factor in history. It is necessary to
avoid construing these materialist and ideological factors too
crudely.   Marxian materialism is not the simple notion that human
history consists in the production of wealth; it is the project of
creating a human environment which reflects the historical
development of human sensibility.   Similarly, the Marxist claim
that ideological systems are related to economic factors is not a
simple reductionist argument; it is the claim that ideological
factors and the mode of production are mutually determining
expressions of a given social order.   At any given moment the
mode of production may be the expression of the ideological
superstructure just as the physical movements of the body may
express a person's life-style.   But in the long run it is the
economic infrastructure which is the medium of the ideological
message--just as our body is the structure underlying all our
moods.   Because we do not inhabit the present as a region totally
within our survey, nor yet as a zone of pure possibility, history
has familiar contours for us, a feel that we recognize in our daily
lives where others share the same conditions and the same hopes.
This daily life is something we shape through our desires and
which in turn acquires an institutional reality which conditions
the future limits and possibilities that are our life chances.   In
short, we bring a life-style to political action, a lifetime of suffering, with others and for others, and together, for better or
worse, we decide to act.   But it is neither an open nor a closed
calculation.   It is more like the decision to live from which we
cannot withdraw, a decision which we never make once and for all
and yet for which we are uniquely responsible.   And like the
decision to live, the choice of a politics entails the responsbility
for the contingency of violence which is the 'infantile disorder' in
our private and public lives.

One can no more get rid of historical materialism than of
psychoanalysis by impugning 'reductionist' conceptions and
casual though in the name of a descriptive and phenomenological method, for historical materialism is no more linked to

21.   John O'Neill, MAKING SENSE TOGETHER, An introduction to Wild
Sociology, New York: Harper and Row and London: Heinemann, 1974.

such 'causal' formulations as may have been given than is psychoanalysis, and like the latter it could be expressed in another language . . .

There is no one meaning of history; what we do always has several meanings, and this is where an existential conception of history is distinguishable from materialism and spiritualism. But every cultural phenomenon has, among others, an economic significance, and history by its nature never transcends, any more than it is reducible to, economics . . . It is impossible to reduce the life which involves human relationships either to economic relations, or to juridical and moral ones thought up by men, just as it is impossible to reduce individual life either to bodily functions or to our knowledge of life as it involves them. But in each case one of the orders of significance can be regarded as dominant: one gesture as 'sexual', another as 'amorous', another as 'warlike', and even in the sphere of coexistence, one period of history can be seen as characterized by intellectual culture, another as primarily political or economic. The question whether the history of our time is pre-eminently significant in an economic sense, and whether our ideologies give us only a derivative or secondary meaning of it is one which no longer belongs to philosophy, but to politics, and one which will be solved only by seeking to know whether the economic or ideological scenario fits the facts more perfectly. Philosophy can only show that is it <u>possible</u> from the starting point of the human condition.[22]

The foundations of Marxian history and politics are grounded in the dialectic between man and nature (domination) and between man and his fellow men (recognition). It is the nature of human consciousness to realize itself in the world and among men; its embodiment is the essential mode of its openness towards the world and to others. The problems of conflict and coexistence only arise for an embodied consciousness driven by its basic needs into the social division of labor and engaged by its deepest need in a life and death struggle for identity through mutual recognition and solidarity. Embodied consciousness never experiences an original innocence to which any violence would do irreparable harm; we experience only different kinds of violence. For consciousness only becomes aware of itself as already engaged in the world, in definite and specific situations in which its resources are never entirely its own but derive from the exploitation of its position as the child of these parents, the incumbent of such and such a role, or the beneficiary of certain class and national privileges. We rarely act as isolated individuals and

22.   Maurice Merleau-Ponty, PHENOMENOLOGY OF PERCEPTION, Translated by Colin Smith, London: Routledge and Kegan Paul, 1962, pp. 171-173.

even when we seem to do so our deeds presuppose a community which possesses a common measure of the good and evil it experiences.

The problem which besets the Marxist theory of the proletariat is that the emergence of truth and justice presuppose a community while at the same time the realization of a genuine community presupposes a concept of truth and justice. The Marxist critique of the liberal truth as a mystification which splits the liberal community starts from the exposure of its lack of correspondence with the objective relations between man in liberal society. By contrast, Marxism claims to be a truth in the making; it aims at overthrowing liberal society in the name of an authentic community. However, the birth of communist society is no less painful than the birth of man himself and from its beginnings communism is familiar with violence and deception. It might be argued that the violence of Marxist revolutionary politics arises because the Party forces upon the proletariat a mission for which history has not prepared it. The proletariat is thus the victim of the double contingency of bourgeois and communist deception and exploitation. The constant shifts in Party directives, the loss of socialist innocence, the reappearance of profit and status in community society may be appealed to as indications of the failure of Marxism to renew human history. Merleau-Ponty was aware of these arguments and indeed explicitly documents them with findings on conditions in the Soviet Union, including the shattering discovery of the labor camps.[23]

Nevertheless, Merleau-Ponty argued that the proper role of Marxist violence is as the midwife of a socialist society already in the womb of capitalist society. The image is essential to his argument. For it was intended to distinguish Marxist violence from historically arbitrary and authoritarian forms of violence.[24] The image of birth suggests a natural process in which there arises a point of intervention which is likely to be painful but is aimed at preserving a life which is <u>already</u> <u>there</u> and not entirely at the mercy of the midwife. In the language of the COMMUNIST MANIFESTO, the argument is that the birth of socialist society depends upon the full maturation of capitalism which engenders a force whose transition from dependency to independence is achieved through a painful transition in which dramtic roles are assigned to the bourgeoisie, the proletariat, and the Party. There are, of course, features of the imagery of birth that lead to outcomes rather different from those which Merleau-Ponty wishes to draw. The human infant achieves maturity only after a

23. "The U.S.S.R. and the Camps", SIGNS, pp. 263-273.

24. "There is indeed a Sartrean violence, and it is more highly strung and less durable than Marx's violence." ADVENTURES OF THE DIALECTIC, p. 159.

long period of tutelage in which if anything social dependency becomes far more burdensome than umbilical dependency, as we have learned from Freud. Understood in this way the image involves a greater political dependency of the proletariat upon the Party and its commissars than is compatible with the aims of socialist humanism. Merleau-Ponty's ideal for the childhood of the revolution is the period of Lenin's frank and open discussions with the proletariat concerning the reasons for NEP. This was a time when words still had their face meaning, when explanations for changes of tactics were given which left the proletariat with an improved understanding of events and with heightened revolutionary consciousness.

> . . . Marxist Machiavellianism differs from Machiavellianism insofar as it transforms compromise through awareness of compromise, and alters the ambivalence of history through awareness of ambivalence; it makes detours knowingly and by announcing them as such; it calls retreats retreats; it sets the details of local politics and the paradoxes of strategy in the perspective of the whole.[25]

Marxist violence is thus an integral feature of the theory of the proletariat and its philosophy of history. To be a Marxist is to see meaning taking shape within history. Anything else is to live history and society as sheer force. To be a Marxist is to believe that history is intelligible and that it has a direction which encompasses the proletarian control of the economic and state apparatus, along with the emergence of an international brotherhood. Whatever the lags on any of these fronts, it is the Marxist persuasion that these elements delineate the essential structure or style of communist society. It is this structure of beliefs which determines the Marxist style of historical analysis and political action.

Even before he turned to Max Weber for his conception of responsible history, Merleau-Ponty had anticipated those adventures of the dialectic which had made it necessary to rethink Marxism as a philosophy of history and institutions. Unless this task is undertaken, Marxism must either continue to hide from its own history or else see its universal hopes thrown into the wasteland of historical relativism. Only an absolutely relativist conception of history as the milieu of our own living can keep alive what Merleau-Ponty called 'Western' Marxism.

> History is not only an object in front of us, far from us, beyond our reach: it is also our awakening as subjects. Itself a historical fact the true of false consciousness that we have of our history cannot be simple illusion. There is a

25. HUMANISM AND TERROR, p. 129.

mineral there to be refined, a truth to be extracted, if only
we go to the limits of relativism and put it, in turn, back
into history. We give a form to history according to our
categories; but our categories, in contact with history, are
themselves freed from their partiality. The old problem of
the relations between subject and object is transformed, and
relativism is surpassed as soon as one puts it in historical
terms, since here the object is the vestige left by other
subjects, and the subject--historical understanding--held in
the fabric of history, is by this very fact capable of self-
criticism. [26]

We have to understand how it is that Marxism which arises as a
movement within history can be the fulfillment of history rather
than a phase subject to its own laws of historical transition. How
is it possible that men who are driven by material circumstances
in general and the protetariat in particular are capable of the
vision of humanity freed from exploitation and alienation? However these questions are answered, we have to face the fact that
the proletariat is given direction by the Communist Party and that
with respect to this relationship we face new questions about
Marxist knowledge and the freedom of the masses. In his
analysis of these questions Merleau-Ponty extended his reading of
Weber through Lukács' studies in Marxist dialectics. [27] In terms
of this reading Merleau-Ponty came to a reformulation of Marx's
historical materialism. If materialism were a literal truth it is
difficult to see how the category of history could arise. For
matter does not have a history except by metaphorical extension.
Men live in history. But their history is not external to themselves in the same sense that the history of geological strata
might be available to observation. Men inhabit history as they do
language. [28] Just as they have to learn the specific vocabulary
of Marxism, so they have to bring their everyday experience of
poverty, power and violence under the notion of the 'proletariat'
and to interpret their experiences through the projection of class
consciousness' and 'revolution'. Thus 'class consciousness' does
not inhere in history either as a preexisting idea or as an inherent environmental force. What we can say is that despite all
its contingencies the history of society gathers into itself the
consciousness that is dispersed in all its members so that it
fosters their consciousness as civic knowledge:

26. ADVENTURES OF THE DIALECTIC, pp. 30-31.

27. Georg Lukács, HISTORY AND CLASS CONSCIOUSNESS, Studies in Marxist
Dialectics, Translated by Rodney Livingstone, London: Merlin Press, 1971.

28. John O'Neill, "Institution, Language and Historicity", in PERCEPTION,
EXPRESSION AND HISTORY, pp. 46-64.

As a living body, given its behavior, is, so to speak, closer to consciousness than a stone, so certain social structures are the cradle of the knowledge of society. Pure consciousness finds its "origin" in them. Even if the notion of interiority, when applied to a society, should be understood in the figurative sense, we find, all the same, that this metaphor is possible with regard to capitalist society but not so with regard to precapitalist ones. This is enough for us to say that the history which produced capitalism symbolizes the emergence of a subjectivity. There are subjects, objects, there are men and things, but there is also a third order, that of relationships between men inscribed in tools or social symbols. These relationships have their development, their advances and their regressions. Just as in the life of the individual, so in this generalized life there are tentative aims, failure or success, reaction of the result upon the aim, repetition or variation, and this is what one calls history.[29]

Despite its detours and regressions, Merleau-Ponty retains his conviction of the overall meaning of human history as an emancipatory process but allows for the successes and failure in this project to lie in one and the same historical plane. History is the growing relationship of man to man. This does not mean that all previous societies are to be judged by today's standards because at every stage history is threatened with loss and diversion. What we can properly regard as today's developments really only take up problems that were immanent in the previous period. Hence the past is not merely the waste of the future. If we can speak of an advance in history it is perhaps only in the negative sense that we can speak of the elimination of non-sense rather than of the positive accumulation of reason. The price we must pay for history's deliverance of reason and freedom is that freedom and reason never operate outside of the constraints of history and politics. Therefore Marxism cannot simply claim to see through all other ideologies as though it alone were transparent to itself. Indeed, Marxism is itself open to the danger of becoming the most false ideology of all inasmuch as its own political life will require changes of position that can hardly be read from the state of its economic infrastructure.

If Marxism is not to degenerate into a willful ideology and yet not claim absolute knowledge, it must be geared to the praxis of the proletariat. But this is not an easy matter since the proletariat does not spontaneously realize its own goals and by the same token the Party cannot easily avoid a specious appeal to the allegedly objective interests of the proletariat. If like Sartre we force the distinction between theory and praxis, then the Party is

29. ADVENTURES OF THE DIALECTIC, pp. 37-38.

either reduced to a democratic consultation of the momentary thoughts and feelings of the proletariat or else to bureaucratic cynicism with regard to the gap between the present state of the proletariat and the Party's idea of its future. So long as we think of consciousness as a state of individual minds then we cannot get around the problem of locating the synthesis of knowledge in an absolute consciousness, called the Party. This means that the proletariat is really not the subject of its own deeds but the object of what the Party knows on its behalf. To understand Merleau-Ponty's critique of Sartre's 'ultrabolshevism' we need to have some notion of how they were divided even over a common philosophical background. The opposition between Sartre and Merleau-Ponty derives in the first place from their fundamentally opposite phenomenologies of embodiment. For Sartre the body is a vehicle of shame, nausea and ultimate alienation caught in the trap of the other's look.[30] In Merleau-Ponty the body is the vehicle of the very world and others with whom together we labor in love and understanding and the very same ground to which we must appeal to correct error or overcome violence. In Sartre the body is the medium of the world's decomposition, while in Merleau-Ponty the body symbolizes the very composition of the world and society. In each case there follows radically different conceptions of political life. In Merleau-Ponty, the extremes of collectivism and individualism, labor and violence are always historical dimensions of our basic social life. To Sartre, nothing unites us with nature and society except the external necessity of scarcity which obliges us to join our labor and individual sovereignty into collective projects which are always historically unstable.

> The "master", the "feudal lord", the "bourgeois", the "capitalist" all appear not only as powerful people who command but in addition and above all as Thirds; that is, as those who are outside the oppressed community and for whom this community exists. It is therefore for them and in their freedom that the reality of the oppressed class is going to exist. They cause it to be born by their look. It is to them and through them that there is revealed the identity of my condition and that of others who are oppressed; it is for them that I exist in a situation organized with others and that my possibiles as dead-possibles are strictly equivalent with the possibles of others; it is for them that I am a worker and it is through and in their revelation as the Other-as-a-look that I experience myself as one among others. This means that I discover the "Us" in which I am integrated or "the class" outside, in the look of the Third,

30.   Jean-Paul Sartre, BEING AND NOTHINGNESS, Translated and with an Introduction by Hazel E. Barnes, New York: Washington Square Press, 1969, Part III.

and it is this collective alienation which I assume when
saying "Us". From this point of view the privileges of the
Third and "our" burdens, "our" miseries have value at first
only as a signification; they signify the independence of the
Third in relation to "Us"; they present our alienation to us
more plainly. Yet as they are nonetheless endured, as in
particular our work, our fatigue are nonetheless suffered, it
is across this endured suffering that I experience my being-
looked-at-as-a-thing-engaged-in-a-totality-of-things. It is in
terms of my suffering, of my misery that I am collectively
apprehended with others by the Third; that is, in terms of
the adversity of the world, in terms of the facticity of my
condition. Without the Third, no matter what might be the
adversity of the world, I should apprehend myself as a
triumphant transcendence; with the appearance of the Third,
"I" experience "Us" as apprehended in terms of things and
as things overcome by the world.[31]

In Sartrean Marxism it is therefore the role of the Party to unite
an ever disintegrating proletariat to which it plays the role of the
other or Third analogous to the role of the capitalist as the Other
who unites the atomized labor of the workshop or assembly line.
In effect, sartre constructs the Party as the sole source of
historical intelligibility because he denies any basis for intersubjectivity to arise at other levels of conduct. The result is
that Sartre is obliged to idealize the notions of fact, action and
history as nothing but what is determined by the Party. Hence
the Party is subject to permanent anxiety since it is deprived of
any middle ground between itself and a proletarian praxis from
which it might learn to formulate, revise and initiate plans that
do not risk its whole life. Because he can only understand
expression as pure creation or as simple imitation, Sartre loses
the real ground of political communication.

If one wants to engender revolutionary politics dialectically
from the proletarian condition, the revolution from the rigid-
ified swarm of thoughts without subject, Sartre answers with
a dilemma: either the conscious renewal alone gives its
meaning to the process, or one returns to organicism. What
he rejects under the name of organicism at the level of
history is in reality much more than the notion of life: it is
symbolism understood as a functioning of signs having its
own efficacy beyond the meanings that analysis can assign to
these signs. It is, more generally, expression. For him
expression either goes beyond what is expressed and is then
a pure creation, or it copies it and is then a simple unveiling. But an action which is an unveiling, an unveiling

31. BEING AND NOTHINGNESS, pp. 544-545.

which is an action--in short, a dialectic--this Sartre does
not want to consider.[32]

Properly speaking, praxis is not divided between theory and
practice but lies in the wider realm of communication and expression.   Here Merleau-Ponty's argument already anticipates
Habermas' later correction of Marx's confusion of the emancipatory
orders of labor and symbolic interaction.[33]   The everyday life
of the proletariat makes the notion of a class a possibility long
before it is formulated as such.   When the occasion for the
explicit appeal to class consciousness arises, its formal possibility
does not lie in the power of the Party's theoreticians but in the
ordinary capacity of men to appraise their situation and to speak
their minds together because their thoughts are not locked behind
their skulls but are near enough the same in anyone's experience
of exploitation and injustice.   Of course, the Party has to give
these thoughts a political life, to realize their truth as a common
achievement in which the proletariat and the Party are mutually
enlightened.   'This exchange, in which no one commands and no
one obeys, is symbolized by the old custom which dictates that,
in a meeting, speakers join in when the audience applauds.   What
they applaud is the fact that they do not intervene as persons,
that in their relationship with those who listen to them a truth
appears which does not come from them and which the speakers
can and must applaud.   In the communist sense, the Party is this
communication; and such a conception of the Party is not a
corollary of Marxism--it is its very center.'[34]   Thus we see
that the heart of Marxism is not just the communalizing of
property but the attainment of an ideally communicative or educa-
tive society whose icon is the Party.   At the same time, this ideal
society of labor and speech is obliged to resort to violence since
its truths reflect only a reality that has to be brought into
being.   Marxist truth is not hidden behind empirical history
waiting to be deciphered by the Party theoreticians.   Ultimately,
the issue here is the question of the education of the Party itself
in its role of educating the masses.   It was first raised by Marx

32.   ADVENTURES OF THE DIALECTIC, p. 142.

33.   "In his empirical analyses Marx comprehends the history of the species
under the categories of material activity <u>and</u> the critical abolition of ideologies, of
instrumental action <u>and</u> revolutionary practice, of labour <u>and</u> reflection at once.   But
Marx interprets what he does in the more restricted conception of the species' self-
reflection through work alone.   The materialist concept of synthesis is not conceived
broadly enough in order to explicate the way in which Marx contributes to realizing
the intention of a really radicalized critique of knowledge.   In fact, it even
prevented Marx from understanding his own mode of procedure from this point of
view."   Jürgen Habermas, KNOWLEDGE AND HUMAN INTERESTS, Translated by
Jeremy J. Shapiro, Boston: Beacon Press, 1971, p. 42.   Cf. Jürgen Habermas,
THEORY AND PRACTICE, Translated by John Viertel, Boston: Beacon Press, 1973,
Ch. 4, Labor and Interaction: Remarks on Hegel's Jena PHILOSOPHY OF MIND.

34.   ADVENTURES OF THE DIALECTIC, p. 52.

himself in the Third Thesis on Feuerbach. If the Party is not above history then it is inside history like the proletariat itself. The problem is how to relativize the opposition between Party and proletarian consciousness so that their mutual participation in history is not organized in terms of a (Party) subject and (proletariat) object split. The argument between Sartre and Merleau-Ponty parallels the difference between the political practices of Lenin and Stalin, at least insofar as Merleau-Ponty like Lukács can argue for a period in Lenin's own use of the Party as an instrument of proletarian education and party self-critique. In his book, Lenin,[35] Lukács argues with respect to Lenin's political practice much the same thesis that Merleau-Ponty later espoused, namely, that it must not be confused with realpolitik. 'Above all, when defining the concept of compromise, any suggestion that it is a question of knack, of cleverness, of an astute fraud, must be rejected. "We must," said Lenin, "decisively reject those who think that politics consists of little tricks, sometimes bordering on deceit. Classes cannot be deceived." For Lenin, therefore, compromise means that the true developmental tendencies of classes (and possibly of nations--for instance, where an oppressed people is concerned), which under specific circumstances and for a certain period run parallel in determinate areas with the interests of the proletariat, are exploited to the advantage of both.'[36] In the postscript to his essay on Lenin, Lukács repeats the argument for the unity of Lenin's theoretical grasp of the political nature of the imperialist epoch and his practical sense of proletarian politics. In trying to express the living nature of that unity in Lenin's own life, Lukács describes how Lenin would learn from experience or from Hegel's LOGIC, according to the situation, preserving in himself the dialectical tension between particulars and a theoretical totality. As Lenin writes in his PHILOSOPHIC NOTEBOOKS: 'Theoretical cognition ought to give the Object in its necessity, in its all-sided relations, in its contradictory movement, in- and for-itself. But the human Concept "definitively" catches this objective truth of cognition, seizes and masters it, only when the Concept becomes "being-for-itself" in the sense of practice.'

It was by turning to Hegel that Lenin sought to find a way to avoid making theory the mere appendage of state practice, while reserving to practice a more creative political role than the retoactive determination or revision of ideology. But this meant that Marxist materialism could never be the simple enforcement of political will, any more than political will could be exercised without a theoretical understanding of the specific class relations it presupposed. Thus Lenin remarks that 'The standpoint of life,

35.   Georg Lukács, LENIN, A STUDY ON THE UNITY OF HIS THOUGHT, London: NLB, 1970.

36.   LENIN, p. 79.

of practice, should be first and fundamental in the theory of knowledge . . . Of course, we must not forget that the criterion of practice can never, in the nature of things, either confirm or refute any idea <u>completely</u>. This criterion too is sufficiently "indefinite" not to allow human knowledge to become "absolute", but at the same time it is sufficiently definite to wage a ruthless fight against all varieties of idealism and agnosticism.' Of course, in these later Hegelian formulations Lenin is modifying his own version of Engels' dialectical materialism as set forth in MATERIALISM AND EMPIRIO-CRITICISM, thereby rejoining the challenge set to this work by Lukács own HISTORY AND CLASS CONSCIOUSNESS, as well as by Karl Korsch's MARXISM AND PHILOSOPHY, both published in 1923. Lukács' essay on Lenin was published on the occasion of Lenin's death in 1924. What died with Lenin was orthodox Marxism, although its dead hand was to be upon socialism for another thirty years or more. But while it is clear that scientific socialism was not ready for Lukács, the same must be said of the West, where only today is the critique of scientific praxis entering into a properly reflexive or critical social science. What HISTORY AND CLASS CON-SCIOUSNESS made clear was that living Marxism is inseparable from its idealist and Hegelian legacy. The Hegelian concept of totality furnishes a matrix for the integration of ethics and politics through the restless dynamics of man's attempt to measure his existential circumstances against the ideal of his human essence, which he achieves through the struggle against self and institutional alienation. The Hegelian Marxist totality is thus the basis for the integral humanism of Marxist social science.[37]

What Merleau-Ponty adds to Hegelian Marxism from his own phenomenology of perception is an unshakable grasp of the 'inter-world' (<u>intermonde</u>) of everyday living and conduct which is far too dense and stratified to he a thing of pure consciousness. This is the world of our species-being, a corporeal world whose deep structures of action and reflection are the anonymous legacies of the body politic.[38] The interworld is never avail-able to us in a single unifying moment of consciousness or as a decision whose consequences are identical with the actor's inten-tions. But then none of us thinks or acts outside of a life whose ways have moulded us so that what 'we' seek is never entirely our own and therefore borrows upon the very collective life which

---

37.   This much has bee.. established in the academic debate over the early and later writings of Marx.   One would have thought that it is no longer arguable that Marxism can be separated from its Hegelian sources.   Yet, recently this argument has reappeared in the influential contributions to critical theory developed by Habermas and by the structuralist readings of Marx fostered by Althusser. I have considered these arguments in Chapters 2 and 8.

38.   John O'Neill, "Authority, Knowledge and the Body Politic", in SOCIOLOGY AS A SKIN TRADE, pp. 68-80.

it advances or retards. Thus we never have anything like
Sartre's absolute power of decision to join or withdraw from
collective life. What we have is an ability to shift institutions off
center, polarizing tradition and freedom in the same plane as
creativity and imitation. Our freedom, therefore, never comes to
us entirely from the outside through the Party, as Sartre would
have it. It begins inside us like the movements of our body in
response to the values of a world which opens up through its own
explorations and accommodations. It follows that Sartre's conception of the party expropriates the spontaneity of all life in the
name of the proletariat, having first separated the proletariat
from what it shares with men anywhere engaged in the struggle
for life.

> The question is to know whether, as Sartre says, there are
> only _men_ and _things_ or whether there is also the interworld,
> which we call history, symbolism, truth-to-be-made. If one
> sticks to the dichotomy, men, as the place where all meaning
> arises, are condemned to an incredible tension. Each man,
> in literature as well as in politics, must assume all that
> happens instant by instant to all others, he must be im-
> mediately universal. If, on the contrary, one acknowledges
> a mediation of personal relationships through the world of
> human symbols, it is true that one renounces being instantly
> justified in the eyes of everyone and holding oneself re-
> sponsible for all that is done at each moment. But since
> consciousness cannot in practice maintain its pretension of
> being God, since it is inevitably led to delegate responsi-
> bility--it is one abdication for another, and we prefer the
> one which leaves consciousness the means of knowing what it
> is doing.[39]

The universality and truth towards which political consciousness
aims are not an intrinsic property of the Party. They are an
acquisition continuously established and reestablished in a community and tradition of knowledge for which individuals in
specific historical situations call and to which they respond.
Understood in this way, history is the call of one thought to
another, because each individual's work or action is created
across the path of self and others towards a public which it
elicits rather than serves. That is, history is the field which
individual effort requires in order to become one with the community it seeks to build so that where it is successful its invention appears always to have been necessary. Individual action,
then, is the invention of history, because it is shaped in a
present which previously was not just a void waiting to be
determined by the word or deed but in a tissue of calling and
response which is the life of no one and everyone. Every one of

39. ADVENTURES OF THE DIALECTIC, p. 200.

life's actions, insofar as it invokes its truth, lives in the expectation of a historical inscription, a judgement not only of its
intention or consequences but also of its fecundity which is the
relevance of its 'story' to the present.

> History is the judge--not History as the Power of a moment
> or of a century--but history as the space of inscription and
> accumulation beyond the limits of countries and epochs of
> what we have said and done that is most true and valuable,
> taking into account the circumstances in which we had to
> speak. Others will judge what I have done because I
> painted the painting to be seen, because my action committed
> the future of others; but neither art nor politics consists in
> pleasing or flattering others. What they expect of the artist
> or politician is that he draw them toward values in which
> they will only later recognize their own values. The painter
> or politician shapes others more than he follows them. The
> public at whom he aims is not given; it is a public to be
> elicited by his work. The others of whom he thinks are not
> empirical "others", nor even humanity conceived as a
> species; it is others once they have become such that he can
> live with them. The history in which the artist participates
> (and it is better the less he thinks about "making history"
> and honestly produces his work as he sees it) is not a
> power before which he must genuflect. It is the perpetual
> conversation woven together by all speech, all valid works
> and actions, each according to its place and circumstance,
> contesting and confirming the other, each one recreating all
> the others.[40]

Merleau-Ponty returns Marxist politics to the flux of the natural
and historical world, rejecting its compromise with the ideals of
objectivism which have made the tradition of rationality an enigma
to itself. Henceforth, politics must abide in the life-world where
Husserl found its roots and from there it must recover its own
ontological history.

Today history is hardly more meaningful because of the advent of
socialism in the Soviet Union or elsewhere. Indeed, the potential
nuclear confrontation of world ideologies has brought human
history to new heights of absurdity. Marxism has become a truth
for large parts of the world but not in the sense it intended.
The question is what conclusion we should draw from this.
Writing in 1947 and the decade following, Merleau-Ponty was
afraid that the West would try to resolve the Communist problem
through war. To this he argued that the failures of Communism

    40. Maurice Merleau-Ponty, THE PROSE OF THE WORLD, Translated and with
an Introduction by John O'Neill, Evanston: Northwestern University Press, 1973, p.
86.

are the failures of Western humanism as a whole and so we cannot
be partisan to it, far less indifferent. The Marxist revolution
can lose its way. This is because, as Merleau-Ponty puts it, it
is a mode of human conduct which may be true as a movement but
false as a regime. But it is the nature of political action to offer
no uniquely happy solution. Political life involves a fundamental
evil in which we are forced to choose between values without
knowing for certain which are absolutely good or evil. In the
Trojan wars the Greek gods fought on both sides. It is only in
modern politics that, as Camus remarks, the human mind has
become an armed camp. In this situation Merleau-Ponty wrote to
overcome the split between good and evil which characterizes the
politics of crisis and conflict. Above all, he raised the voice of
reason which despite scepticism and error achieves a truth for us
that is continuous with nothing else than our own efforts to
maintain it.

> For the very moment we assert that unity and reason do not
> exist and that opinions are carried along by discordant
> options which remain below the level of reason the conscious-
> ness we gain of the irrationalism and contingency in us
> cancels them as fatalities and opens us to the other person.
> Doubt and disagreement are facts, but so is the strange
> pretension we all have of thinking of the truth, our capacity
> for taking the other's position to judge ouselves, our need
> to have our opinions recognized by him and to justify our
> choices before him, in short, the experience of the other
> person as an alter ego in the very course of discussion.
> The human world is an open or unfinished system and the
> same radical contingency which threatens it with discord also
> rescues it from the inevitability of disorder and prevents us
> from despairing of it, providing only that one remembers
> that its various machineries are actually men and tries to
> maintain and expand man's relations to man.

> Such a philosophy cannot tell us that humanity will be
> realized as though it possessed some knowledge apart and
> were not itself embarked upon experience, being only a more
> acute consciousness of it. But it awakens us to the im-
> portance of daily events and action. For it is a philosophy
> which arouses in us a love for our times which are not the
> simple repetition of human eternity nor merely the conclusion
> to premises already postulated. It is a view which like the
> most fragile object of perception--a soap bubble, or a
> wave--or like the most simple dialogue, embraces indivisibly
> all the order and all the disorder of the world.[41]

41. HUMANISM AND TERROR, pp. 188-189.

CHAPTER 10

MARXISM AND THE TWO SCIENCES

I.--THE DEMARCATION PROBLEM

The problem we wish to identify is an ambiguity in the demarcation of the sociology of science as understood by Marx and
followers. The 'two sciences' problem, incidentally, does not
refer to the demarcation of the natural and social sciences--nor to
the <u>double</u> <u>hermeneutic</u> of the natural and social sciences.[1] It
refers to the inadequacy of the Marxist topology of superstructure and substructure to accommodate a sophisticated understanding of scientific inquiry. The result is that:

(a) the natural sciences are both subject to and exempt
from social determination;

(b) function in both the substructure and the superstructure according to historicized stages of capitalist
development;

(c) a Marxist sociology of science, in view of (a) and (b),
cannot avoid the problem of its own demarcation.

While it is generally conceded that Marxism has given a considerable impetus to the sociology of science, it is undeniable that
the Marxist conception of science is ambiguous--if not ambivalent.
In very simple terms, Marx launched what we may call an
<u>externalist</u> <u>sociology</u> <u>of</u> <u>science</u> inasmuch as he stressed the social
determination of knowledge and belief, rejecting the idealist or
ideological view that society is driven by dominant ideas and
values:

Political, juridical, philosophical, religious, literary, artistic,
etc., development is based on economic development. But all
these react upon one another and also upon the economic
base. It is not that the economic position is the <u>cause and</u>
<u>alone active</u>, while everything else has only a passive effect.
There is, rather, interaction on the basis of the economic
necessity, which ultimately always asserts itself. [2]

1. Anthony Giddens, NEW RULES OF SOCIOLOGICAL METHOD, A Positive
Critique of Interpretative Sociologies, London: Hutchinson, 1976.

2. Friedrich Engels, "Letter to Heinz Starkenburg, 25 January," in
SELECTED WORKS, by Karl Marx, Moscow: Foreign Languages Press, 1935.

Whether Marx or Engels is to blame for the equivocation here, we have not to decide. Engels' recognition of the interaction between the ideological superstructure and the economic infrastructure--even with a certain primacy accorded to the economic base--makes it necessary to draw further analytic distinctions in order to construct a working sociology of science within which a place is provided for the distinctive analytic enterprise of Marxism as a science of society. Otherwise, an ambiguity dogs Marxist sociology, namely, the uncertainty of whether to locate itself as a relatively autonomous ideological enterprise, or to ground itself in the deterministic springs of the economic infrastructure. The seriousness of this ambiguity appears once we also see that Marx was tempted both to exempt the natural sciences from economic determinism and to claim that the Marxist analysis of the economic infrastructure was itself a natural science:

> With the change of the economic foundation the entire immense superstructure is more or less rapidly transformed. In considering such transformations the distinction should always be made between the material transformation of the economic conditions of production which can be determined with the precision of natural science, and the legal, political, religious, aesthetic or philosophic--in short, ideological forms in which men become conscious of this conflict and fight it out.[3]

The ambiguity we refer to as the 'two sciences' stand consists in the sociology of science having to define science as both the object of its study and as its own method of research.[4] The demarcation of the sociology of science vis à vis the natural sciences is only resolved by the 'two sciences' stand if we can assume that the philosophy of science is more descriptive of scientific practice than prescriptive; or that scientific practice is to be treated as an approximation to its idealized methods; or, finally, that the social sciences in principle, if not in practice, aspire to meet the standards of the natural sciences characterized in either of the preceding ways.[5] The 'two sciences' stand settles the demarcation problem by trading upon a realist and empiricist view of science grounded in a correspondence theory of

3.   Karl Marx, ECONOMIC AND PHILOSOPHICAL MANUSCRIPTS OF 1844, Moscow: Foreign Languages Press, 1956.

4.   Barry Gruenberg, "The Problem of Reflexivity in the Sociology of Science," PHILOSOPHY OF THE SOCIAL SCIENCES, 8, 1978, pp. 321-43; Jonathan R. Cole and Harriet Zuckerman, "The Emergence of a Scientific Specialty: The Self-Exemplifying Case of the Sociology of Science," in THE IDEA OF SOCIAL STRUCTURE, Papers in Honor of Robert K. Merton, New York: Garden City, 1975.

5.   Barry Barnes, SCIENTIFIC KNOWLEDGE AND SOCIAL THEORY, London: Routledge and Kegan Paul, 1974.

truth.   According to this view, scientists seek causal relationships that hold with respect to man and nature independently of
their procedures for constructing contexts in which these relationships are found to have local dominance.   However, this is
seriously challenged wherever it can be argued that the categories through which we construct facts are not context-free with
respect to their usage.[6]   This does not rule out objectivity in
science.   Rather, it calls for an empirical study of the constitutive practices and conventions of scientific inquiry as a laboratory and literary enterprise.   A difficulty here for sociologists of
science who presume upon their own grounding in the methods of
science is that the practice of the natural and social sciences
differes widely from its members' own idealized accounts of their
procedures.   We consider that, if the 'two sciences' stand is to
be avoided, then the sociology of science must drop any distinction between the natural and social sciences inasmuch as each
offers a domain of interpretative and discursive inquiry whose
practical adequacy furnishes the sociology of science with its
topics of investigation.[7]   On this view the phenomena for sociological study are the linguistic, conceptual and technical practices
that are for practitioners of disciplinary-specific domains of
inquiry pragmatically adequate and competent achievements of
sense, fact, generalization, confirmation, refutation and the
like.[8]   It is premature, if not mistaken, to tax such practices
and their study with claims for absolute internal consistency since
this only reintroduces the demarcation problem regarding the
ultimate grounds for the distinction between rational and nonrational beliefs in purely metaphysical terms.   The paradox here
is that we are committed in the name of empirical science to an a
priori conception of what shall count as science.   Perhaps it is
this score that we can be sympathetic to the efforts by

6.   Ludwig Wittgenstein, ON CERTAINTY, New York: Harper, 1969; Aaron V.
Cicourel, METHOD AND MEASUREMENT, New York: Free Press of Glencoe, 1964;
Harold Garfinkel, STUDIES IN ETHNOMETHODOLOGY, Englewood Cliffs: Prentice-
Hall, 1967.

7.   Edward Michael Lynch, "Art and Artifact in Laboratory Science: A Study
of Shop Work and Shop Talk in a Research Laboratory," Unpublished Ph.D. Dis-
sertation in Social Sciences, University of California, Irvine, 1979; Karin D. Knorr,
FROM SCENES TO SCRIPTS, On the Relationship Between Laboratory Research and
Published Paper in Science, Research Monograph No. 132, Vienna, Institute for
Advanced Studies, 1978,

8.   John O'Neill, "The Literary Production of Natural and Social Science
Inquiry," THE CANADIAN JOURNAL OF SOCIOLOGY, 6, 1981, pp. 105-20; Kenneth
L. Morrison, "Some Researchable Recurrences in Social Science and Science Inquiry,"
Paper presented at SSRC/BSA International Conference on Practical Reasoning and
Discourse Processes, Oxford, St. Hugh's College, 1979; Bruno Latour and Steve
Woolgar, LABORATORY LIFE, The Social Construction of Scientific Facts, Beverly
Hills, Sage Publications, 1979.

9.   John O'Neill, "Historian's Artifacts: Some Production Issues in Ethno-
History," Paper presented SSRC/BSA International Conference on Practical Reasoning
and Discourse Processes, Oxford, St. Hugh's College, 1979.

Habermas[10] and Apel[11] to historicize the grounds of the natural and social sciences in a hierarchy of human knowledge interests and ideological criticism.

II.--PARSONIAN EXCURSUS ON THE SUBSYSTEM OF SCIENCE

On the strong externalist-program of the sociology of science, Marxist sociology and political economy is itself subject to determinism from the economic infrastructure. But this renders superfluous the distinctively political and voluntarist nature of Marxist social science. However, if we weaken the Marxist program to a thesis on the interactive nature of ideology and the material substructure of society, Marxism is reduced to a hermeneutical exercise without benefit of the claim to constitute a scientifc reading of social structure and historical process. It is here that the Weberian option for a historical- hermeneutical sociology of science opens up. Thus Parsons[12] argues that, rather than debate whether or not ideas in general determine, or are determined by the material substructure, we need to distinguish three types of ideas which will then allow us to adjudicate between a Marxist and a Weberian sociology of science:

(I)   Existential Ideas: These are frameworks for the analysis of the external world. They may be divided into (a) empirical ideas, verifiable by scientific method, and a residual class (b) nonempirical, existential ideas;

(II)   Normative Ideas: These refer to valued states of affairs which an actor may seek to preserve or to bring into existence. Normative ideas may not be verifiable in terms of empirical scientific method;

(III) Imaginative Ideas: These are possible states of affairs that no actor, however, is obliged to realize; for example, Marcuse's idea of a 'New Science' which we shall take up later.

With regard to existential ideas, there exists a large consensus that valid empirical knowledge is best achieved, for given ends, by means of instrumentally rational action. This is the dominant scheme in economics and technology and even in commonsense, nonscientific knowledge. It was Weber's contribution to show that

10.   Jürgen Habermas, COMMUNICATION AND THE EVOLUTION OF SOCIETY, Boston: Beacon Press, 1979.

11.   Karl-Otto Apel, ANALYTIC PHILOSOPHY OF LANGUAGE AND THE GEISTESWISSENSCHAFTEN, Dordrecht: Reidel, 1964.

12.   Talcott Parsons, "The Role of Ideas In Social Action," in ESSAYS IN SOCIOLOGICAL THEORY, edited by Talcott Parsons, New York: The Free Press, 1949.

certain nonempirical existential ideas (the interest in salvation) could favor empirically rational-legal accounting behavior. The question of the relative causal status of normative and existential empirical ideas in the relation between Protestantism and capitalism is itself decidable in principle through the comparative method of empirical social science and, as Parsons would claim, a generalized theory of action. On this basis, then, Parsons argues that Marx's super/substructure scheme is too simple. It is incapable of differentiating the role of empirically verifiable ideas at work in the processes of technology as well as in the processes of law, art and science which it is obliged to locate in the ideological superstructure.

Just as the division between superstructure and substructure proves to be too rough to handle the differentiation of meaning-systems, so we need to refine the distinction we began with, namely, that between the externalist and internalist programs in the sociology of science. These labels will undoubtedly remain useful as broad characterizations of contemporary directions of research. But each is capable of overlapping with the other at so many points, as well as at different levels of analysis, and with respect to quite different subsystems of the institutions and conduct of science. It may be useful, therefore, to offer at least a brief summary and map of the domain of inquiry that occupies the sociology of science. Whatever its own interpretative biases, the Parsonian schema of of science as a cultural system[13] permits us to identify the analytic sense in speaking of the internal and external economy of science or of the internal and external values of science as a social system. Readers can check for themselves the ways in which the various arguments we shall deal with make adequate analytic distinctions or presume upon boundary exchanges within the sub-system of science without articulating what levels of the system are in question. We are not, of course, proposing to settle differences through this device. Rather, we think it may serve to identify both persistent differences of approach and areas of complementary inquiry.

We do not require an instant master of the Parsonian four-function scheme. Here it has no other purpose than to facilitate recognition of the 'boxes' left in the dark if one tries to trace the specific analytic domains recognized in any particular argument drawn from either an internalist or externalist sociology of

13.   Thomas J. Fararo, "Science as a Cultural System," in EXPLORATIONS IN GENERAL THEORY IN SOCIAL SCIENCE, Essays in Honor of Talcott Parsons, edited by Jan J. Loubser, Rainer C. Baum, Andrew Effrat, Victor Meyer Lidz, New York: The Free Press, 1976.

science.[14] To speak of overlaps or gaps between these two approaches is a clumsy way of trying to identify their specific capacities for dealing with subsystem processes of differentiation and boundary exchanges between science as a subsystem and its environment of cultural, economic and political subsystems. This system of exchanges can, of course, be addressed from the standpoint of any other subsystem, thereby relativizing the others as environmental exchange subsystems. This contingency bears, for example, on the issue of whether we regard science as dependent upon politics and technology, or vice-versa. It also allows us to see that we need to be clear that science as a subsystem has its own economic and political subsystems, to which we refer later. We therefore cannot presume that the internal and external subsystems of science are the same thing throughout.

THE SUBSYSTEMS OF SCIENCE

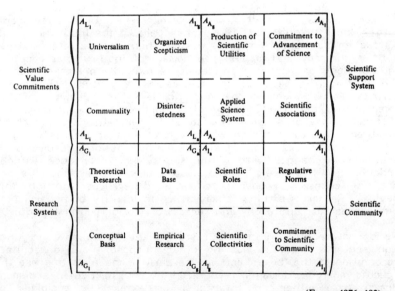

(Fararo 1976: 192)

14.   Richard D. Whitley, "Black Boxism and the Sociology of Science: A Discussion of the Major Developments in the Field," in THE SOCIOLOGY OF SCIENCE, The Sociological Review Monograph No. 18, edited by Paul Halmos, Keele: University of Keele, 1972.

What the four-by-four system of functions reveals to us is that we cannot regard science in abstraction from such other elements of the cultural system of a society as its arts, law, religion and cosmology. Thus science is an adaptive system (A) analogous to the economy in its standing to society. As such, it has its own fourfold structure. Its primary goal (G) will be the production of knowledge. This subsystem of science is the research subsystem (AG). This system requires whatever resources are needed for its function and this provision constitutes the adaptive scientific support subsystem (AA). Faced with the integration (I) of its internal goals and its need for external resources, there is a need to integrate the units involved and this falls to the scientific community (AI). Finally, there is a need for an overall normative structure (L) to preserve the commitment to science within its members and within the broader society. This identifies the fourth subsystem of scientific value commitments (AL).

Each of the four subsystems of science may be further differentiated according to the four-function (A, G, I, L) system. Thus, with respect to the subsystem of scientific value-commitment, we can identify the specifically integrating values described by Merton--universalism, organized scepticism, communality and disinterestedness--which may be at odds with, or enhanced by, the wider cultural value system. Similarly, the cognitive values of the science subsystem may be threatened by the values at work within its own adaptive quest for research money and by the external economy's or the political system's adaptive quest for scientific knowledge of one sort or another. Here we can identify a number of issues with respect to claims for the 'public' and/or 'autonomous' nature of scientific inquiry. We can differentiate either claim with respect to its ideological, adaptive and community functions. More important we can imagine that any of these issues will have empirically distinctive features as soon as we differentiate field-specific sciences with their respective technologies and adaptative systems which will certainly offer variable degrees of immunity and dependence in regard of 'influence.' Again, therefore, if we differentiate the research subsystem into its fourfold component functional systems, any assertion regarding the political or economic determinism of science will have to be made specifically with regard to either or all of its theoretical research, its data base, its conceptual basis or its empirical research, as we shall see in the final section of this paper. Likewise, it is with respect to the scientific support system that we look for factors shaping how the science community sets itself problems and research programs, how it acquires its hardware, socializes its research personnel--in general, how it translates general societal needs for knowledge into specific science research problems that motivate and reward science personnel. Finally, the science system maintains more or

less permeable boundaries with the rest of the sociocultural
system of arts, law and cosmology and with the social, political
and economic subsystems which surround it. In the following
sections of this paper we propose to take up these abstracted and
generalized considerations in the context of arguments over the
internal and external relations between science, technology and
politics in Marxist and Mertonian sociology of science.

III.--SCIENCE, TECHNOLOGY, AND IDEOLOGY

Modern technology is largely based upon scientific knowledge.
Thus, we may infer that Marxists would have to save their own
theory of ideology by arguing that in 'advanced capitalism' the
relation of super- to substructure is 'reversed', namely, that the
economy and technology become 'science driven', operated and
managed by 'intellect workers'.[15] But then, apart from its obvious difficulties as an explanatory variable that moves back and
forth from substructure to superstructure, natural science loses
the <u>exemption</u> accorded to it in a Marxist sociology of science
which, in turn, needs this exemption for its own identity. That
this is not a purely imaginative possibility is to be seen in
Habermas'[16] attempt to remedy the Marxist schema through a
corrective move which nevertheless preserves the 'two sciences'
distinction. The difficulty in this is that the natural sciences, on
the one hand, are exempt from a sociology of science, while
Marxism itself as a critical science is confined to a superstruc-
tural activity of communicative and emancipatory hermeneutics
designed to contain the disembedded logic of a science-driven
technical and instrumentally rational political economy.

Habermas has argued that Marx failed to develop a unified critical
science of man because, in splitting the natural and social
sciences, he reduced historical materialism to the laws of the
<u>natural science</u> of production and failed to develop any adequate
<u>theory of ideologycritique</u> other than a simplistic materialism
reduction of knowledge interests:

> If Marx had reflected on the methodological presuppositions
> of social theory as he sketched it out and not overlaid it
> with a philosophical self-understanding restricted to the
> categorial framework of production, the difference between
> vigorous empirical science and critique would not have been
> concealed. If Marx had not thrown together interaction and

15.   Alvin W. Gouldner, THE DIALECTIC OF IDEOLOGY AND TECHNOLOGY,
The Origins, Grammar, and Future of Ideology, New York: The Seabury Press,
1976; and his THE FUTURE OF THE INTELLECTUALS AND THE RISE OF THE NEW
CLASS, New York: The Seabury Press, 1979.

16.   Jürgen Habermas, KNOWLEDGE AND HUMAN INTERESTS, Boston: Beacon
Press, 1971.

work under the label of social practice (Praxis), and had he instead related the materialist concept of synthesis likewise to the accomplishments of instrumental action and the nexuses of communicative action, then the idea of a science of man would not have been obscured by identification with natural science.[17]

Here, then, we must notice a distinctive version of the 'two sciences' argument. Habermas sees in Marx only one science of man reduced to a materialist science of the forces of production, ultimately the natural sciences. We have cited Marx to show that he held the 'two sciences' view, i.e., that science is socially determined and that the natural sciences are exempt from social determination. Moreover, in a later citation we shall show that Marx also held out the possibility of the historical unification of the natural sciences and the social sciences of man. Against this view, and in particular against Marcuse's remarks on the third option of a 'New Science', Habermas himself holds to the 'two sciences' view, arguing that human knowledge is guided by a triple structure of technical, hermeneutic and emancipatory interests. At the technical level, scientific rationality is exempt from strictly sociological determination, although at the transcendental level of the constitutive interests of knowledge science appears to lose its exemption.[18]

We propose now to examine this argument to show that it misses the opportunity to treat science as a single but highly differentiated communicative meaning-system analyzable without any exemption clause to set it apart from other subsystems of society. In short, a Marxist sociology of science cannot exempt the natural sciences from sociological analysis and at the same time try to embed science inquiry with the hermeneutical, emancipatory pragmatics of universal communication.[19] Rather, we think that recent developments in the sociology of science indicate that once we adopt an antirealist view of science, thereby becoming fully conscious of the socially constructed nature of science, the exemption clause is removed and the 'two sciences' become one community of science. It is with respect to this single community of science that a Marxist sociology of science must propose studies of science inquiry and social policy.

It is always possible to assemble texts from Marx in order to refine what we have called the 'two sciences' problem. To avoid

17.   IBID., p. 62.

18.   Tronn Overend, "Enquiry and Ideology: Habermas' Trichotomous Conception of Science," PHILOSOPHY OF THE SOCIAL SCIENCES, 8, 1978, pp. 1-35.

19.   Apel, ANALYTIC PHILOSOPHY OF SCIENCE AND THE GEISTESWISSENSCHAFTEN; Alvin W. Gouldner, THE TWO MARXISMS, Contradictions and Anomalies in the Development of Theory, New York: The Seabury Press, 1980.

such assembly, we propose the following schema:

MARX'S SYSTEM OF SCIENCE AND ECONOMY

(I) tools   } Technology
(II) technology (applied science)
(III) theoretical natural sciences ─────────────────── } Science*
(IV) economic relations of production (economic science) } Economy
(V) social relations of production (law) ──────────
(VI) political relations of production/reproduction   } State

[See also Model on
p. 168 below]

We then have in Marx a functionalist schema of four subsystems, technology, science, economy and state, each with obvious overlaps or boundary exchanges, and with no subsystem reducible to a simple sub- and superstructure dichotomy between the processes of transforming nature and the transformations of ideas. However, it is hard to deny that Marx tends to identify science and technology as a system of man's domination over nature that reinforces (causes or is caused by?) the social domination of man by man.[20] Yet, insofar as Marxism is the social science that looks to man's social emancipation, it looks toward the end of science:

> Industry is the real historical relationship of nature, and therefore of natural science, to man. If then it is conceived of as the open revelation of human faculties, then the human essence of nature or the natural essence of man will be understood. Natural science will then lose its one-sidedly materialist, or rather idealistic, orientation and become the basis of human science as it has already, though in an alienated form, become the basis of actual life. And to have one basis for life and another for science would be in itself a falsehood.[21]

20.   Kostas Axelos, ALIENATION, PRAXIS, AND TECHNE IN THE THOUGHT OF KARL MARX, Austin: University of Texas Press, 1976.

21.   Marx, ECONOMIC AND PHILOSOPHIC MANUFSCRIPTS, p. 154, my emphasis.

The end of science flies in the face of the end of ideology[22] not only because it rejects the ideology that science ends ideologies, but also because it envisages a new science which would not be the instrument of the scientization of social and political life. It is over this 'imaginative idea' of science that Marcuse differs equally with Parsons and Habermas. Marcuse, then, proposes that in any Marxist redefinition of social labor, it would be necessary to redefine not only economic and political labor but also scientific labor. In other words, he challenges the residual 'two sciences' thesis in Marx, as well as in Habermas, since he proposes to take science out of the realm of necessity. According to Marcuse, natural science is part of our historical amnesia.[23] The 'two sciences' stand represents an unnecessary concession to surplus repression and alienation. Unfortunately, Marcuse himself was not consistent in his conception of science. He had only the shakiest idea of the actual practice of the natural sciences.[24] Yet he is of interest to us because he tried to bring the 'two sciences' argument to a utopian solution in his vision of a 'new science' made possible by the very social dominance of positive science:

> The point which I am trying to make is that science, by virtue of its own method and concepts, has projected and promoted a universe in which the domination of nature has remained linked to the domination of man--a link which tends to be fatal to his universe as a whole. Nature, scientifically comprehended and mastered, reappears in the technical apparatus of production and destruction which sustains and improves the life of the individuals while subordinating them to the masters of the apparatus. Thus the rational hier-archy merges with the social one. If this is the case, then the change in the direction of progress, which might sever this fatal link, would also affect the very structure of science--the scientific project. Its hypotheses, without losing their rational character, would develop in an essentially different experimental context (that of a pacified world); science could arrive at essentially different concepts of nature and establish essentially different facts.[25]

22.   Daniel Bell, THE END OF IDEOLOGY, New York: Free Press, 1961.

23.   Charles Rachlis, "Marcuse and the Problem of Happiness," CANADIAN JOURNAL OF SOCIAL AND POLITICAL THEORY, 2, 1978, pp. 63-88.

24.   Peter Sedgwick, "Natural Science and Human Theory: A Critique of Herbert Marcuse," in THE SOCIALIST REGISTER, edited by Ralph Miliband and John Saville, New York: Monthly Reveiw Press, 1966.

25.   Herbert Marcuse, ONE-DIMENSIONAL MAN, Studies in the Ideology of Advanced Industrial Society, Boston: Beacon Press, 1964.

Here is is not to the point to explain in any detail how Marcuse's reduction of the methods of the natural sciences to behaviorism, operationalism, functionalism and instrumentalism needs to be complemented by more contemporary research into the conduct of scientific research. What is to be remarked in the preceding passage is how Marcuse seems to move the natural sciences from the substructure into the superstructure. He attributes social domination to the method and concepts of science, while it is substructural force, and then tries to reverse the process, calling for a socially emancipated science that would, nevertheless, not lose its conceptually rational character. This equivocation is a perfect example of what we have called the 'two sciences' stand in Marxism.

Now Habermas[26] rejects out of hand any notion of a unified science of man and nature. Interestingly enough, his argument against Marcuse also preserves the 'two sciences' stand. Habermas argues that the psycho-somatic organization of man makes it historically impossible for us to conceive of an end to instrumentally rational action. In other words, we cannot conceive of science and technology as anything else but natural science. Consequently, Marcuse's proposal, if any sense is to be made of it, requires a distinction between two subsystems of society-- work (instrumental action, typically science and technology) and language (symbolic action, typically politics and ethics). The two subsystems are defined in terms of a gloss upon the Parsonian/Weberian schema of rational and nonrational orientations which yields the following contrastive structure:

26.   Jürgen Habermas, TOWARD A RATIONAL SOCIETY, Student Protest, Science and Politics, Boston: Beacon Press, 1970.

	Institutional frame-work: symbolic inter-action	Systems of purposive-rational (instrumental and strategic) action
action-orienting rules	social norms	technical rules
level of definition	intersubjectively shared ordinary language	context-free language
type of definition	reciprocal expecta-tions about behavior	conditional predictions conditional imperatives
mechanisms of acquisition	role internalization	learning of skills and qualifications
function of action type	maintenance of insti-tutions (conformity to norms on the basis of reciprocal enforce-ment)	problem-solving (goal attainment, defined in means-ends rela-tions)
sanctions against violation of rules	punishment on the basis of conventional sanctions: failure against authority	inefficacy: failure in reality
"rationalization"	emancipation, individ-uation; extension of communication free of domination	growth of productive forces; extension of power of technical control

[Habermas 1970: 93]

It should be noted that Habermas' own schema preserves the exemption of scientific rationality from the rationality of language. Scientific discourse and communicative discourse are separable sub-systems of meaning-production. It is an error to address either system in terms of the logic and relevances of the other:

> The alternative to existing technology, the project of nature as opposing partner instead of object, refers to an alterna-tive structure of action: to symbolic interaction in distinc-tion to purposive-rational action. This means, however, that the two projects are projections of work and language, i.e., projects of the human species as a whole, and not of an individual epoch, a specific class, or a surpassable situation. The idea of a New Science will not stand up to logical scrutiny any more than that of a New Technology, if indeed science is to retain the meaning of modern science inherently

oriented to possible technical control. For this function, as for scientific-technical progress in general, there is no more 'humane' substitute.[27]

Like Parsons, Habermas finds the superstructure distinction too unwieldy. Rather, he historicizes it. In early capitalism, science and technology may be said to drive the social system from below. In late capitalism[28] science enters the 'steering-system' as the principal arm of the legitimacy function, redefining all the ethical problems of the communicative subsystem in terms of the technical problem--focus of the subsystem of science and technology. Critical theory resists the scientization of politics.[29] But it is not our present task to follow these arguments.[30] It is the other side of the coin with which we have to deal. Is critical theory concerned to analyze the politicization of science, or is that the same thing as the scientization of politics, and these two phenomena together the basic issues in Marxist critical sociology of science? There is much to be said for this conclusion. Thus, it can be argued that the positivist methodology of the natural sciences functions not only to demarcate the technical rationality of science from the interpretative understanding proper to the historical and social 'sciences' but also, through the program of unified science, to recommend the scientization of politics and society:

> . . . it is its (instrumental) conception of the relation of theory to practice that gives the scientific conception of truth its meaning and therefore sets the conditions for the validity of a scientific explanation. It is just this conclusion which supports my claim that a positivist conception of the knowledge of social life contains within itself an instrumentalist-engineering conception of the relation of this knowledge to social action; for one is committed to this engineering view of theory and practice in the very act of adopting the postivist view of theory--indeed, it is this engineering view which supports and gives meaning to this view of social theory.[31]

27. IBID., p. 88.

28. Jürgen Habermas, LEGITIMATION CRISIS, Boston: Beacon Press, 1975.

29. Theodor Albert Hans Adorno, Ralf Dahrendorf, Jürgen Habermas, Harold Pilot, Karl R. Popper, THE POSITIVIST DISPUTE IN GERMAN SOCIOLOGY, translated by Glyn Adey and David Frisby, London: Heinemann, 1976.

30. John O'Neill, "Scientism, Historicism and the Problem of Rationality," in MODES OF INDIVIDUALISM AND COLLECTIVISM, edited by John O'Neill, London: Heinemann, 1973.

31. Brian Fay, SOCIAL THEORY AND POLITICAL PRACTICE, London: Allen & Unwin, 1975, p. 43.

That this is not a one-sided Marxist view is clear enough from the Popperian counterclaim that all that stands between an 'open society' and totalitarianism is a commitment to a 'falsificationist' view of science.[32]   The consequence of this view, is that politics is defined as a field for 'piecemeal' social engineering rather than for any holistic planning.   At issue, too, is a definite sociology of science, inasmuch as Popperians consider the scientific community to be the heart of liberal social values as well as the seat of the Western commitment to critical rationality.   By contrast, Marxism only imagines it is a science--or a policial science, for that matter--because it has a mistaken view of the concepts and procedures of the natural sciences and a wholly erroneous view of the kind of lawful system a society might be. Indeed, there are others[33] who would argue that inasmuch as a modern society is definitionally a 'knowledgeable society', any form of ideology and dogmatism such as Marxism ought to recede in favor of the rule of scientific logic and evaluation.   In other words, the critics of Marxism and Marxists themselves seem to agree that to have any notion of an alternative sociology of science than a descriptive version of the knowledgeable society is sheer utopianism.   Habermas rejects this agreement, yet he is unwilling to support the Marcusean alternative of a New Science[34] because, although he is critical of the positivist program in the social sciences, he nevertheless uncritically accepts it as an adequate version of the natural sciences.   He therefore remains caught in the 'two sciences' stand.   By contrast, Popper has a subtly differentiated view of the unified science approach which allows the method of science to vary with its specific subject matter, but is always consistent with a critically rationalist view of science as an antirealist or constructionist enterprise. This means, however, that Popper also rejects the instrumentalist view of science which goes unchallenged in the 'two sciences' view adopted by Marxists:

> Popper is firmly against the instrumentalist view of the role of theories in science which argues that theories ought to be regarded as tools in research, and judged strictly in terms of their differential utility or functional capacity to this end.

32.   Karl R. Popper, THE POVERTY OF HISTORICISM, New York: Harper and Row, 1944; and his THE OPEN SOCIETY AND ITS ENEMIES, 2 vols., London: Routledge and Kegan Paul, 1945.

33.   Robert Lane, "The Decline of Politics and Ideology in a Knowledgeable Society," AMERICAN SOCIOLOGICAL REVIEW, 31, 1966, pp. 647-61; Daniel Bell, THE COMING OF POST-INDUSTRIAL SOCIETY, New York: Basic Books, 1973.

34.   Ben Agger, "Marcuse and Habermas on New Science," POLITY, 10, 1976, pp. 158-81; William Leiss, "Technological Rationality: Marcuse and his Critics," in THE DOMINATION OF NATURE, New York; George Braziller, 1972; Norman Stockman, "Habermas, Marcuse and the Aufhebung of Science and Technology," PHILOSOPHY OF THE SOCIAL SCIENCES, 8, 1978, pp. 15-35.

He believes that such a focus is appropriate only to technological rules, where this sort of success orientation is war-
ranted. With Bunge, he views the long-term effects of this
attitude as potentially and actually injurious to science, and
therefore technology as well.[35]

Whether or not one accepts the details of Popper's philosophy of
science, it is important to see that without the distinction it
draws between theoretical science and applied science Marxists are
driven to locate the instrumentalism of applied science in science
generally. They are then caught in the dilemma of a sociological
critique of applied science that seems to involve a rejection of
scientific rationality as such. Science rationality and science
practice may in fact each be open to a constructionist or antirealist sociology of science, for which there is much contemporary
evidence. If Marxists were not obliged to the 'two sciences'
stand, they could then avail themselves of a unified constructionist interpretation of scientific inquiry and social inquiry.
They could recognize a subsystem of applied science and
technology whose instrumentalism may well be its defining methodology. However, where the subsystem of applied science and
technology exchanges with other subsystems of science, economy,
society and politics, they could properly avoid any scientistic
formulation of the logic of these discourse systems. Incidentally,
this is precisely what is involved in the critique of Marxist
scientism.[36]

IV.--THE MERTONIAN ECONOMY OF SCIENCE

We may speak generally of the social factors in the vocation of
science,[37] or else we may wish to argue that the cognitive
procedures, hypotheses, methods as well as the objects/ objectives of scientific research are also socially, economically and
politically determined. Here sociologists of knowledge (Mannheim
1952) have generally backed off into what we have called the 'two
sciences stand', i.e., the position that the natural sciences are
exempt from social determination, at least with respect to their
cognitive structure, if not in respect of their community
structure. Yet, as Merton observes, the social sciences, with the

35. H. T. Wilson, "Science, Critique and Criticism: The 'Open Society'
Revisited," in ON CRITICAL THEORY, edited by John O'Neill, New York: The
Seabury Press, 1976, p. 84.

36. John O'Neill, "Merleau-Ponty's Critique of Marxist Scientism," CANADIAN
JOURNAL OF SOCIAL AND POLITICAL THEORY, 2, 1978, pp. 31-62; Albrecht
Wellmer, CRITICAL THEORY OF SOCIETY, New York: The Seabury Press, 1974;
Wilson, "Science, Critique and Criticism: The 'Open Society' Revisited", LOC. CIT.

37. Max Weber, "Science as a Vocation," in FROM MAX WEBER, Essays in
Sociology, edited by Hans Gerth and C. Wright Mills, New York: Oxford University
Press, 1958.

possible exception of 'proletarian science', are not accorded any
similar exemption.   They are identified with the sphere of ideological   knowledge--despite   the   difficulties   this   raises   for   the
conceptual   status   of   the   sociology   of   knowledge   itself.   In
practice, Merton has himself shaped most of the working options:

    (I)   The Sociology of Knowledge
   (II)   The Sociology of Scientific Knowledge
  (III)   The Normative Structure of Science
  (IV)   The Reward System of Science
   (V)   The Processes of Evaluation in Science [Merton 1973,
          pp. vii-viii]

Thus, at the level of general social determinism of science, he
showed the nonlogical (not irrational) sources of science in Puri-
tanism. [38]   Then, with reference to the community of science,
Merton initiated an internalist or interactionist sociology of science
built upon the 'two sciences' exemption clause with respect to the
cognitive structure of science (logical positivism) but otherwise
opening up the sociological study of the conduct of science.   This
made   it   possible   to   ignore   cognitive   questions   regarding   the
production   of   knowledge   in   general   and   in   the   particular
sciences. [39]   Today,   however,   these   are   areas   of   concern   for
several   sociologists   of   science. [40]   Meantime,   Mertonians   could
construct a sociology of science as a <u>social institution</u>.   Here the
emphasis lay in spelling out the functional relationships between
the   conduct   of   critical,   empirical   science   and   its   institutional
norms   of   universalism,   communism,   disinterestedness,   and
organized scepticism (Merton 1942).   A next major step lay in the
study of the <u>internal economy of science</u>, so to speak.   Here we
refer   to   studies   by   Merton   and   many   others[42]   which   have

38.   Robert K. Merton, "Paradigm for the Sociology of Knowledge," in THE
SOCIOLOGY OF SCIENCE, Theoretical and Empirical Investigations, Chicago: The
University of Chicago Press, 1973, pp. 173-90.

39.   M. D. King, "Reason, Tradition and the Progressiveness of Science,"
HISTORY AND THEORY, 10, 1971, pp. 3-32.

40.   M. J. Mulkay, "Conformity and Innovation in Science," in THE SOCIOLOGY
OF SCIENCE, The Sociological Review Monograph No. 18, Keele: University of
Keele, 1972; Richard D. Whitley, "Black Boxism and the Sociology of Science"; Rolf
Klima,   "Scientific   Knowledge   and   Social   Control   in   Science: The   Application of a
Cognitive Theory of Behaviour to the Study of Scientific Behaviour," in SOCIAL
PROCESSES OF SCIENTIFIC DEVELOPMENT, edited by Richard Whitley, London:
Routledge and Kegan Paul, 1974; Gernot Bohme, "The Social Function of Cognitive
Structures: A Concept of the Scientific Community Within a Theory of Action," in
DETERMINANTS AND CONTROLS OF SCIENTIFIC DEVELOPMENT, edited by Karin D.
Knorr, Harman Strasser and Hans Georg Zilian, Dordrecht: Reidel, 1975.

41.   Robert K. Merton, "The Normative Structure of Science" in Merton, OP.
CIT.

42.   Warren O. Hagstron, THE SCIENTIFIC COMMUNITY, New York: Basic
Books, 1965; Norman W. Storer, THE SOCIAL SYSTEM OF SCIENCE' New York:
Holt, Rinehart and Winston, 1966; Diana Crane, INVISIBLE COLLEGES: Diffusion of

analyzed the problems of scientific priority, recognition, unequal reward, competition and deviancy, evaluation procedures and related topics. This is a huge literature. It is easily available to anyone interested in the sociology of science. Here we seek only to characterize it as a 'rival enterprise' which Marxist sociologists of science cannot afford to ignore. We think this is so, because the Mertonian approach confronts Marxists with a concrete version of the economy of science analyzable in terms of specific schemas of the production of knowledge and status which go far beyond any programmatic invocation of the economic determinism of science.

Thus, in an approximation to the model economy of science, we may understand science as the socially organized production and consumption of knowledge and recognition according to a schema that we offer as a device for bridging Mertonian and Marxist sociology of science:

MODEL OF SCIENCE PRODUCTION AND REPRODUCTION

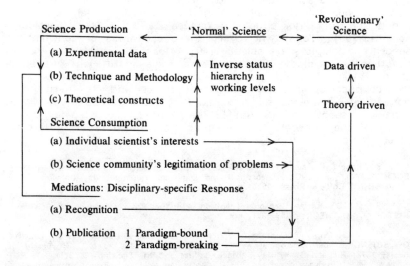

Knowledge in Scientific Communities. Chicago: University of Chicago Press, 1972. Harriet Zuckerman, "The Code of Science," STUDIUM GENERALE, 23, 1970, pp. 942-61; Derek J. de Solla Price, LITTLE SCIENCE, BIG SCIENCE, New York: Columbia University Press, 1963; Jerry Gaston, ORIGINALITY AND COMPETITION IN SCIENCE, A Study of the British High Energy Physics Community, Chicago: University of Chicago, 1973; Jonathan R. Cole and Stephen Cole, "Scientific Output and Recognition: A Study in the Operation of the Reward System in Science," AMERICAN SOCIOLOGICAL REVIEW' 32, 1967, pp. 377-90.

It is clear from the literature that science theories are not easily abandoned merely on account of disturbing facts. The scientific community, particularly at field-specific levels, or within heavily capitalized research programs, will hold tenaciously to paradigm-bound inquiry.[43]   None of this rules out science opportunism,[44] competition, secrecy, ambition, exclusivity.   In short, the science community is not nearly so 'free floating' as Mannheim claimed.   Rather it reflects the average vices and virtues of the general community, while nevertheless getting the business of science done.   To the extent that we accord any autonomy to science that is not simply due to our ignorance of its practice, we refer to what Hagstrom[45] calls the 'gift' in science.   That is, we recognize that the production of scientists is to a certain extent self-generated in its choice of problems, its methods and procedures for evaluation.   Even in the worst of science-fiction this is a recognized attribute of science--though sometimes equated with its madness and open capacity for good and evil.

It should be noted that Merton generally presumes upon the 'two sciences' exemption clause with respect to the cognitive structure of science.   In terms of the more recent sociology of science, it is questionable to what extent the philosophy of science describes or prescribes the actual pragmatics of science inquiry.   Here it suffices to refer to the argument over the critical and consensus oriented functions of scientific paradigms,[46] falsificationism[47] or research programs.[48]   As a matter of fact, Merton is committed both ways, that is, both to Popper and to Kuhn, although the Popperians reject any sociology of science.   Of course, Popper's situational logic of scientific conduct presupposes the values of individualism and critical rationality in the open society. Yet, Popper's view of science is decidedly anti-psychologistic, at the same time that it is opposed to Kuhnian consensualism as a potentially irrational sociologism.[49]   The Mertonian accommodation, however, is managed by allowing Popper's critical positivism

43. Thomas S. Kuhn, THE STRUCTURE OF SCIENTIFIC REVOLUTIONS, Chicago: University of Chicago, 1972.

44. Karin D. Knorr, "Producing and Reproducing Knowledge: Descriptive or Constructive? Towards a Model of Research Production," SOCIAL SCIENCE INFOR- MATION, 16, 1977, pp. 969-96.

45. Hagstrom, THE SCIENTIFIC COMMUNITY.

46. Kuhn, THE STRUCTURE OF SCIENTIFIC REVOLUTIONS.

47. Karl R. Popper, THE LOGIC OF SCIENTIFIC DISCOVERY, New York: Harper and Row, 1959.

48. Imre Lakatos, "Falsification and the Methodology of Scientific Research Programmes," in CRITICISM AND THE GROWTH OF KNOWLEDGE, edited by Imre Lakatos and Alan Musgrave, Cambridge: Cambridge University Press, 1970.

49. Herminio Martins, "The Kuhnian 'Revolution' and Its Implications for Sociology," in IMAGINATION AND PRECISION IN POLITICAL ANALYSIS, Essays in Honour of Peter Nettl, London: Faber, 1972.

to rule in the validating processes of science and regarding the Kuhnian program as a natural ally in the sociology of discovering science. [50]

V.--THE POLITICAL ECONOMY OF SCIENCE AND SCIENCE POLICY

Following Bourdieu,[51] Knorr has argued that scientific inquiry when studied through an ethnography of practices of a large research laboratory is best viewed as a constructive process aimed at 'successful' research careers. The pragmatics of science opportunism are not caught by the perspective of a correspondence or realist theory of knowledge. Rather, the scientific field must be regarded as locus for the competitive struggle to achieve recognition while the laboratory is then understood as the investment site for the symbolic and material capital accumulated by means of successful scriptural recognition (publication). The input-output relationships in the production and reproduction of scientific knowledge my then be formulated in the way shown in the chart on the page following.

The benefit of Knorr's model is that it permits us to focus empirical research in the sociology of science on three levels:

(a) Laboratory Production: the pragmatics of laboratory inquiry.[52]

(b) Literary Production: the pragmatics of written inquiry in the sciences.[53]

(c) Historiographical Reproduction of Science: the historicity of science achieved through literary reconstruction.[54]

50. Abraham Kaplan, THE CONDUCT OF INQUIRY, San Francisco: Chandler Publishing, 1964.

51. Pierre Bourdieu, "The Specificity of a Scientific Field and the Social Conditions of the Progress of Reason," SOCIAL SCIENCE INFORMATION, 14, 1975, pp. 19-47.

52. Knorr, FROM SCENES TO SCRIPTS; Lynch, "Art and Artifact in Laboratory Science"; Latour and Wooldgar, LABORATORY LIFE, LOC. CIT.

53. Joseph Gusfield, "The Literary Rhetoric of Science: Comedy and Pathos in Drinking Driver Research," AMERICAN SOCIOLOGICAL REVIEW, 41, 1976, pp. 339-65; O'Neill, The Literary Production of Natural and Social Science Inquiry"; Kenneth L. Morrison, "Some Properties of 'Telling-Order Designs' in Didactic Inquiry," PHILOSOPHY OF THE SOCIAL SCIENCES, 11, 1981, pp. 245-62; Morrison, "Some Researchable Recurrences in Social Science and Science Inquiry", LOC. CIT.

54. Kuhn, THE STRUCTURE OF SCIENTIFIC REVOLUTIONS; Gerald Holton, "Themata in Scientific Thought," in THE SCIENTIFIC IMAGINATION, Case Studies, edited by G. Holton, Cambridge: Cambridge University Press, 1978.

It is at the first level that we discover the 'two sciences' stand to be misconceived. It is not necessary to concede either simple realism or simple idealism in order to account for science's work- ing relation with the world it simultaneously constructs.[55] Similarly, at the scriptural level, the literary production of natural and social science inquiry turns upon local laboratory interpretations of a disciplinary-specific literature as well as upon intertextual practices that call for empirical study as the organ- izational matter of public knowledge. It is only on the basis of such studies that we may be able to fill out the Kuhnian paradigm as something more than a gloss upon the scriptural regulation of science. Needless to say, such studies would differ entirely from studies of written inquiry as an organizational object.[56]

It cannot be denied that there is a tendency in the Mertonian program to concede a certain autonomy to the science subsystem analogous to the autonomy of the self-regulating competitive market system. This is so, even though everyone knows, Parsons and Merton included, that the subsystems of science, politics and economics have highly permeable boundaries (though not unregulated exchange in terms of the norms ruling each subsystem). Similarly, although Habermas speaks of the scientiza- tion of politics, it is probably erroneous to see this in terms of a conspiracy of scientists rather than as the divisive effect of the particular political objectives upon specific fields and technologies of science.[57] Here it is possible to argue that the professional and technical expertise of the sciences, so far from being the arm of democratic enlightenment, render them less and less account- able to lay political authority.[58] This is aggravated to the extent that politicians turn more and more to the social sciences rather than to the natural sciences, though there are powerful and dangerous bio-social cross-fertilizations that have even more frightening prospects for the citizenry.

55. Bernard d'Espagnat, "The Quantum Theory and Reality," SCIENTIFIC AMERICAN, 241, 1979, pp. 158-81.

56. Morrison, "Some Researchable Recurrences in Social Science and Science Inquiry"; Morrison, "Some Properties of 'Telling-Order Designs' in Didactic Inquiry"; O'Neill, "Historians Artifacts: Some Production Issues in Ethno-History"; O'Neill, "The Literary Production of Natural and Social Science Inquiry", LOC. CIT.

57. Yaron Ezrahi, "The Political Resources of Science," in SOCIOLOGY OF SCIENCE, Selected Readings, Harmondsworth: Penguin Books, 1972.

58. John O'Neill, "The Mutuality of Accounts: An Essay on Trust," in THEORETICAL PERSPECTIVES IN SOCIOLOGY, edited by Scott G. McNall, New York: St. Martin's Press, 1979.

A MODEL OF RESEARCH PRODUCTION*

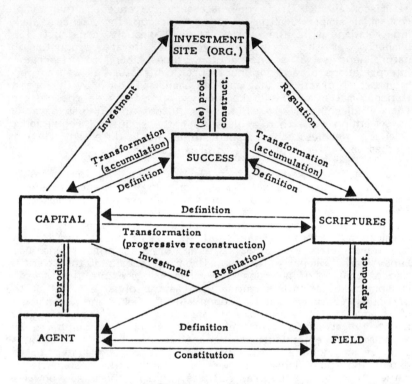

* The model represents the predominant relationships as seen from the respective entry.   E.g. the scientific field is <u>constituted</u> by the agents, while the position of the agents is <u>defined</u> by the field.   Double lines represent relationships of <u>production</u>, single arrows represent phenomena in the area of <u>production</u>, and arrows combining relationships of transformation with those of definition represent the level of <u>historicity</u> (see below).   The model is proposed as an analytical tool to facilitate our understanding of the relationships between the concepts chosen and <u>not</u> as a somewhat mechanistic description of research production.

(Knorr 1977:   671)

In this regard, Van den Daele and Weingart[59] distinguish
between the external influence of social policy upon science,
aimed at promoting science on its own terms with a general pre-
sumption of its influence say, on the quality and productivity of
manpower, and policy controls which bear directly upon a specific
science discovering process, say, cancer research. The latter
direction offers the possibility of pursuing in some detail the
otherwise general but nonspecific claims of the externalist
program in the sociology of science. To render adequately the
case where social policy seeks to foster a specific science
specialty, Van den Daele and Weingart,[60] point to a triple
structure of analysis:

(i)   the policy level--definition of science policy objectives;
(ii)   the cognitive level--definition of the structures of
       science as a working enterprise;
(iii) the institutional level--definition of science in terms of
       a system of social action.

It then becomes possible to locate the influence of social policy
upon science in terms of the empirically specific receptivity or
resistance of a given specialty enterprise in cognitively and in-
stitutionally specific terms. Thus, at the policy level we may
distinguish whether the objective is, for example, to facilitate
description or assessment of the demographic or health characteristics of the population. Alternatively, the policy objective may
be for the production of constructed theory and data in the
implementation of some systems' control operation, for example,
water fluoridation or pest control. At the cognitive level, exchanges with the policy level requirements may be generalized,
specific, possible or severely restrictive, or else unattainable
without redefinitions and negotiations on either side. Within the
cognitive level, it would be necessary to examine, for a given
specialty, the extent to which change or resistance to policy
directives affect singly or cumulatively its subdimensions of
method and technology, theory construction and disciplinary
relations with other fields of research. Finally, at the institutional level, the strong sense of policy influence exists when we
have evidence of a science specialty with distinctive differentiation of its research area, membership and reproduction
mechanisms. Clearly, the process of differentiation in each
subsystem on the institutional level involves exchange differentiation on each of the other levels and their specific sub-systems.

59. Wolfgang Van den Dael and Peter Weingart, "Resistance and Receptivity of
Science to External Direction: The Emergence of New Disciplines Under the Impact
of Science Policy," in PERSPECTIVES ON THE EMERGENCE OF SCIENTIFIC
DISCIPLINES' edited by Gerald Lemaine, Roy Macleod, Michael Mulkay, and Peter
Weingart, The Hague: Mouton, 1976.

60. IBID., p. 248.

In order, then to speak of the social policy determination of science, Van den Daele and Weingart argue that it is necessary to be able to demonstrate a mutual convergence, so to speak, of politics and science. In other words, political objectives must increasingly adopt the form and methodology of technical or applied science, while science itself must be correspondingly organized to be capable of servicing policy demands for description, measurement, functional and causal explanations. The following typology may then be sketched as a device for locating the differentiation of levels of policy and science exchange.

TYPOLOGY OF DEGREES OF 'SCIENTIFICATION' OF POLITICAL PROBLEMS, FUNCTIONS OF KNOWLEDGE AND LEVELS OF DEVELOPMENT OF SCIENCE

Political objectives of control according to the degree of 'scientification' of political problems	Scientific capacity (cognitive level of development)	Political objective of control according to function of demanded knowledge
'analytical politics (rationalizing initial conditions of political problem-solving)	assessment (description)	basic structural concepts operationization analysis and measurement
'means-end' rationalization (production of technical means of political intervention)	systems control	functional explanation, macro-theory of the subject matter
	construction	causal explanation micro-theory of the subject matter
systems politics (reflexive process of goal definition for political intervention)	systems formation	integrated science fusion of natural and social sciences theory of complex system

[Van den Daele and Wingart 1976: 265]

What this typology permits is the location of specific areas in which it is possible to analyze, with respect either to policy objectives or to the distinctive activities within a given science specialty, the factors that bear upon desired or undesired chances of influence, cooperation, lag, and resistance. It remains to be said that thereafter it is a question of empirical ethnographic investigation to examine the historical course of the differentiation, demarcation and boundary exchanges institutionalized in specific uses of a policy-fostered science specialty. Moreover, such studies would not only contribute to deepen our sense of the sociology of science. Due to their power to pursue the system exchanges between levels of policy objectives and science practice, they promise to demonstrate the reciprocal scientization of politics.   They thereby fulfill an important part of the program of a critical theory of science discourse and practice.

CONCLUSION

The Marxist and Weberian traditions in the sociology of science treat science as socially determined while nevertheless according it a sociological exemption.   This practice--the 'two sciences' stand--and it subsequent reformulations in Habermas and Marcuse, was examined with the aid of Parsons and Merton, in order to connect it with more recent work which differentiates the analysis of scientific production, and its subsystem exchanges with the economic and social policy domains.   We have argued that in future the sociology of science does not need to respect the distinction between superstructure and substructure in analyzing the domains of science, technology and polity.   Indeed, any attempt to preserve such a distinction leads only to a 'surplus of difficulty' (Morrison) pointed to in such practices as the exemption clause, demarcation problem, reflexive question, and the utopianization of science.   We consider that the 'two sciences' stand can be avoided if the sociology of science drops any distinction between the natural and the social sciences inasmuch as each activity offers a domain of interpretive and discursive inquiry whose practical adequacy furnishes the sociology of science with its proper topics of investigation.

INDEX OF NAMES

INDEX OF TOPICS

The Author

John O'Neill is Professor of Sociology at York University in
Canada. He has translated HUMANISM AND TERROR and THE
PROSE OF THE WORLD, both by Maurice Merleau-Ponty, and
STUDIES ON MARX AND HEGEL by Jean Hyppolite. He is also
the editor of THE INTERNATIONAL LIBRARY OF PHENOMENOLOGY
AND THE MORAL SCIENCES and co-editor of PHILOSOPHY OF THE
SOCIAL SCIENCES. Additionally, he is the editor of the books
MODES OF INDIVIDUALISM AND COLLECTIVISM and ON CRITICAL
THEORY. His numerous articles appear in various learned
journals. His is the author of PERCEPTION, EXPRESSION, AND
HISTORY: THE SOCIAL PHENOMENOLOGY OF MAURICE MERLEAU-
PONTY, SOCIOLOGY AS A SKIN TRADE: ESSAYS TOWARD A RE-
FLECTIVE SOCIOLOGY, and MAKING SENSE TOGETHER: AN INTRO-
DUCTION TO WILD SOCIOLOGY. ESSAYING MONTAIGNE: A STUDY
OF THE RENAISSANCE INSTITUTION OF WRITING AND READING is
his most recent work.

F